GREENHOUSE AUSTRALIAN CRAFTS

CROSS STITCH DESIGNS

GRAEME ROSS

GREENHOUSE

Greenhouse
Penguin Books Australia Ltd
487 Maroondah Highway, PO Box 257
Ringwood, Victoria 3134, Australia
Penguin Books Ltd
Harmondsworth, Middlesex, England
Viking Penguin, A Division of Penguin Books USA Inc.
375 Hudson Street, New York, New York 10014, USA
Penguin Books Canada Limited
10 Alcorn Avenue, Toronto, Ontario, Canada M4V 3B2
Penguin Books (N.Z.) Ltd
182–190 Wairau Road, Auckland 10, New Zealand

First published by Penguin Books Australia 1993

10 9 8 7 6 5 4 3 2 1

Copyright © Graeme Ross, 1993

All rights reserved. Without limiting the rights under copyright reserved above, no part of this publication may be reproduced, stored in or introduced into a retrieval system, or transmitted, in any form or by any means (electronic, mechanical, photocopying, recording or otherwise) without the prior written permission of both the copyright owner and the above publisher of this book.

Produced by Viking O'Neil
56 Claremont Street, South Yarra, Victoria 3141, Australia
A Division of Penguin Books Australia Ltd

Design by Karen Trump
Photography by Feiko Ruedisulj
Charts by Diana Murray, DiZign
Chart font design by Peter and Diana Murray using Adobe Illustrator
Typeset in Sabon and Helvetica by Bookset, Melbourne
Printed and bound through Bookbuilders Limited, Hong Kong

National Library of Australia
Cataloguing-in-Publication data

Ross, Graeme.
  Cross stitch designs.

  ISBN 0 86436 418 0.

  1. Cross-stitch – Patterns. I. Title.

746.443041

CONTENTS

Introduction   1

The Basics   4
Cross Stitch   4
Tapestry   4
Count   4
Petit Point, Gros Point   5
Thread   5
Needles   5
Frames   6
Washing   7

Let's Start   8
Before Starting   8
How to Start   8
Stitching a Horizontal Row   9
Stitching a Vertical Row   9
Finishing a Thread   9
Backstitching   10
Fractional Stitches   10
Unpicking   10
Knots   11

Using this Book   12

DESIGNS

Australiana   14
Cloncurry Parrot   14
Variegated Wren   16
Regent Parrot   19
Big Greasy   23
Red Lacewing   26
Australian Plane   29
Eastern Grey   33
Poinciana   38

Japanese Fashions   44
Ippitsusai   44
Eiri   50
Chobunsai   54
Torii   58
Kaigetsudo   63
Kitao   68

French Fashions 72
Lucy Ellen 72
Stella Adele 76
Alice May 82
Lynly Elliott 87

Papua New Guinea Collection 93
Era River Figure 94
Gulf Province Figure 98
Tami Island Mask 102
Abelam Mask 106
West Sepik Mask 110

Faces 114
Marilyn 114
Sarah 119
Woman Weeping 126
Tutankhamen 138

INTRODUCTION

My interest in cross stitch is relatively recent. The first piece I am aware of really noticing was in September 1987. This was at an Arts and Craft Exhibition at the Waigani Arts Centre in Papua New Guinea. The very next day I bought a chart, some fabric, threads and a needle and the rest is history – I was hooked! There was no going back. Do one piece of cross stitch and you're addicted for life.

In the five years since that day I have stitched innumerable pieces, designing in excess of one hundred and thirty of them so far. I am constantly being asked how I go about designing. It seems that I work completely in reverse to the way that is usually taught. I design by stitching first, charting what I have done as each thread or area of colour is completed. It never ceases to amaze me that, when sitting with pen on graph paper, so many people will ask: 'Do you work all that out on computer first?' But then again, I am often asked if I am working in acrylics or watercolours. Have I tried oils? Have I ever tried designing anything original? And there am I sitting outside my little gallery that is crammed with all the originals that I have managed to keep my hands on.

It has been suggested that I have the largest range of cross stitch originals on display anywhere, but I am not able to confirm or refute this.

I dearly love detail. Possibly this stems from a life-time involvement with art. A letter to my parents from a United States marine shortly after the end of the Second World War asked: 'Does little Graeme still keep up his interest in art?' And that was when I was still in my early teens.

I was born in Ballarat, Victoria, in December 1932 and my childhood was spent on the family property of Avondale at Miners Rest. Two of my cross stitch designs, 'Early Avondale' and 'The Hayshed', were inspired by this period of my life.

The last year of my schooling was spent at the Arts Faculty of the School of Mines, Ballarat. Here the greater part of the year was spent designing such items as toothpaste packets and lettering our names over and over and over in precise detail. I found it all most uninspiring.

After joining the workforce at the age of fourteen, I became a window dresser where, once again, artistic flair and attention to detail were the all-important factors.

In 1961 I answered the call of the wild and flew off to distant shores to train as a teacher of English as a foreign language in Rabaul, then in the Territory of Papua and New Guinea. After graduation I was posted to Manus Island. It was then that my interest in needlework began, with my first piece being worked on hessian, using any form of thread that I could obtain in the village trade store.

In 1968 I resigned from teaching and moved to the national capital of Papua New Guinea, Port Moresby. There I began working on insect screen, once again using any form of thread I could lay my hands on. During this period I also illustrated five children's books, created a deck of playing cards with all the court cards featuring warriors and women of Papua New Guinea, and held an exhibition of traditional designs worked on stained and carved plywood, which was a great success and sold out.

At this stage I came upon my first genuine canvas and tapestry wools. From that day until the time I discovered cross stitch, I designed needlepoint pieces. Three of these were purchased by the Governor-General and were hung in Government House in Port Moresby.

I find that designing and stitching in public has its amusing moments, some of the comments I hear are really worth repeating. During my very first week of stitching in public, when I was still feeling particularly embarrassed about it all, a woman came along and said: 'You look stupid sitting there doing that!' I could feel myself shrinking when she added: 'That's woman's work!'

There was the dear old soul in Melbourne who walked right up, looked me directly in the eyes, and said: 'You don't do cross stitch on a tapestry frame'. Maybe she does not, but I do, and I prefer it that way. My work never needs washing, and I find it easier, quicker and far neater.

Of course, there are the argumentative ones, like a woman in Cairns who asked: 'Is that long stitch or needlepoint you're doing?' I replied that it was cross stitch. 'I know it's cross stitch', she snapped, 'What I want to know is, is it petit point or gros point?'

And then there was the day when I had a deaf and mute friend sitting beside me. A woman was deeply engrossed in conversation with him, a fact of which he was unaware. I excused myself and said: 'Pardon me, madam, but he's totally deaf. He can't hear a thing.' Her response was: 'I was talking to him, not you!'

One encounter is particularly memorable. I was verbally abused for asking $8 for a chart of one of my designs. The customer was outraged; she told me so in no uncertain terms. 'I'll buy one cheaper when I get back to England', she said. I mentioned that she would not be able to buy one in England. 'If I want to buy one in England, I will!' I assured her that as the design was very new and had not been released on the market, she could purchase it only from me. 'Well, when I get home I'll buy something else!' and off she stormed.

This is not an Irish joke. I was serving a young Irish tourist who was rapt in my kookaburra design. 'Could I do it smaller?' she asked. I suggested that if she did it on 18 count fabric it would be smaller. 'How much smaller?' she asked. Not being a mathematical genius and not having a calculator on hand, I suggested that it would be approximately 25 per cent smaller. 'Oh, that's good,' she said, 'I certainly wouldn't have time to do anything that big!'

One poor young thing I felt truly sorry for. I was stitching a bought design of a Siamese cat. A young mother and her very small son were walking past behind me when the son, in the shrillest voice imagineable, called: 'Look, Mummy, the lady's knitting a cat!'

I really do like to try and look after my eyes despite all that I subject them to. Daily I hear the comment: 'You must have wonderful eyesight!' In fact, I have wonderful glasses, although they are four years old. What is more wonderful still is the 60-watt daylight globe that I always work under. This gives adequate lighting with no uncomfortable glare. An American tourist recently told me she was having trouble because her eyes weren't what they used to be and I suggested she try working under a light like mine. 'I always work under 300 watts', she informed me. The glare would be unbearable!

All of this leads to the comment I hear almost daily: 'You must have been doing cross stitch all your life'. Possibly my life was leading up to it and I merely traded paints and brushes to paint with a needle and thread. A comment that I treasure came from an American tourist: she told me that I have changed cross stitch from a craft into an art form. I can only hope that you will share her feelings. I dearly love cross stitch; each piece is unique and much love has gone into its creation. I hope you too will grow to feel as I do.

THE BASICS

It is all too easy when you are very familiar with a particular technique to talk about it in terms that may mean a great deal to you, but are quite alien to the public at large. I admit that I can be at fault in this respect, so let's begin with the basic terminology.

Cross Stitch

Cross stitch is a form of embroidery that consists of stitches in the shape of small 'x's. The crosses are worked, in most cases, in horizontal rows, with the first half of the stitches being the diagonals that go from the bottom left to the top right (or vice versa) to the end of that particular area of colour, then working in the opposite direction, that is, from the bottom right to the top left (or vice versa) over the first line of stitches. Individual crosses are worked only when stitching vertical or diagonal lines of a single stitch. It is very important that the first half of the stitch slopes in the same direction throughout the entire design. The background is normally left unworked.

Tapestry

The embroidery that is often called tapestry in Australia and the United Kingdom is known as 'needlepoint' in the United States of America and, to be perfectly honest, the Americans are correct. True tapestries consist of threads woven horizontally through a vertical warp with the cartoon or design sketched or painted onto paper behind the warp as a guide. These woven tapestries are mostly very large and frequently used as wall hangings. Needlepoint is stitched on a fairly coarse canvas and usually worked in wool, with the stitches all sloping in one direction only. All the background in needlepoint is completely covered in stitches.

Count

The size of your stitches is governed by the fabric count, that is, the density of the threads of the fabric you are working on. Most of my designs are worked on 14 count, as this is kind to the eyes when working. 14 count means 14 stitches to the inch;

18 count means 18 stitches to the inch, 22 is 22 stitches to the inch, and so on. The higher the number, the denser the fabric and the smaller the stitches you make. This means that the completed work will be smaller too. Most printed needlepoint (or tapestry) canvases are 10 count.

Petit Point, Gros Point

Petit point is a tent stitch (that is, a single diagonal stitch) worked over a single thread of canvas. 'Petit' is the French word for small. Gros point, as the name implies, is larger, and is tent stitch worked over a double thread of the canvas on the diagonal. It is common for printed canvases to be on Penelope canvas, which has dual threads running both vertically and horizontally. It takes four petit-point stitches to replace one gros-point stitch.

Thread

Cross stitch is normally worked in stranded cotton (also called embroidery thread, depending on which school you went to or where you were brought up). For reasons unknown to me, the English often refer to stranded cotton as 'silk'. Maybe silk has a more prestigious ring to it. The manufacturers, DMC, call it 'Art 117', and that is what I refer to it as in this book.

Stranded cotton is comprised of six individual strands of cotton twisted together and made up into skeins. These skeins will release the thread if you pull gently on one end – and on one end only. This is usually the longer end and easier to locate than the wrong end which, if pulled, will cause headaches and hassles by tangling the skein badly. Hold the skein in one hand and gently pull the end from the skein until the desired length is free. How many strands you should use is normally indicated somewhere on the chart. Grip the required number of strands between your finger and thumb and pull, sliding the unwanted strands away (but make sure to save them for later on).

Needles

Now, it is obvious what a needle is, but for both cross stitch and needlepoint a tapestry needle should be used. This has a blunt tip that will not split the fabric as much as a sharper needle. As for the fabric count, the higher the number for the needle, the smaller it is. I prefer to work with a size 26 but, in many cases, a size 24 is not all that different. The smaller the eye of the needle the better, because it will not enlarge the holes in the fabric too much. This can be important, especially if you make a mistake and work the wrong area and the stitches have to be unpicked, as a large needle will leave unsightly holes that are hard to camouflage.

Why limit yourself to only one needle? This means that you are spending much of your time threading. I keep as many needles going as possible. When I finish an area of colour and have to cut the thread, I then leave that thread in the needle for next time and thread the next colour in another needle. Please do not try to work with several needles at the same time by running threads across the back of your work. You will end up in a tangle and it will surely spell disaster.

Frames

There is a type of frame to suit every taste. If movies are to be believed, in the olden days ladies of leisure sat at their embroidery with the fabric held in a ring that was known as a 'hoop'. A hoop is great for working small pieces, but I find them tiring to hold for long periods, and the work always gets soiled around the outer edges of the ring. The hoop can also stretch the fabric and cause distortion of the stitches if the ring has been placed over a worked area, which happens when the design is too large to fit into the hoop. The hoop is, however, ideal for travellers who like to take their work with them in their bag. Next in size is the lap frame that, as the name implies, is held on the lap. Being rectangular, the lap frame is great for larger pieces as the fabric can be rolled up or down, exposing only the area being worked upon. One up on the lap frame is the table-top model, which can also be used in bed and is, therefore, great for anyone laid up for a few days (or longer). Now we come to the daddy of them all (and my favourite) the floor frame. This is a similar shape to a lap frame but has the added advantage of legs that reach the floor. The floor frame enables the stitcher the luxury of having both hands free at all times. Personally, I would not use anything other than a floor frame. I have a luxury model that stays permanently assembled at all times and a collapsible model that I can pack up and take away with me. There's nothing worse than being stuck in a hotel or motel room with nothing to work on!

It is usual for a frame to have a coarse band of tape over the rollers, and it is to this tape that you attach the fabric. I like to work so that the rollers are uppermost and the fabric below. The reason for this is that, no matter how clean you are, the fabric on the rollers can be become soiled and, if the work is attached in this way, any soiling will be on the back of the work. The correct way to fasten the fabric to the roller is to tack the fabric to the tape with neat little stitches. Always being busy, I cannot find time to stitch mine, so I merely pin it to the tape, ensuring that the pins are close together so that they do not form waves on the fabric when it is tightened. However, there is another reason to stitch it to the tape: in many climates the pins can rust and you will just hate yourself if this happens.

And this reminds me – *never* leave your needle in any part of the fabric that is going to be visible when the work is completed and framed. If you are rushed and cannot finish a thread, then let the needle and thread hang loosely, but better still, complete the thread and leave the needle where you are sure to find it next time.

Washing

Sometimes your work will get soiled and require washing. It is perfectly safe to wash it gently in tepid water with a tiny dash of dishwashing detergent. Gently rub the soiled areas with another piece of the fabric, then rinse it thoroughly in clear water, dry between a folded towel and hang out in the shade. Lightly iron on the reverse side. It is most unlikely that the colour will run, but if it does, soak the piece overnight in clear water.

LET'S START . . .

Before Stitching

It will make your work much easier if you 'grid' the fabric before commencing cross stitch. This will take a little time, but is well worth the effort. Using a single strand of thread, mark out a grid of tiny crosses, each two stitches high by two stitches wide, with the verticals and horizontals being ten rows apart, as shown below. Run your thread loosely from one cross to another at the back. Only mark these crosses in the area to be worked and not on the background, and make sure that you snip and remove each cross as you come to it when actually working the piece.

How to Start

When using a single strand doubled over

Pull the thread from the skein, twice the length you desire for stitching – approximately one metre would be about right. Now select a single strand and pull it gently from the six. Double the strand and thread the two free ends through the needle as shown. Starting from the back of the fabric, stitch upwards through the fabric at the beginning of the first stitch, then down through the fabric in the hole diagonally up from the first hole to complete the first half of your cross. After pulling the needle through the fabric, pass it through the loop in your thread at the back of the fabric. Pull gently on the thread until it tightens onto the fabric without buckling. Now continue the row of half crosses.

When using one or more strands (including two strands that have been cut and have no loop)

There are two ways to start. One is to hold a length of thread 2.5 cm or 1 in at the back of the work and overstitch it as you stitch along the row. The diagram on the left shows what the reverse side of the work will look like.

Alternatively, you may prefer to tie a loose knot in the end of the thread and, commencing a short distance away from where your first stitch will start and in the direction you will be stitching, stitch downwards through the fabric leaving the knot on top of the fabric. Pass across to your starting point and begin stitching, oversewing the loose strand at the back of your work. Snip off the knot when you are satisfied that the thread at the back of the work is held securely in place.

Stitching a Horizontal Row

Work half crosses, that is, bottom right to top left or bottom left to top right diagonal stitches along the row for the whole length of that area of colour, then stitch back in the opposite direction, forming complete crosses. There is no correct direction to work, left to right or right to left. The choice is yours, but it must be maintained consistently throughout the entire design.

Stitching a Vertical Row

Work each cross individually. This also applies when working a diagonal row.

Finishing a Thread

The back of your work will consist of vertical rows of stitches. To finish off a thread neatly, stitch through these back-of-work stitches in a single vertical line, one stitch passing through to the right, the next one to the left and so on for four or five stitches. The work will not come undone, and your finishing off will scarcely be visible.

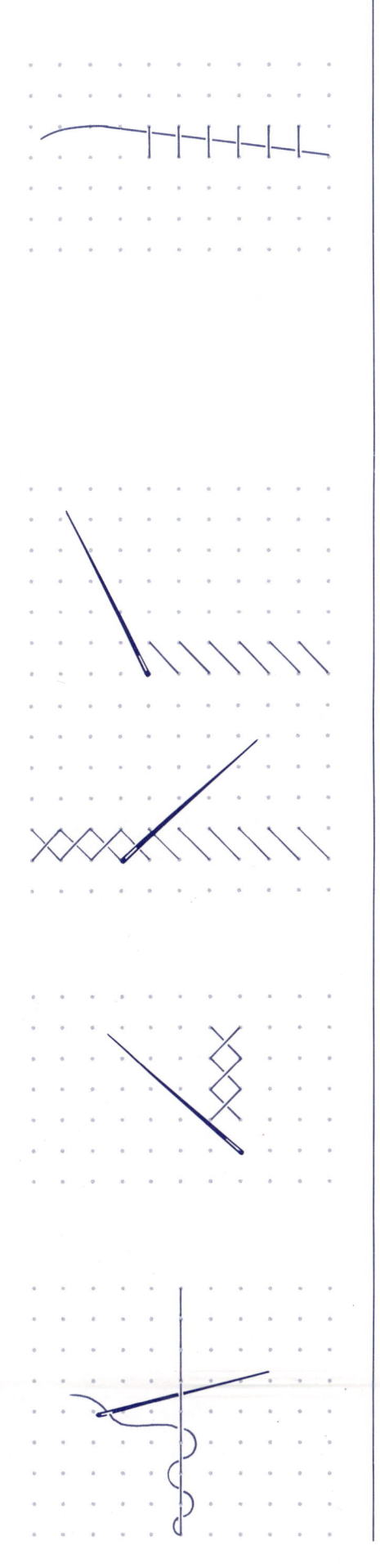

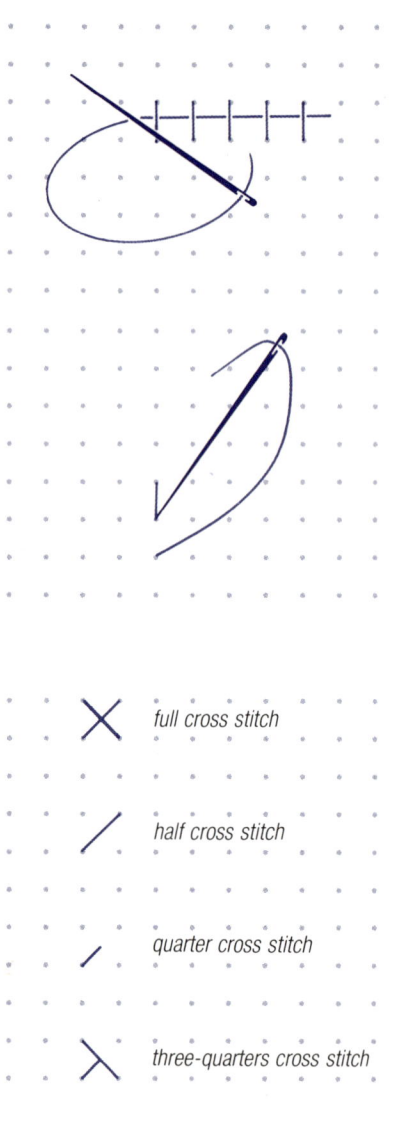

Backstitching

Backstitching is a form of highlighting, usually done using one strand of cotton only. There are cases, however, where two strands may be required. This will always be indicated on your chart. Backstitching is indicated on the chart by a heavier line that can be solid, dotted, dashed, wiggly, etc. indicating which shade of thread is required.

To start backstitching, run through a few stitches at the back of the work, finishing where you wish to commence, then re-stitch through the last stitch again.

Start backstitching by coming up through the fabric, then move forward one stitch on the right side. Go through the fabric, coming up again one stitch back from where you came up the first time; stitch down into the same hole you initially came up through. That is forward one on top of the fabric, backwards two below the fabric, forwards one on top, and so on along the line.

Fractional Stitches

The diagrams on the left show how you work a half cross stitch, a quarter cross stitch and a three-quarter cross stitch.

✕ full cross stitch

╱ half cross stitch

╱ quarter cross stitch

⋋ three-quarters cross stitch

Unpicking

Sorry that this subject has to be mentioned, but we all make mistakes. Yes, even the experts. When you do make a mistake, and I mean when, not if, please do not try and stitch back the way you have been as this will not work. You will foul up by stitching through threads at the back of the work and become hopelessly knotted. I have found there is only one satisfactory way of unpicking and that is to unthread your needle and carefully unpick the offending stitches from the front side of the work. If you happen to damage the thread, unpick a sufficient length so that you can re-thread the needle and finish off at the back.

Knots

Sad to tell, the subject of knotting is one that I cannot satisfactorily solve. I have heard many theories, and tried some of them. I have heard that regardless of how many strands you are using, each should be pulled from the main twist and then the required number put back together again. I have also been told that the strands should be waxed. I couldn't bring myself to do this, as I do not think I could bear the feel of the thread afterwards. I have found, however, that the doubled thread technique I explain in the How to Start section works well and I seldom get any knotting. And always, regardless of what sort of embroidery you are doing, keep a constant check on your thread to ensure that it is not excessively twisted or unravelled. If this is occurring, let the needle hang loosely and it will settle back into its own twist again. The best tip, I find, is to keep a pin handy. When you notice a knot has formed, do not tug on the thread and tighten the knot. Take the pin and insert it into the knot and, in most cases, you will be able to unpick it easily before it tightens into something impossible. It really is a wonderful relief when this happens.

USING THIS BOOK

Many of the charts in this book extend over several pages. To make it easier to follow the design when working your cross stitch, I have included a plan to show the layout of the charts. The numbers in circles indicate pages that link horizontally, while the letters in circles are pages that link vertically. Match the numbers or letters and the whole design will fall into place.

The small black triangles on the charts indicate the centre of the design (these are shown enlarged on the chart below). Use these when marking the grid on your fabric.

Backstitching instructions for each individual design are also given on the chart for that design.

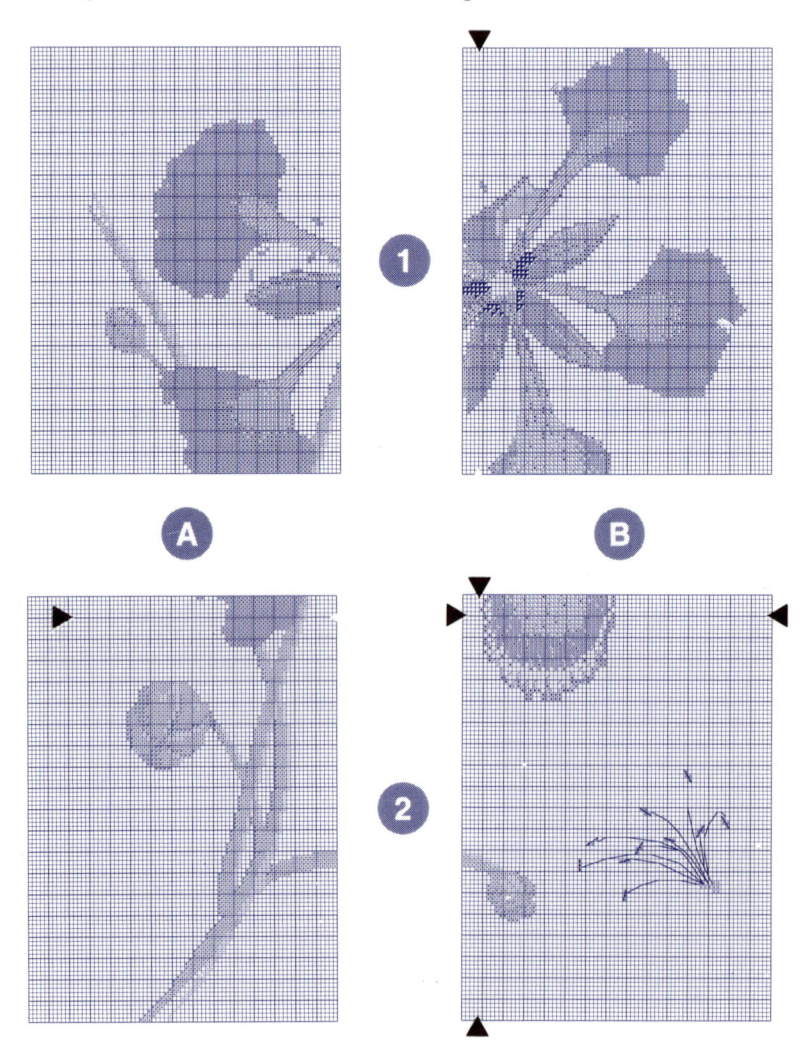

CLONCURRY PARROT

AUSTRALIANA
Cloncurry Parrot

The Cloncurry Parrot is found only in the interior of North Queensland, Australia.

NOTE: The Cloncurry Parrot can be worked as a pair with the Regent Parrot. If you are doing this, one skein of a shade will be sufficient to complete both designs.

Fabric

Count	Centimetres	Inches
10	40 × 29	16 × 12
14	33 × 25	13 × 10
18	30 × 23	12 × 9
22	28 × 22	11 × 9

These measurements give adequate allowance for framing.

This design is 95 stitches high by 56 stitches wide.

The fabric required to work both parrots as one design is given below.

Count	Centimetres	Inches
10	43 × 53	17 × 21
14	35 × 43	14 × 17
18	30 × 36	12 × 15
22	28 × 33	11 × 13

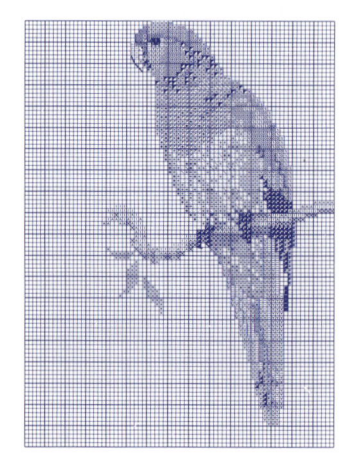

Thread

Use two strands throughout for cross stitch and one strand for backstitching.

DMC Art 117   1 skein each of the following.

Symbol	Code	Colour
·	white	
■	310	(black)
s	367	(green)
⋈	413	(dark steel grey)
⋀	414	(grey)
ı	436	(amber)
×	470	(green)
7	471	(light green)
∴	472	(very light green)
▼	580	(dark green)
\	726	(yellow)
•	729	(dark gold)
—	827	(very light blue)
∧	839	(brown)
⊙	3041	(lilac)
✕	3371	(black/brown)
v	3766	(light blue)
✳	3790	(dark beige)
o	470 & 3766	
+	472 & 729	

Backstitching

Symbol	Code	Strand
——	310	1 strand
══	414	1 strand
--	413	1 strand

AUSTRALIANA

Variegated Wren

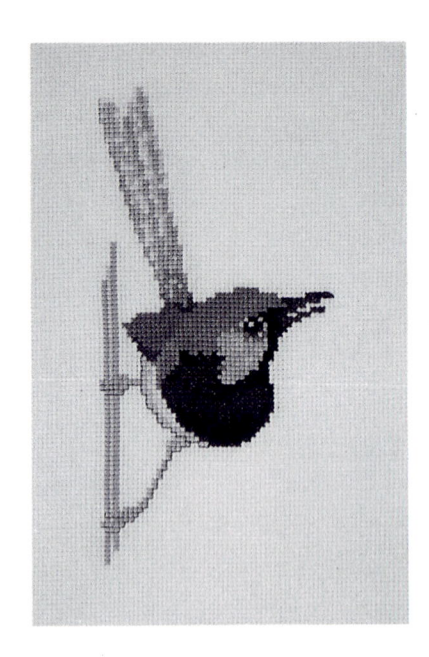

The Variegated Wren is found in coastal districts of southern Queensland and New South Wales.

Fabric

Count	Centimetres	Inches
10	40 × 28	16 × 11
14	34 × 24	14 × 10
18	29 × 23	12 × 9
22	26 × 21	11 × 8

This design is 100 stitches high by 50 stitches wide.

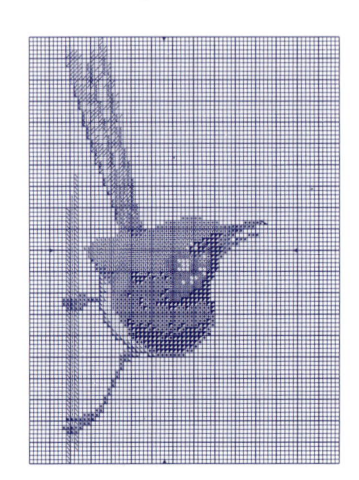

Thread

Use two strands throughout for cross stitch and one strand for backstitching.

DMC Art 117   1 skein each of the following.

	white	
▼	310	(black)
v	334	(blue)
x	340	(lavender)
c	341	(light lavender)
•	413	(dark steel grey)
	414	(grey)
ʞ	415	(light grey)
ı	677	(light gold)
ʌ	721	(tangerine)
L	762	(very light grey)
+	793	(deep blue)
∴	828	(very light blue)
\	834	(gold)
o	3325	(light blue)
/	3747	(very light mauve)
s	3772	(tan)
ĸ	3781	(dark brown)

Backstitching

| — | 414 | 1 strand |
| — | 341 | 1 strand |

VARIEGATED WREN

VARIEGATED WREN

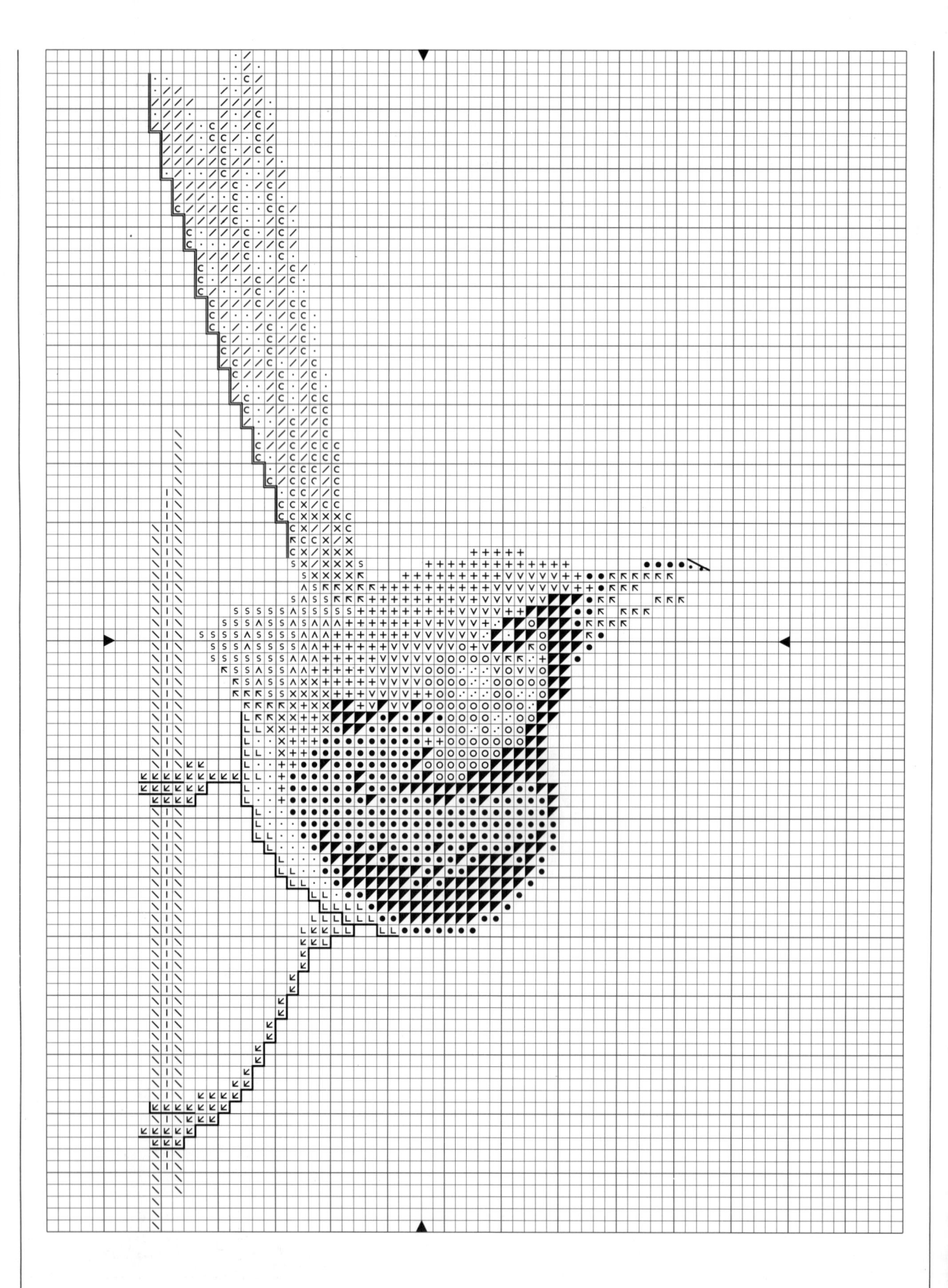

Regent Parrot

The Regent Parrot is common to northern Victoria, southern New South Wales and the south-eastern parts of South Australia.

Fabric

Count	Centimetres	Inches
10	43 × 53	17 × 21
14	35 × 43	14 × 17
18	30 × 36	12 × 15
22	28 × 33	11 × 13

This design is 78 stitches high by 143 stitches wide.

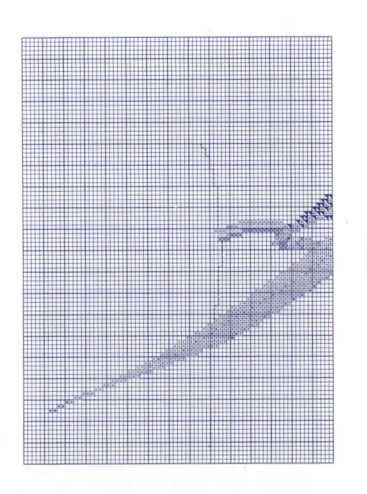

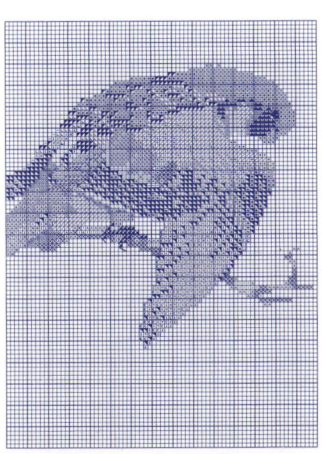

Thread

Use two strands throughout for cross stitch and one strand for backstitching.

DMC Art 117   1 skein each of the following.

/	307	(lemon)
■	310	(black)
⊼	400	(dark tan)
⊿	413	(dark steel grey)
=	414	(grey)
|	436	(amber)
×	470	(green)
▲	471	(light green)
●	580	(dark green)
✕	606	(orange red)
+	676	(light gold)
·	727	(light yellow)
∷	738	(light buff)
v	762	(very light grey)
c	832	(khaki)
^	839	(brown)
⁄	922	(tan)
▼	935	(very dark green)
L	937	(dark green)
−	977	(light tan)
·	3024	(light beige)
✗	3371	(black/brown)
‵	3760	(blue)
т	3766	(light blue)
N	3787	(dark grey)
◣	3799	(very dark grey)
o	307 & 471	

Backstitching

——	310	1 strand
══	3787	1 strand

REGENT PARROT

AUSTRALIANA

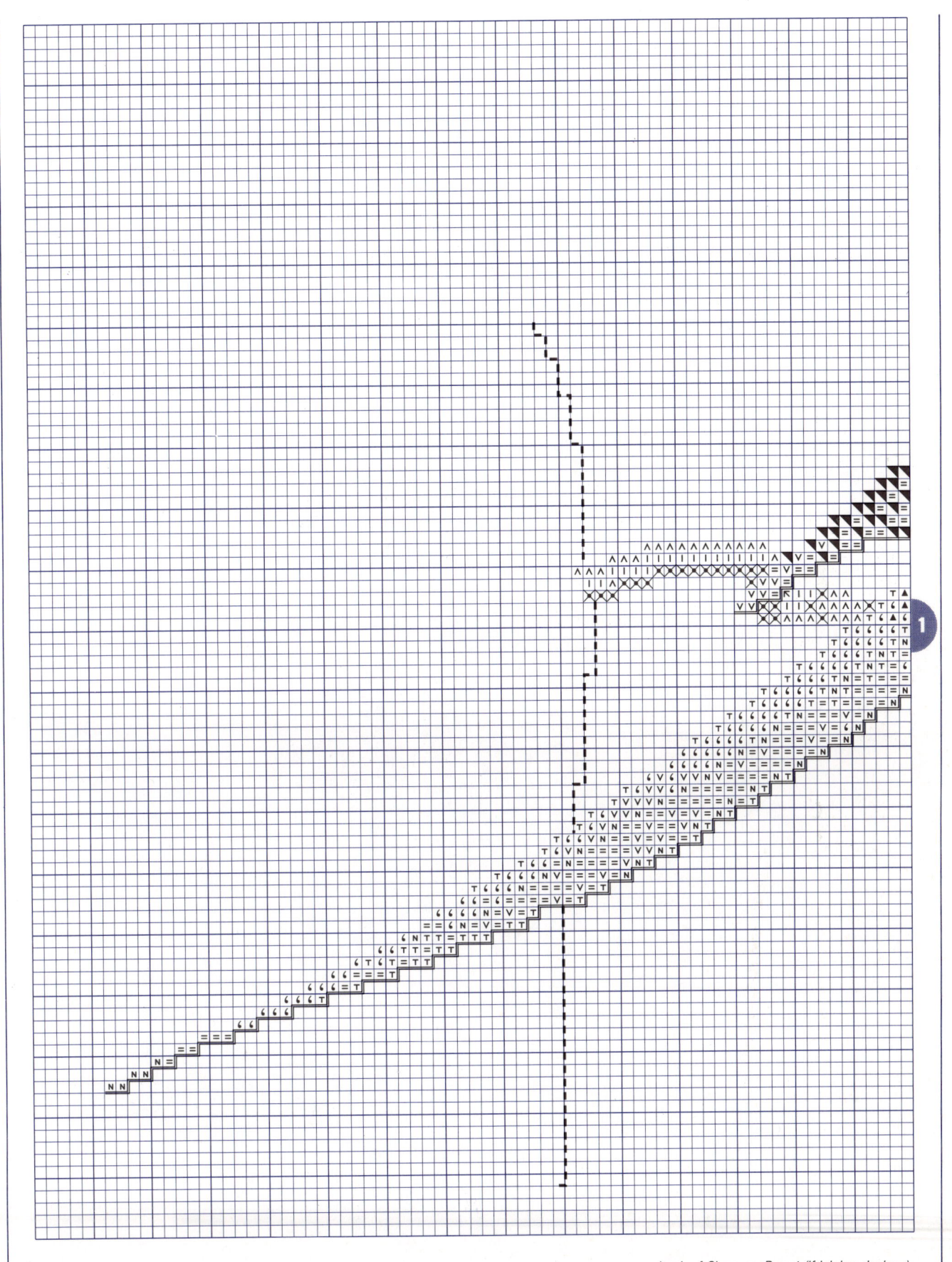

- - - - - - - back of Cloncurry Parrot (if joining designs)

21

REGENT PARROT

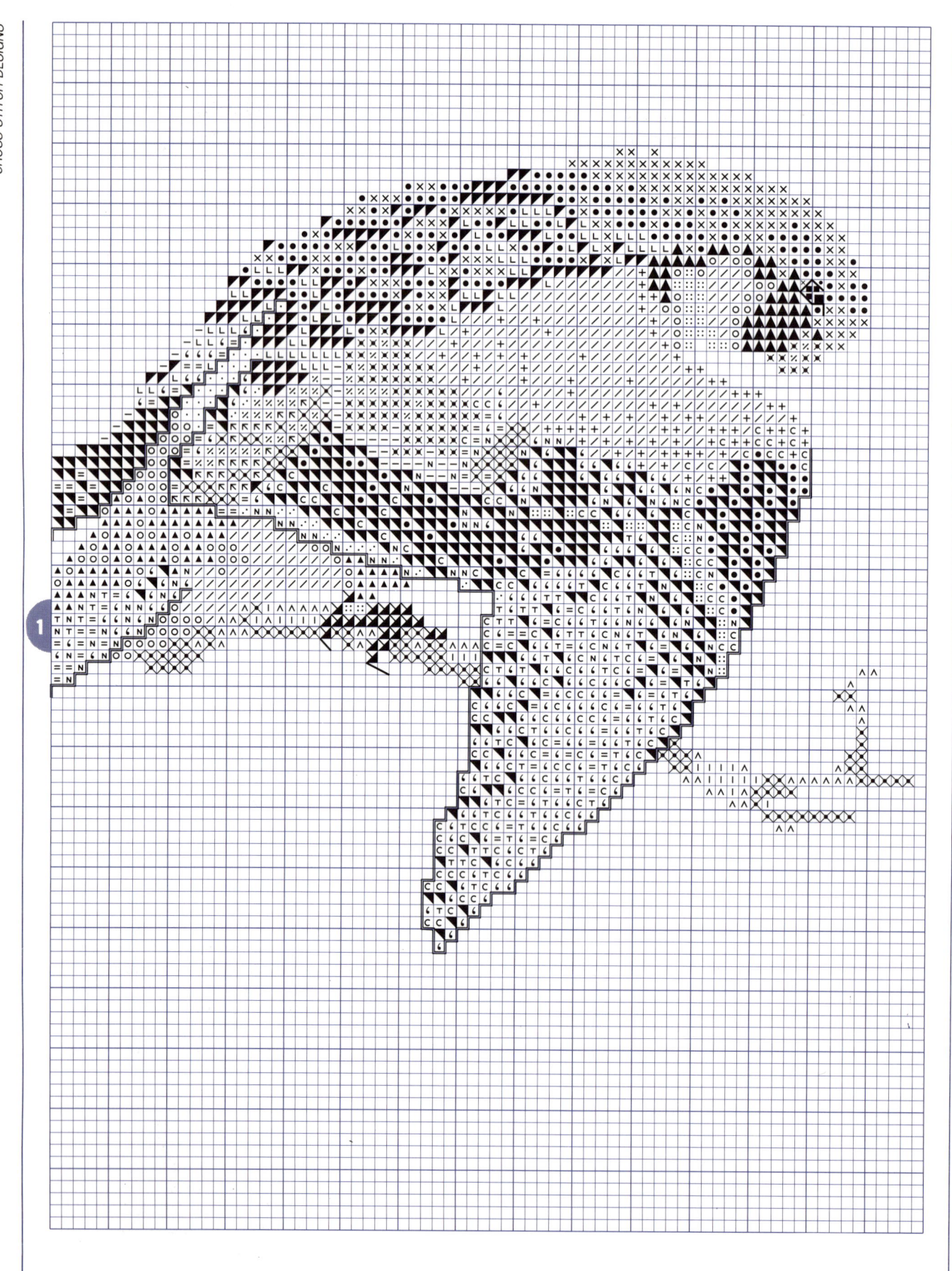

Big Greasy

What a disgusting name for a butterfly – and he really is quite attractive! I have chosen to stitch the male of the species that, together with the female, is found from Sydney all the way north to the islands of Torres Strait.

Fabric

Count	Centimetres	Inches
10	28 × 40	11 × 16
14	25 × 33	10 × 13
18	23 × 29	9 × 12
22	22 × 26	9 × 11

This design is 51 stitches high by 99 stitches wide.

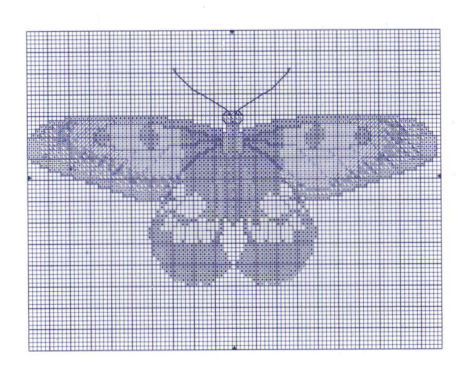

Thread

Use two strands throughout for cross stitch and one strand for backstitching, except for colour 3022 where it is used on the dark brown areas in the middle of the wing, when two strands should be used.

DMC Art 117 1 skein each of the following.

·	white	
×	817	(red)
∕	822	(cream)
v	839	(brown)
+	3022	(dark grey green)
L	3023	(grey green)
o	3024	(light grey green)
•	3371	(black/brown)
−	822 & white	

Backstitching

———	3371	1 strand
═══	839	1 strand
- - -	3022	See chart for details

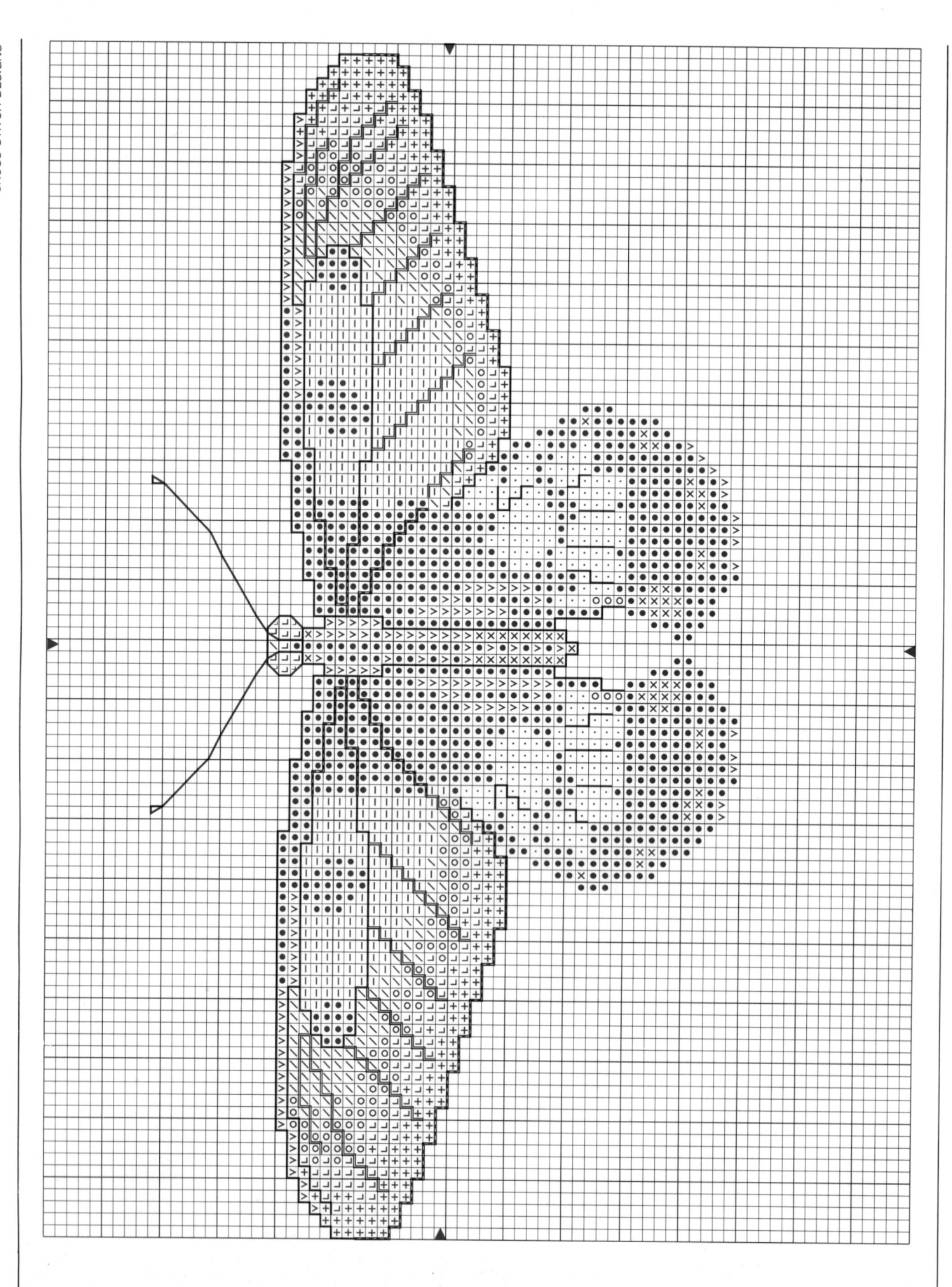

Backstitch with 2 strands of 3022 on the dark brown areas in the middle of the wing. Use only 1 strand under the wing.

BIG GREASY

Red Lacewing

The Red Lacewing is truly a beautiful specimen. It is found in the northern parts of Cape York Peninsula and in parts of Papua New Guinea. This is the male of the species.

Fabric

Count	Centimetres	Inches
10	28 × 36	11 × 15
14	25 × 31	10 × 13
18	23 × 28	9 × 11

This design is 50 stitches high by 89 stitches wide.

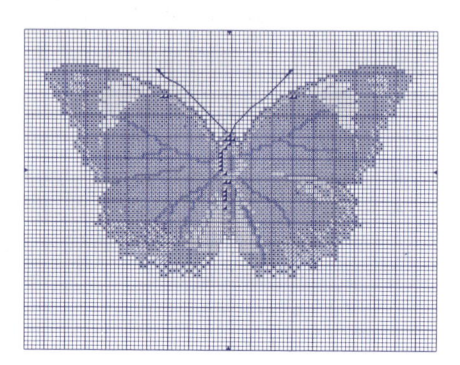

Thread

You will need one skein each of the following if working with two strands throughout. However, I do suggest using three strands for a more brilliant effect, in which case you will need two skeins each of 310 and 666. Backstitch with one strand only.

DMC Art 117

·	white	
•	310	2 skeins (black)
/	327	(lilac)
т	433	(dark tan)
o	435	(tan)
×	666	2 skeins (red)
c	742	(gold)
ı	946	(dark orange)
=	3042	(mauve)
▼	3371	(very dark brown)

Backstitching

| | 3371 | 1 strand |
| | 742 | 1 strand |

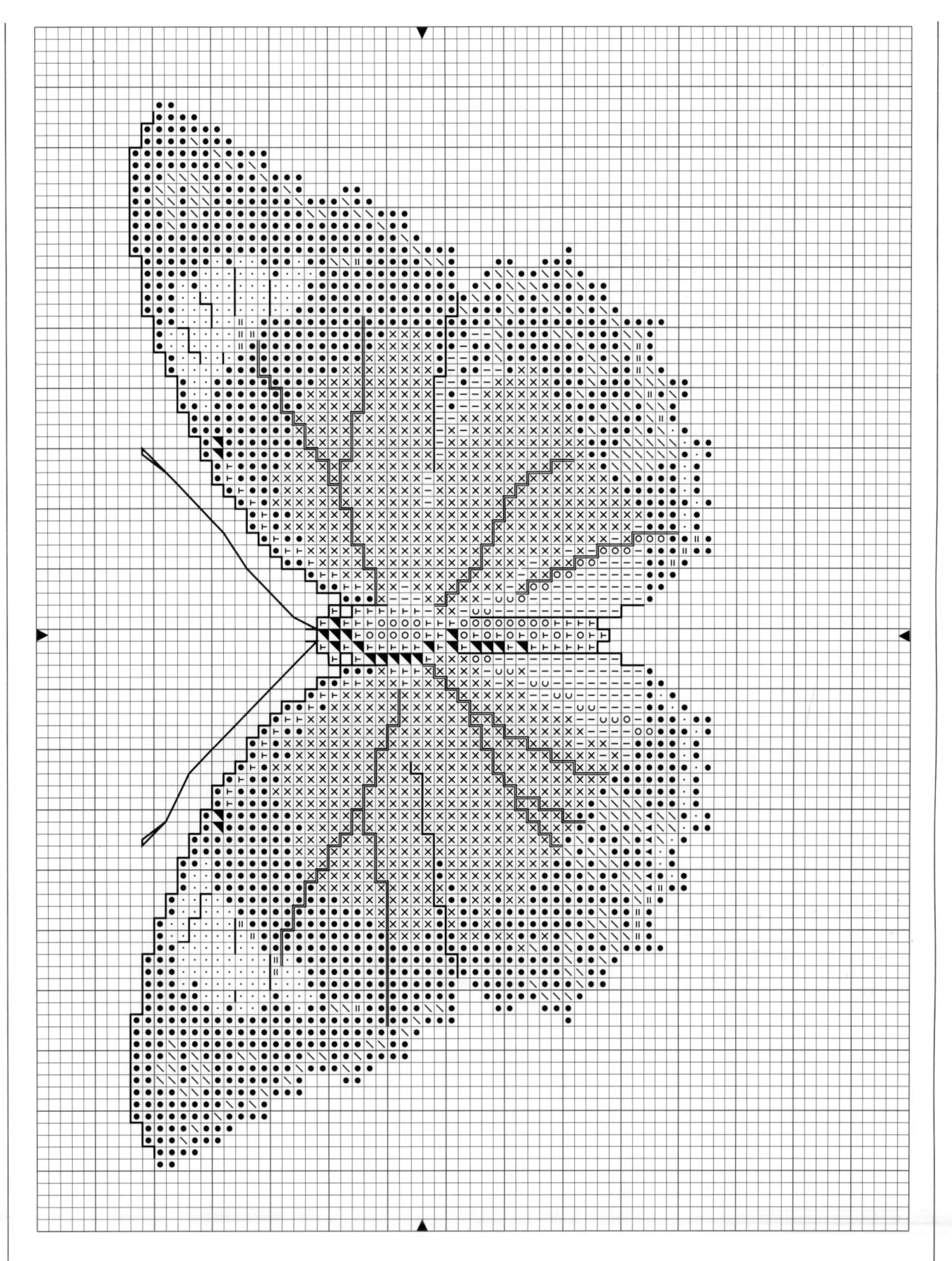

AUSTRALIANA

27

RED LACEWING

Australian Plane

The Australian Plane will appeal to anyone whose colour scheme tends towards blue. This beautiful butterfly is found from Townsville, north to the islands of Torres Strait. As usual, I have chosen the male of the species.

Fabric

Count	Centimetres	Inches
10	40 × 37	16 × 15
14	33 × 31	14 × 13
18	29 × 28	12 × 11
22	26 × 25	11 × 10

This design is 99 stitches high by 90 stitches wide.

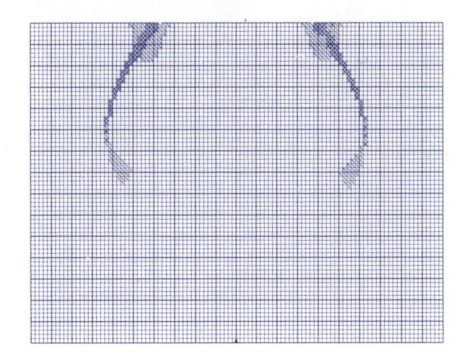

A

Thread

Use two strands throughout for cross stitch and one strand for backstitching.

DMC Art 117   2 skeins of black (310) and 1 skein each of the following unless otherwise stated.

╱	310	(black) 2 strands
▼	310	(black) 3 strands
×	414	(grey)
v	610	(very dark khaki)
=	640	(very dark beige)
.	646	(dark grey)
	806	(teal)
X	922	(rust)
	995	(electric blue)
c	3031	(dark khaki)
\	3045	(dark gold)
•	3371	(black/brown)
o	806 & 995	

Backstitching

——	310	1 strand
═══	646	1 strand
╌╌╌	3371	1 strand

AUSTRALIAN PLANE

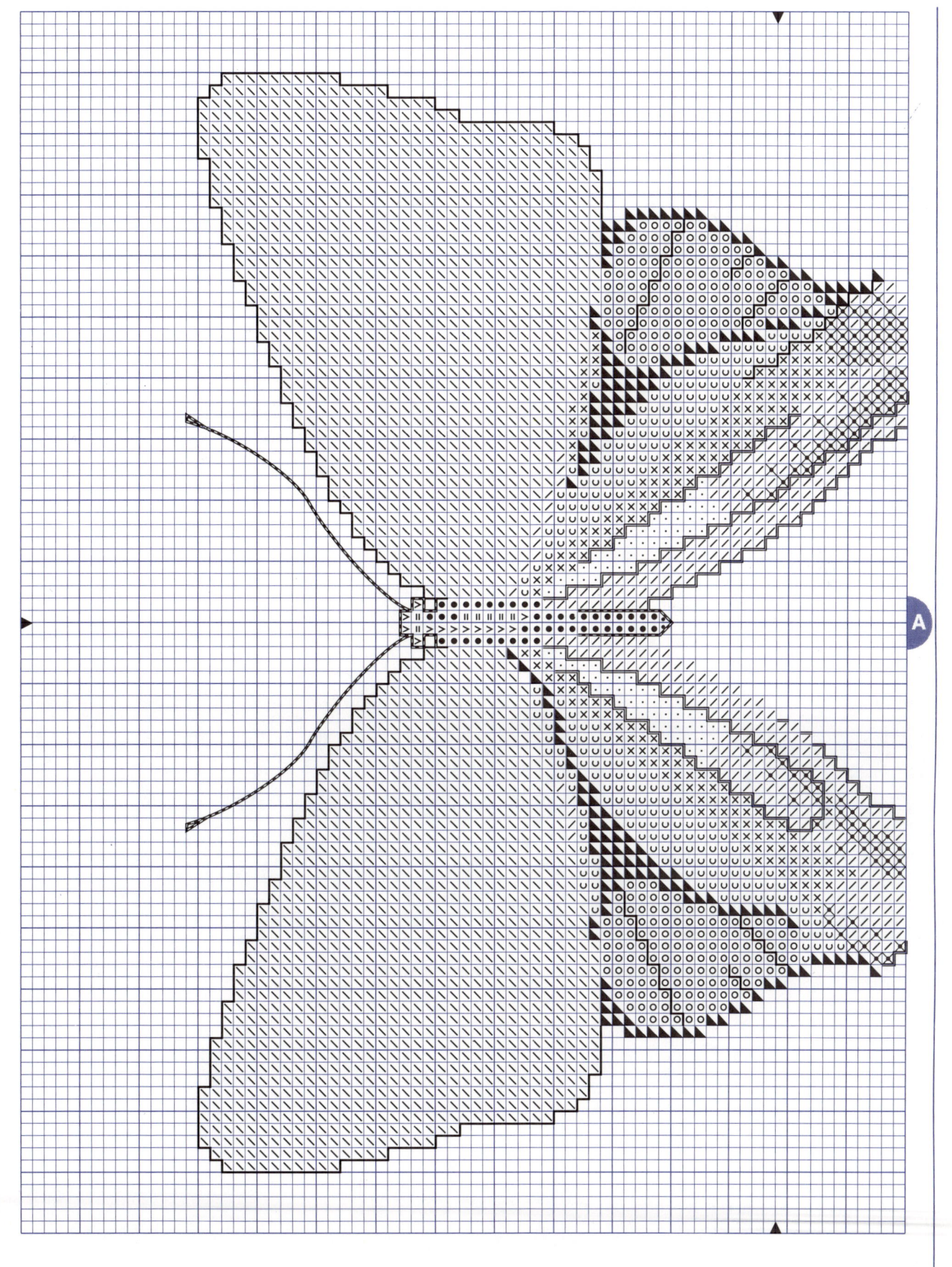

AUSTRALIANA

A

31

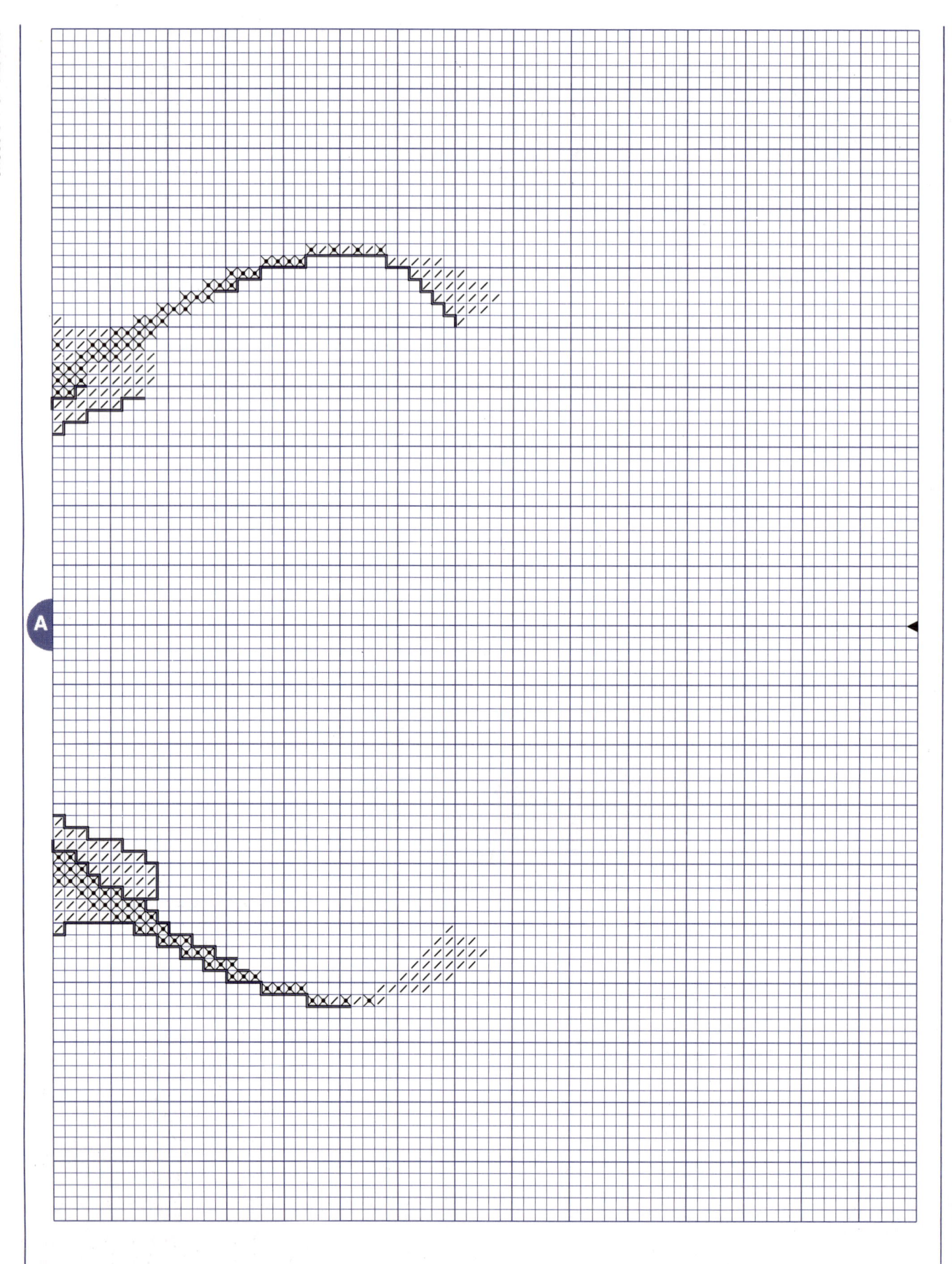

CROSS STITCH DESIGNS

A

32 AUSTRALIAN PLANE

Eastern Grey

The kangaroo is the largest member of the family *Macropodidae*, the herbivorous marsupials of Australia. They have powerful hind legs developed for leaping, a sturdy tail for support and balance, a small head and very short fore limbs.

The kangaroo appears, together with the emu, on the Australian coat-of-arms because neither can move backwards, therefore 'Advance Australia Fair'.

Fabric

Count	Centimetres	Inches
10	53 × 41	21 × 16
14	41 × 33	17 × 13
18	35 × 29	14 × 12
22	28 × 26	11 × 10

This design is 147 stitches high by 100 stitches wide.

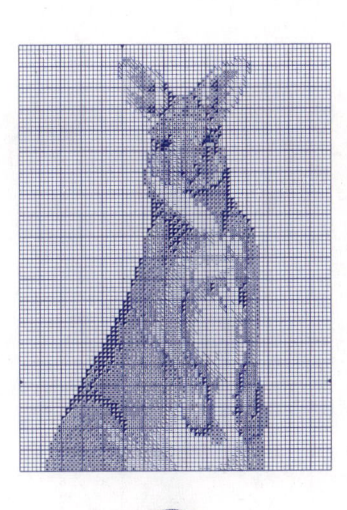

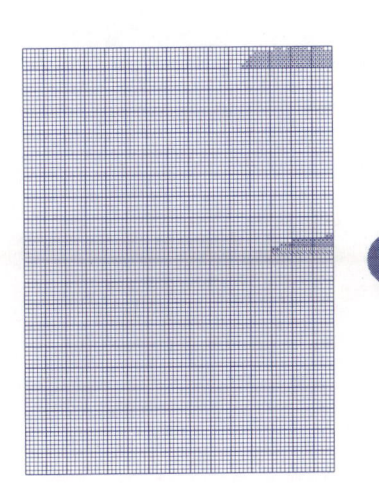

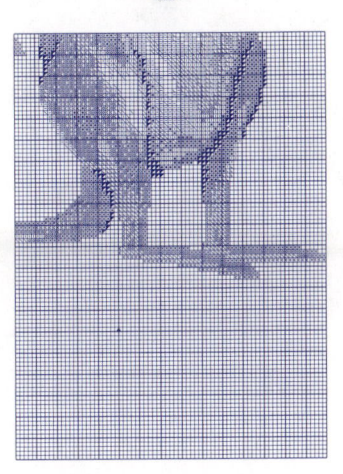

Thread

Use two strands throughout for cross stitch and one strand for backstitching.

DMC Art 117   1 skein each of the following.

.	white	
−	ecru	
■	310	(black)
o	318	(light grey)
×	414	(grey)
ĸ	420	(dark brown)
v	436	(brown)
+	437	(light brown)
c	612	(beige)
L	739	(dark cream)
\	762	(very light grey)
◪	844	(dark pewter)
•	3022	(dark grey green)
ı	3023	(light grey green)
*	3371	(black/brown)
◤	3787	(very dark beige)

Backstitching

═══   844   1 strand

AUSTRALIANA

EASTERN GREY

AUSTRALIANA

EASTERN GREY

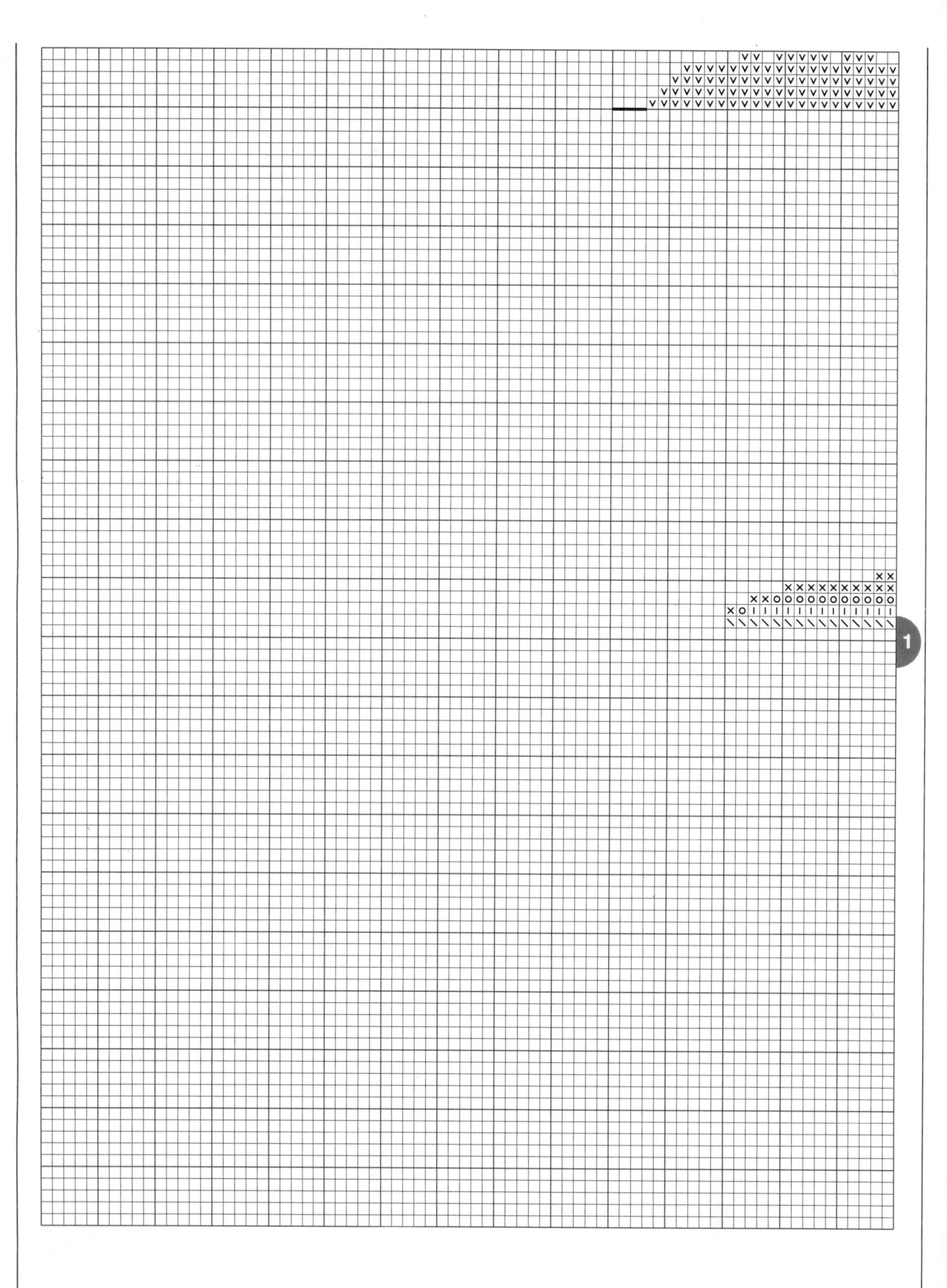

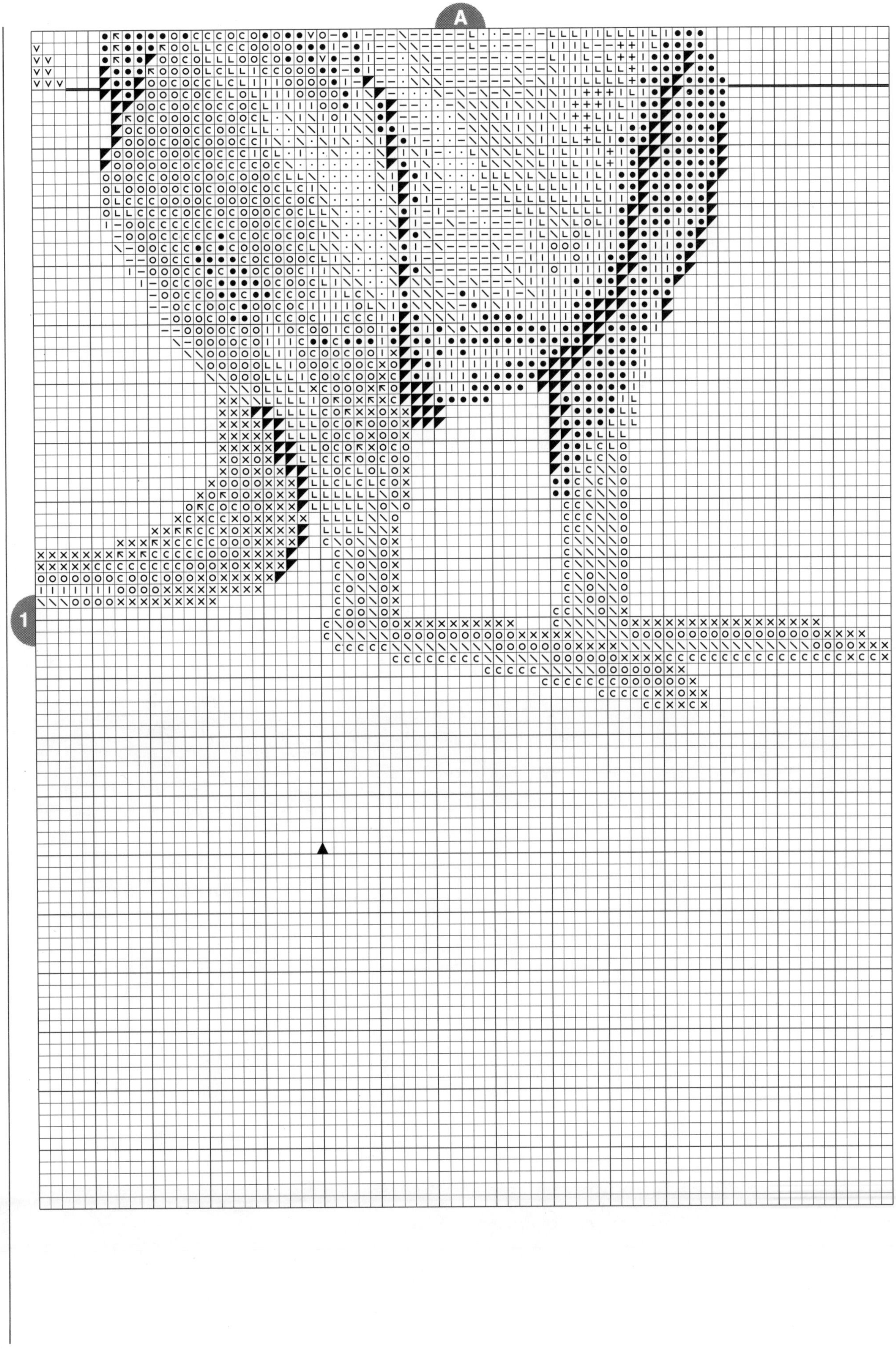
A
1

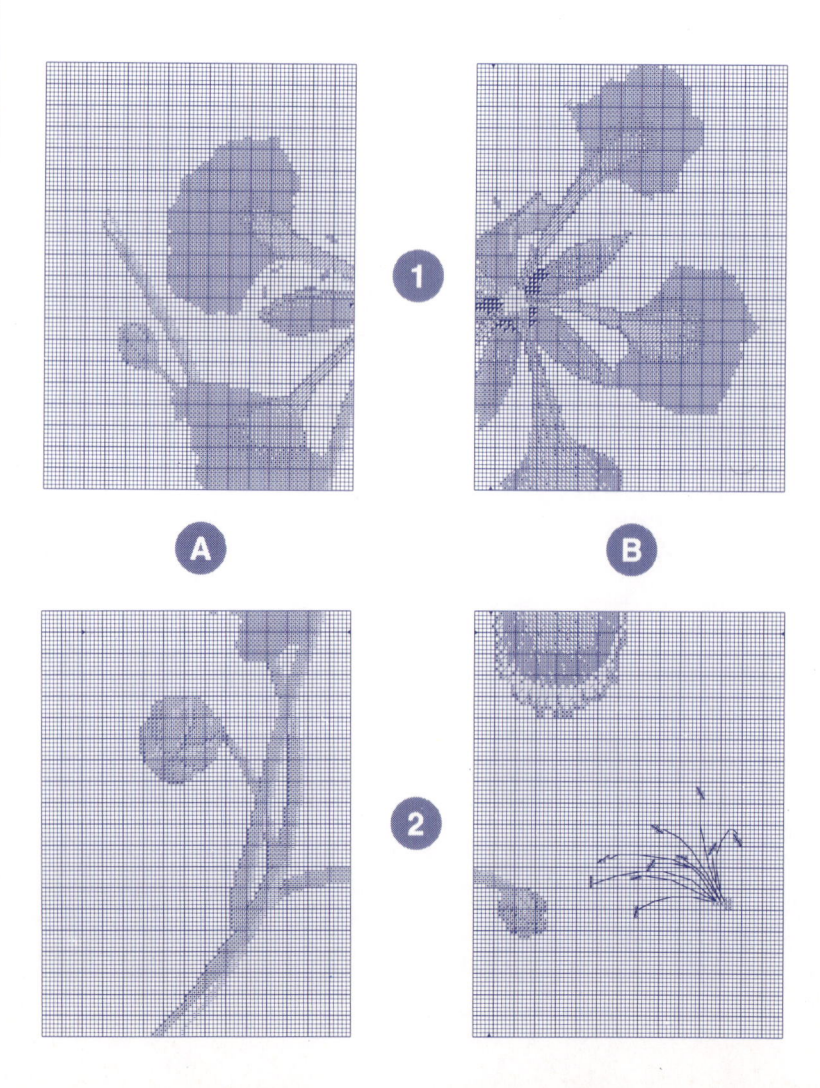

Poinciana

The flamboyant Madagascan Poinciana is a deciduous tree that grows profusely in tropical areas. In season, Cairns comes ablaze with its scarlet blossoms. In Papua New Guinea it is known as 'the Christmas Tree' because it blooms at that time of year.

Fabric

Count	Centimetres	Inches
10	66 × 51	26 × 19
14	54 × 40	22 × 16
18	43 × 33	17 × 13
22	38 × 30	15 × 12

This design is 200 stitches high by 130 stitches wide.

Thread

Use two strands throughout for cross stitch and one strand for backstitching, other than the tips of the stamens, when two strands should be used.

DMC Art 117   1 skein each of the following.

▼	304	(cherry)
•	350	(very dark pink)
c	351	(dark pink)
/	352	(pink)
+	471	(green)
−	472	(light green)
×	666	(red)
L	743	(yellow)
o	744	(light yellow)
.	745	(buttercup)
	844	(yellow)
к	3347	(dark green)
v	471 & 472	

Backstitching

———	3347	(leaves) 1 strand
———	666	(petals) 1 strand

POINCIANA

POINCIANA

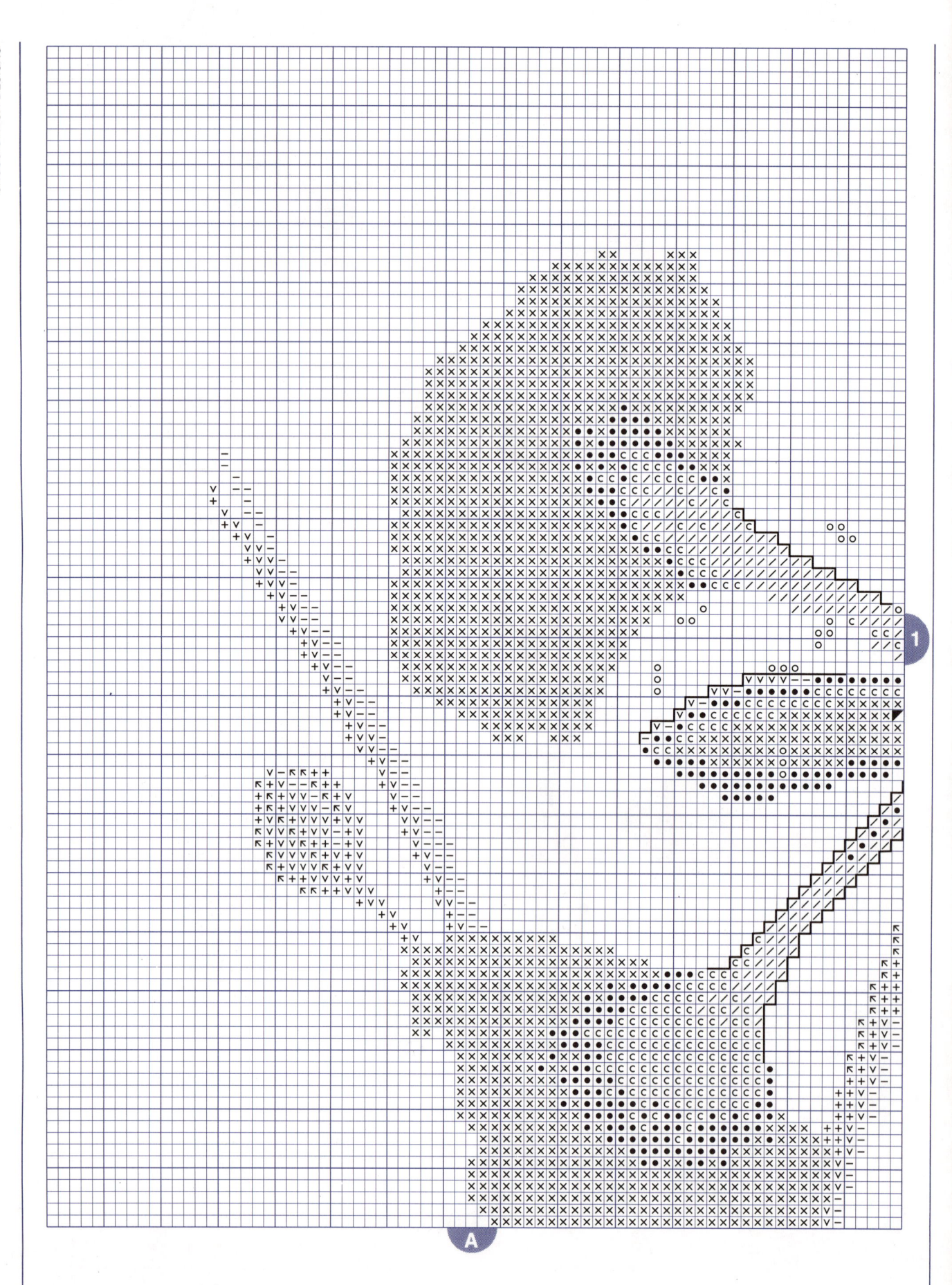

AUSTRALIANA

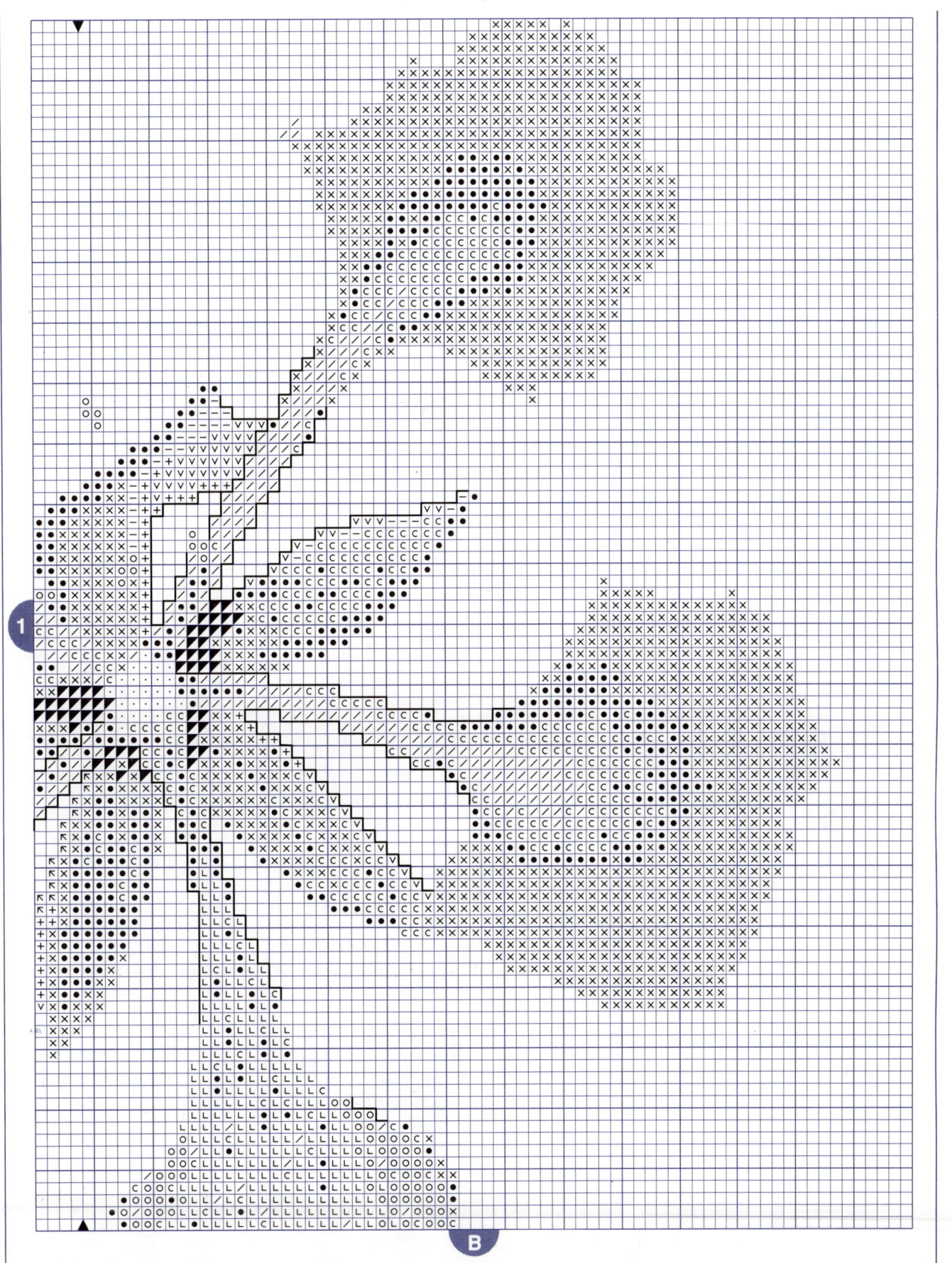

41

42 POINCIANA

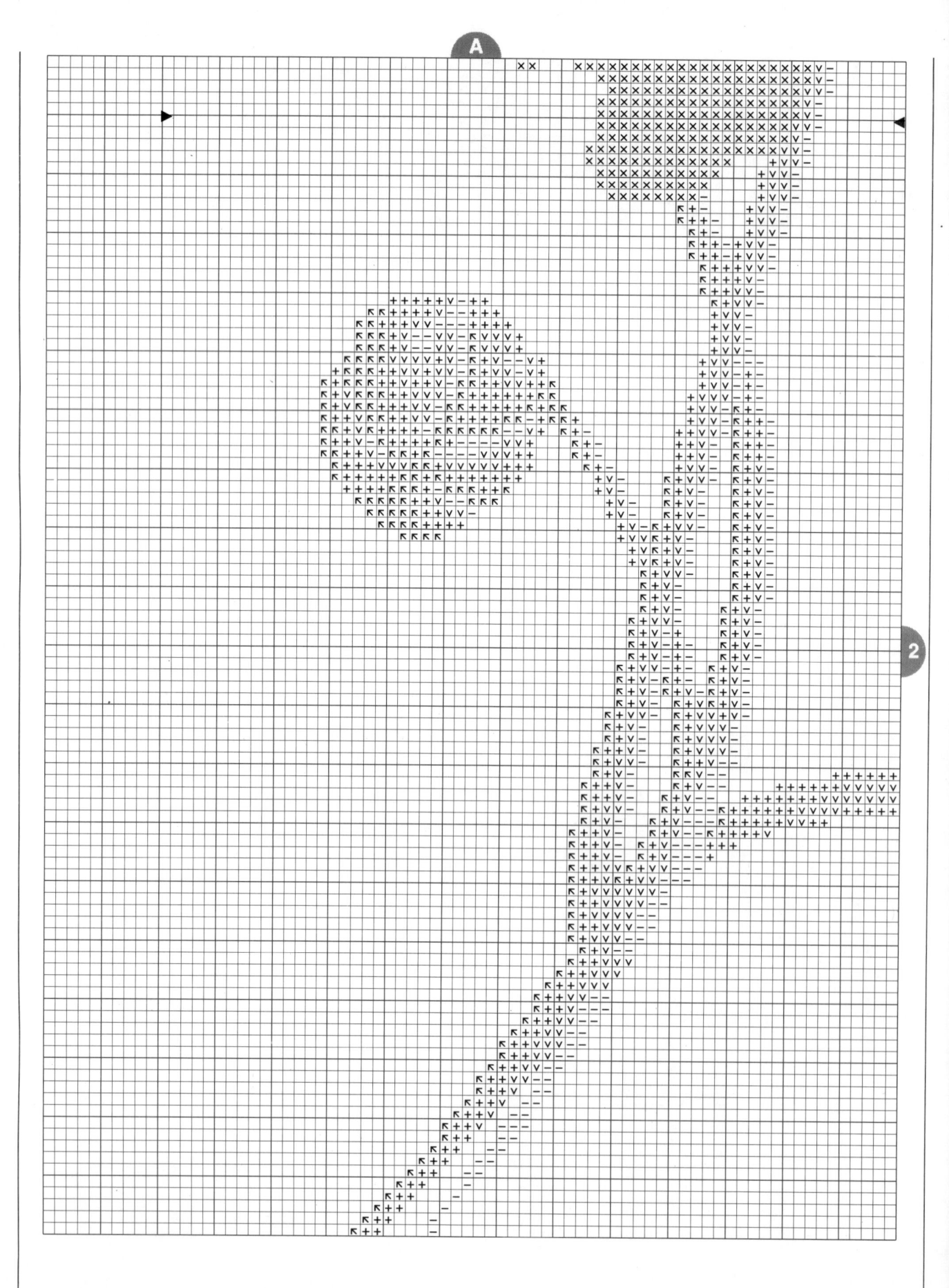

Backstitch the green areas of the flower with 1 strand of 3347.
Backstitch the petals with 1 strand of 666.
Backstitch the tips of the stamens with 1 strand of 844.
Backstitch the stamens with 2 strands of 666.

CROSS STITCH DESIGNS

JAPANESE FASHIONS

The following six designs are based on wood-block prints made in the eighteenth century in Osaka. The fabric patterns have been modified to suit cross stitch but the outline and style are completely authentic.

Ippitsusai (1767)

Fabric

Count	Centimetres	Inches
10	58 × 40	24 × 16
14	46 × 33	19 × 13
18	41 × 28	16 × 11
22	35 × 26	14 × 11

This design is 175 stitches high by 94 stitches wide.

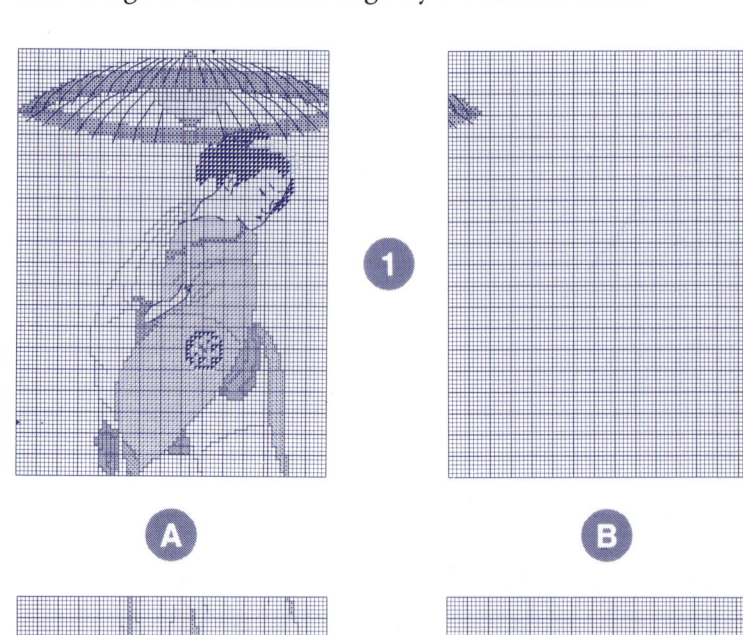

Thread

Use two strands throughout for cross stitch. For details of the backstitching see the instructions on the chart.

DMC Art 117   1 skein each of the following.

⌄ ▼	310	(black)
– •	535	(dark grey)
–	666	(red)
⌄ ∴	676	(gold)
–	712	(cream)
○	741	(light orange)
·	748	(flesh)
∕	962	(pink)
+	991	(teal)
∖	993	(light teal)
×	3350	(dark pink)

Backstitching

——— 535   1 strand

44

IPPITSUSAI

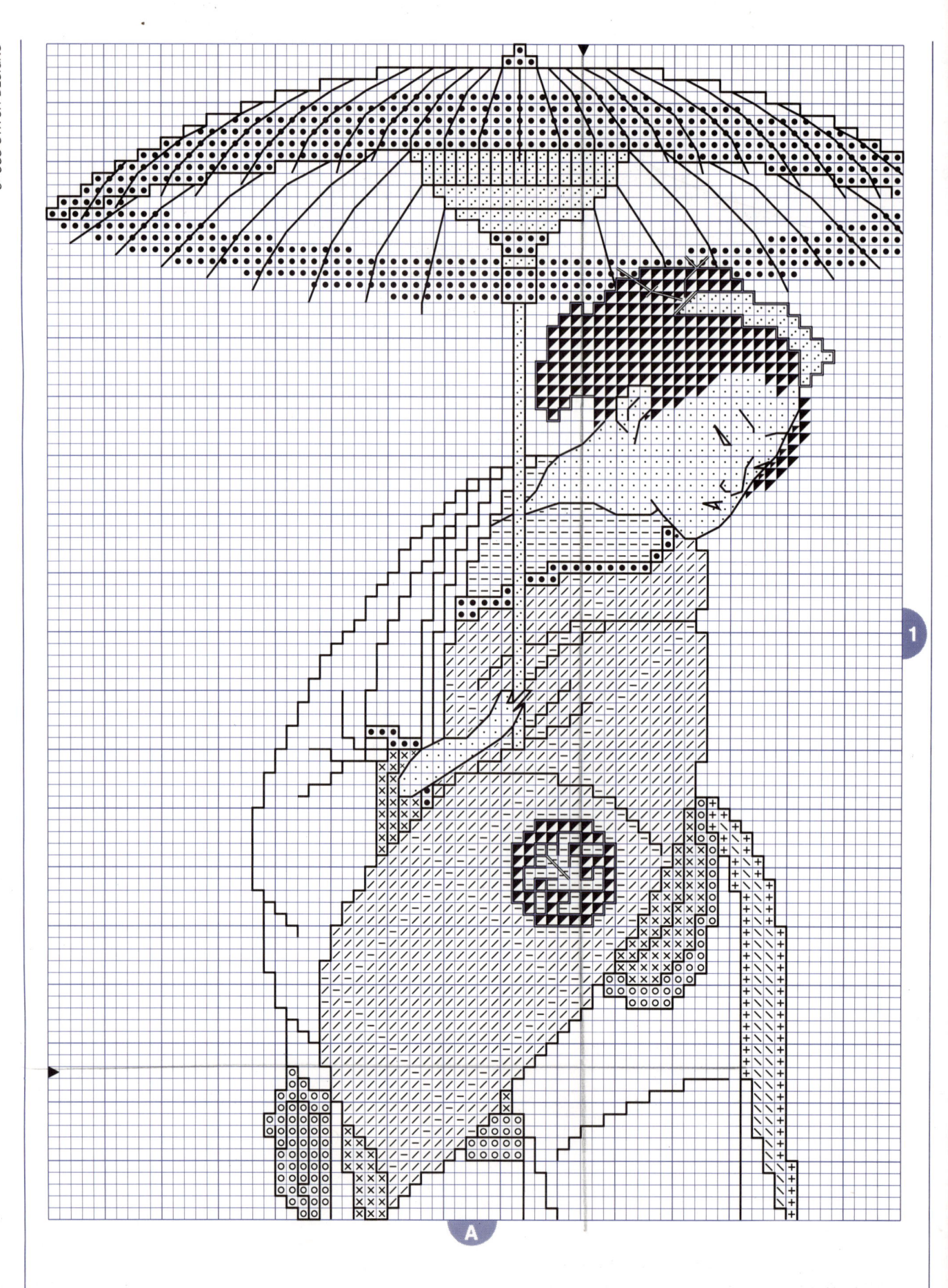

CROSS STITCH DESIGNS

46 IPPITSUSAI

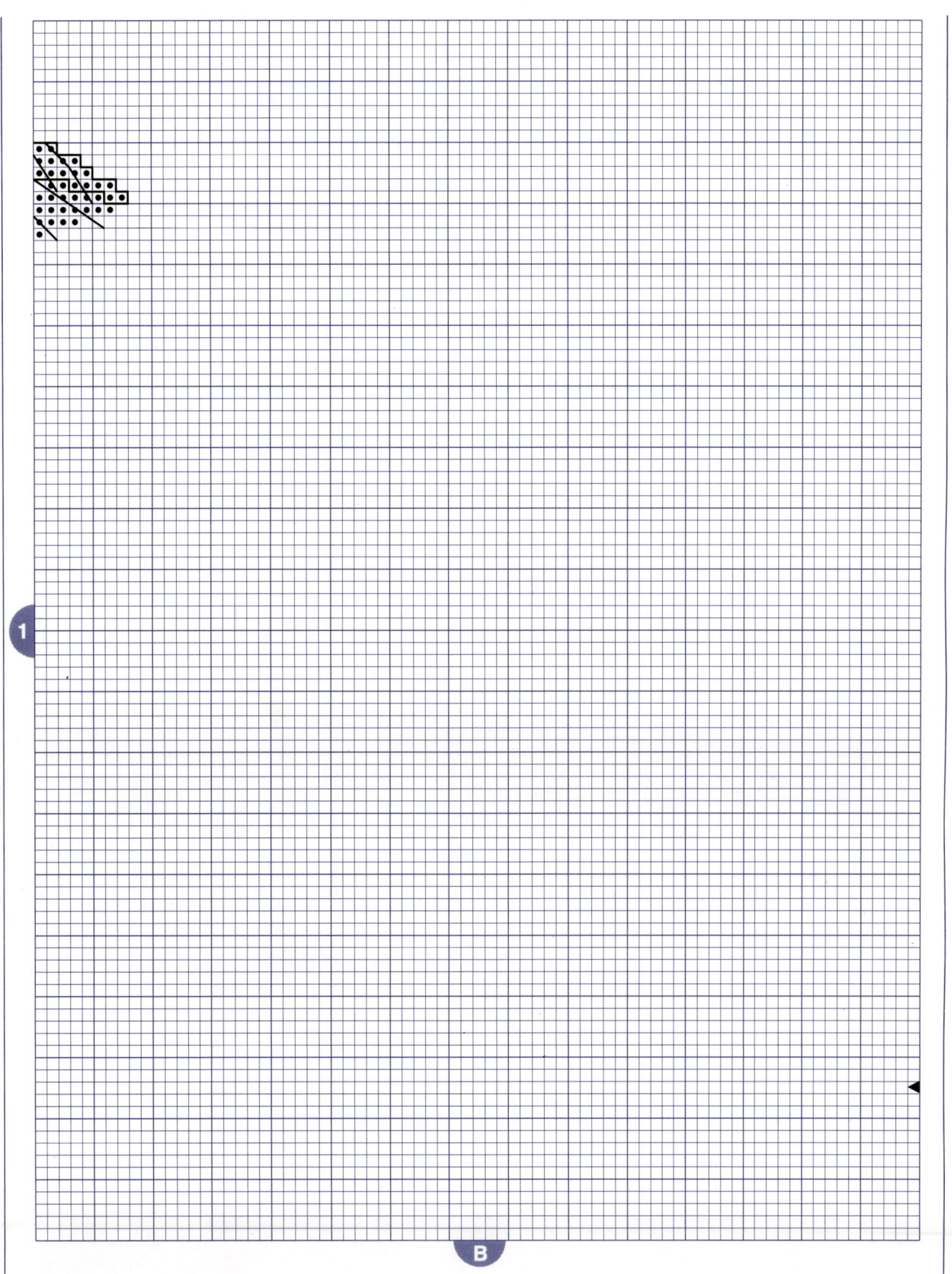

Backstitch hairpins and sandal strap with 2 strands of 676.
Backstitch eyes, brows and sleeve motif with 1 strand of black.
Backstitch mouth with 2 strands of 666 or any red.
Backstitch line at the front of the ear with 2 strands of black.
All other backstitching should be done with 1 strand of 535.

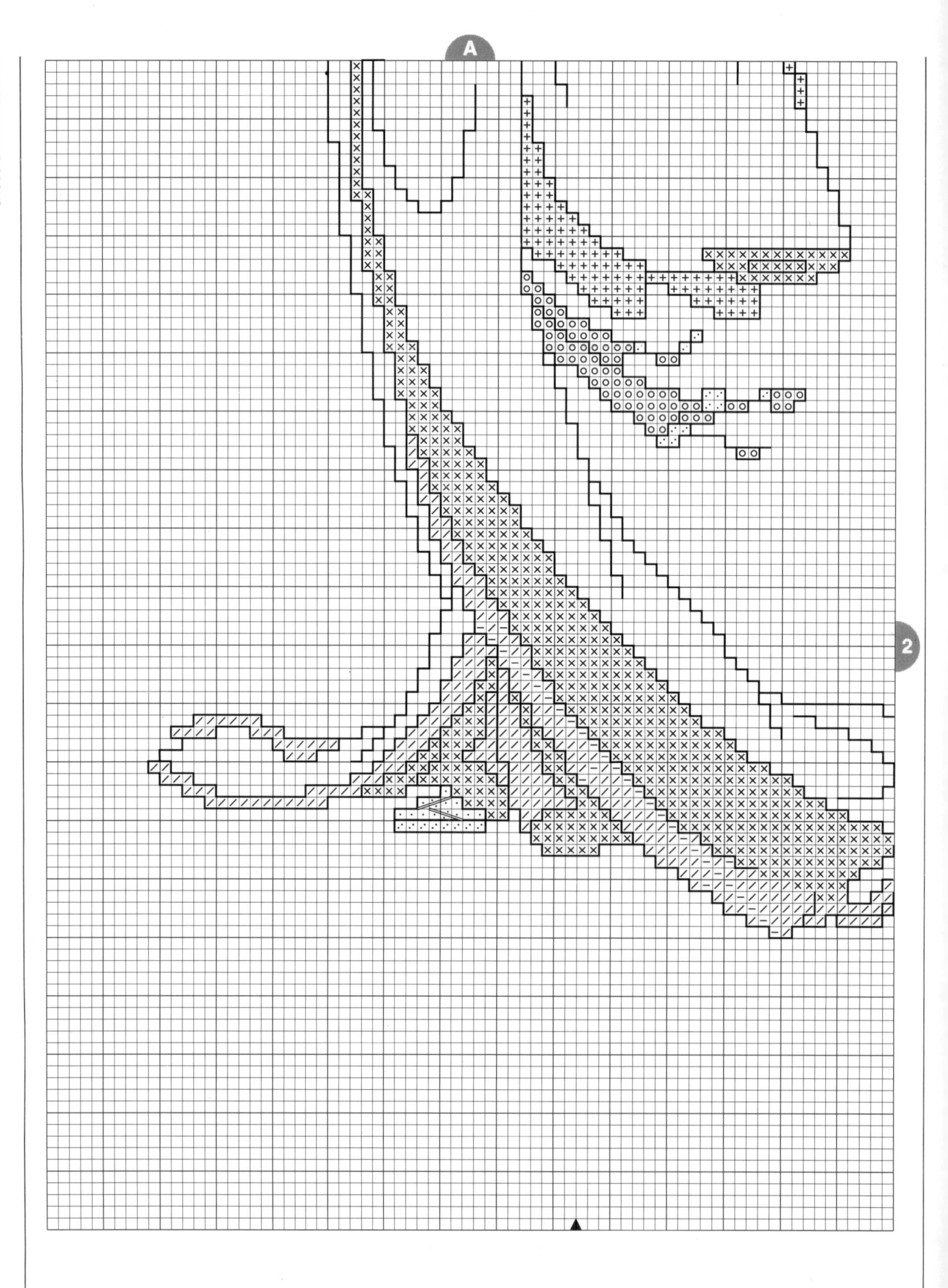

CROSS STITCH DESIGNS

48 | IPPITSUSAI

JAPANESE FASHIONS

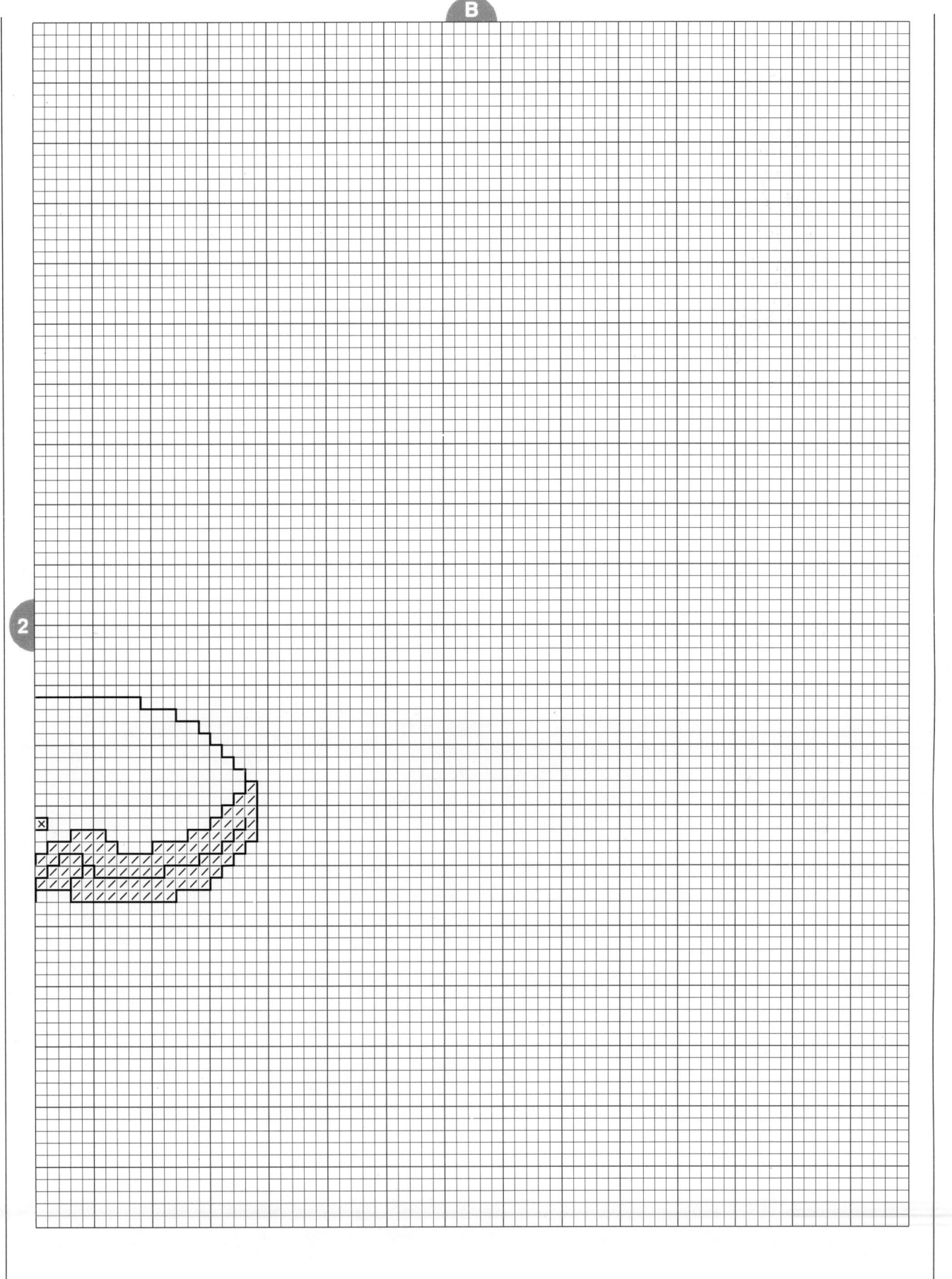

Eiri (1795)

Fabric

Count	Centimetres	Inches
10	55 × 28	22 × 11
14	44 × 25	18 × 10
18	38 × 23	15 × 9
22	33 × 22	13 × 9

This design is 158 stitches high by 51 stitches wide.

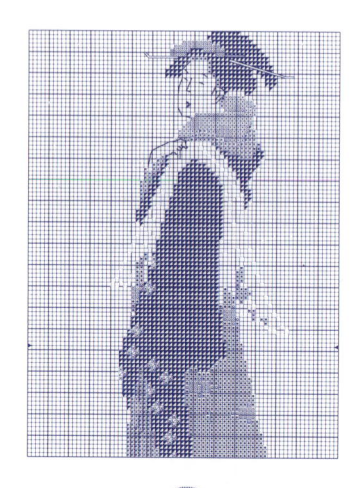

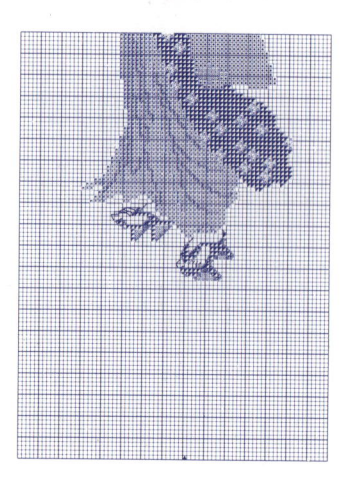

A

Thread

Use two strands throughout for cross stitch. For details of the backstitching see the instructions on the chart.

DMC Art 117   1 skein each of the following.

▼	310	(black)
✱	413	(grey)
•	552	(purple)
×	600	(dark pink)
/	702	(green)
○	726	(yellow)
·	748	(flesh)
ĸ	891	(coral)

Backstitching

▬▬	310	1 strand
▬ ▬	413	1 strand

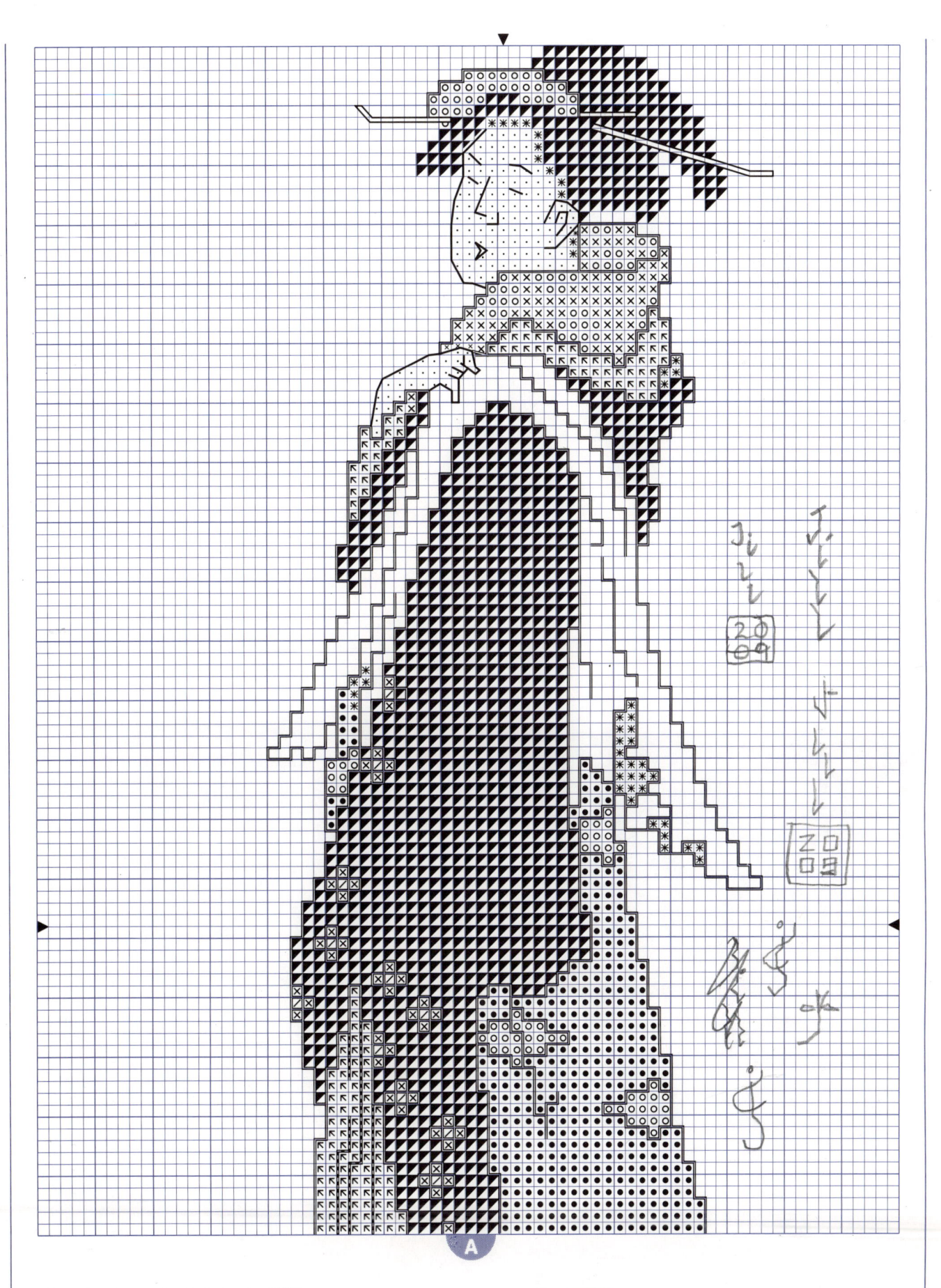

Backstitch the mouth with 2 strands of 600.
Work a long stitch in front of the ear with 2 strands of 310.

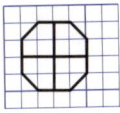

Use this chart to backstitch the yellow flowers on the collar with 1 strand of 600.

JAPANESE FASHIONS

51

Use this chart to backstitch the flowers on the kimono with 1 strand of 310.

Backstitch the eyes and brows with 1 strand of 310.
Backstitch the outline of the flesh with 1 strand of 413.
Use 1 strand for all other backstitching.
If worked on a coloured background, stitch the towel in white.

EIRI

CROSS STITCH DESIGNS

Chobunsai (1794)

Fabric

Count	Centimetres	Inches
10	55 × 38	22 × 15
14	44 × 33	18 × 13
18	38 × 28	15 × 11
22	33 × 25	13 × 10

This design is 159 stitches high by 87 stitches wide.

Thread

Use 2 strands throughout for cross stitch. For details of the backstitching see the instructions on the chart.

DMC Art 117   1 skein each of the following.

▼		310	(black)
✽		317	(grey)
×		318	(light grey)
∕		581	(green) — 372 or 3045
		666	(red)
○		726	(yellow)
−		745 746	(light gold)
·		948	(pink)
●		976	(tan)

Backstitching

═══ 317   1 strand

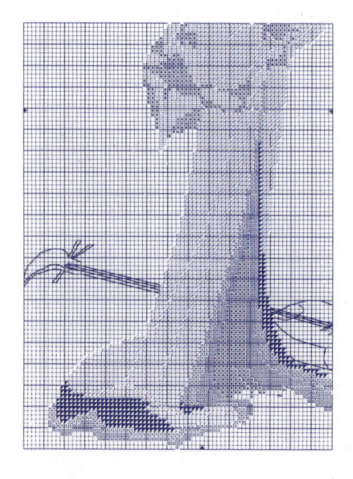

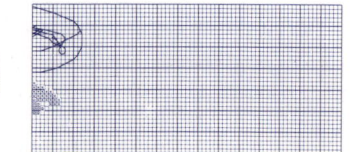

A

1

54

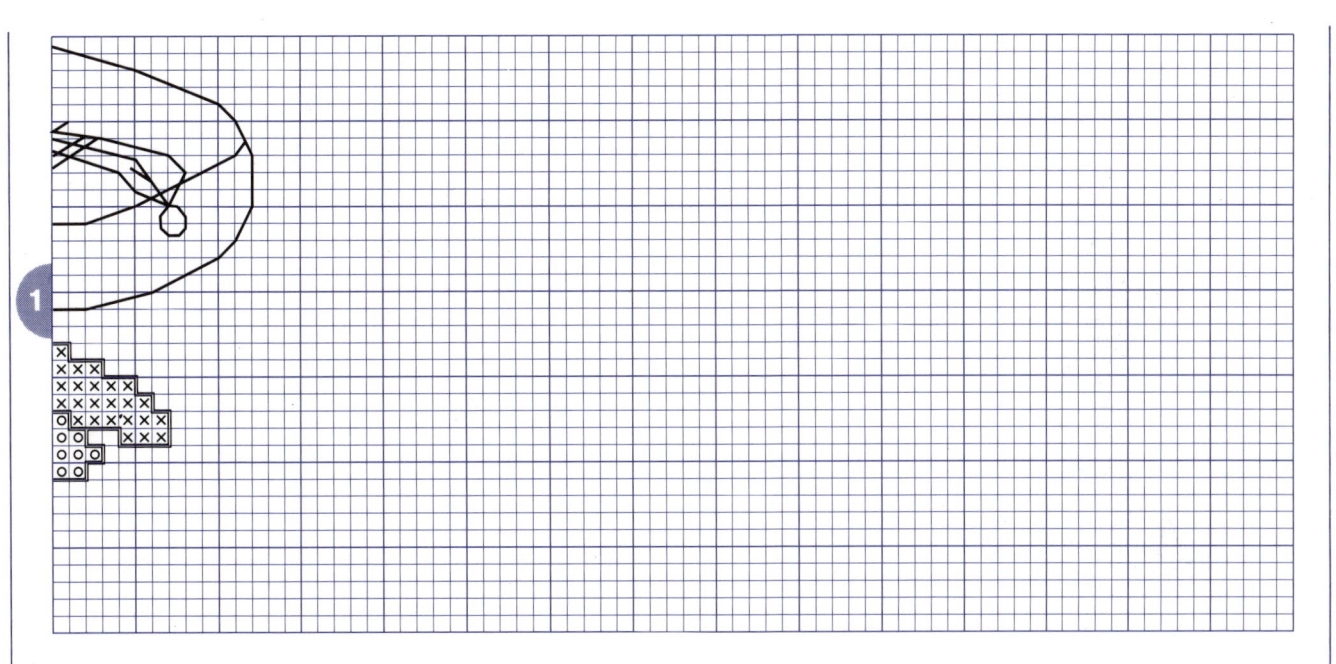

After working the hair, backstitch the hairpins using 2 strands of 726.
Backstitch eyes and brows using 2 strands of black.
Backstitch the mouth using 2 strands of 666 or any red.
All other backstitching should be done with 1 strand of 317.

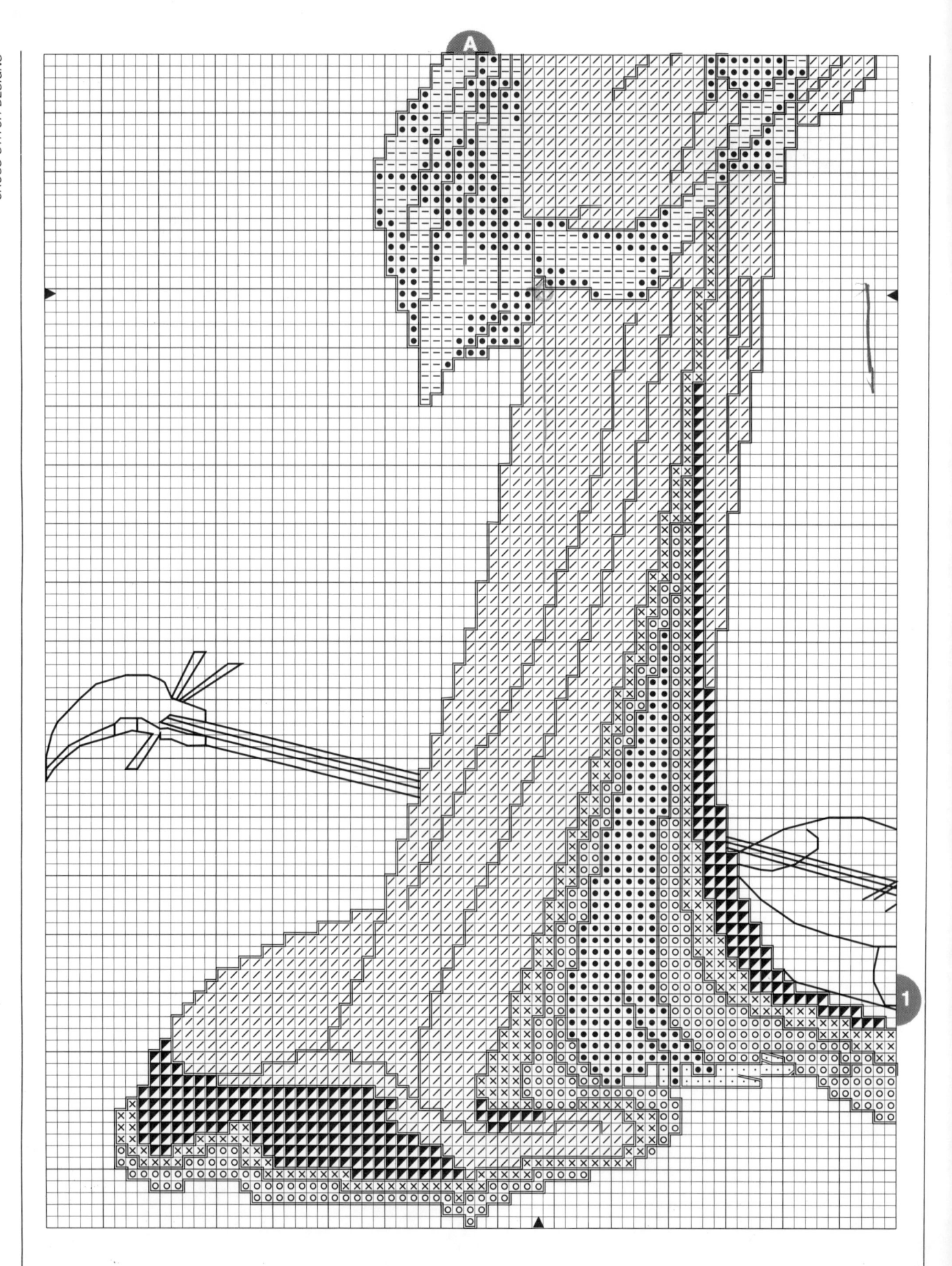

After completing the kimono, overstitch the black areas with 2 strands of 948 in random circles.

CHOBUNSAI

CROSS STITCH DESIGNS

Torii (1762–3)

Fabric

Count	Centimetres	Inches
10	55 × 41	22 × 16
14	44 × 33	18 × 13
18	38 × 29	15 × 12
22	33 × 26	13 × 11

This design is 160 stitches high by 100 stitches wide.

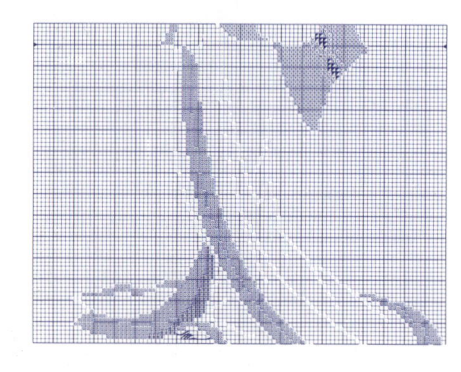

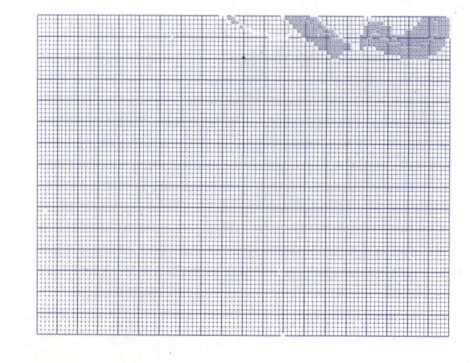

A

B

Thread

Use 2 strands throughout for cross stitch except for colour 975 (see below). For details of the backstitching see the instructions on the chart.

DMC Art 117   1 skein each of the following.

—	○	210	(mauve)
↘	▼	310	(black)
↘	•	414	(grey)
—	φ	552	(purple)
—		666	(red)
↘	v	729	(gold)
—	·	948	(pink)
—	×	975	(brown) 2 strands
—	∕	975	(brown) 1 strand

Backstitching

——	414	v	1 strand
══	310	v	1 strand

58

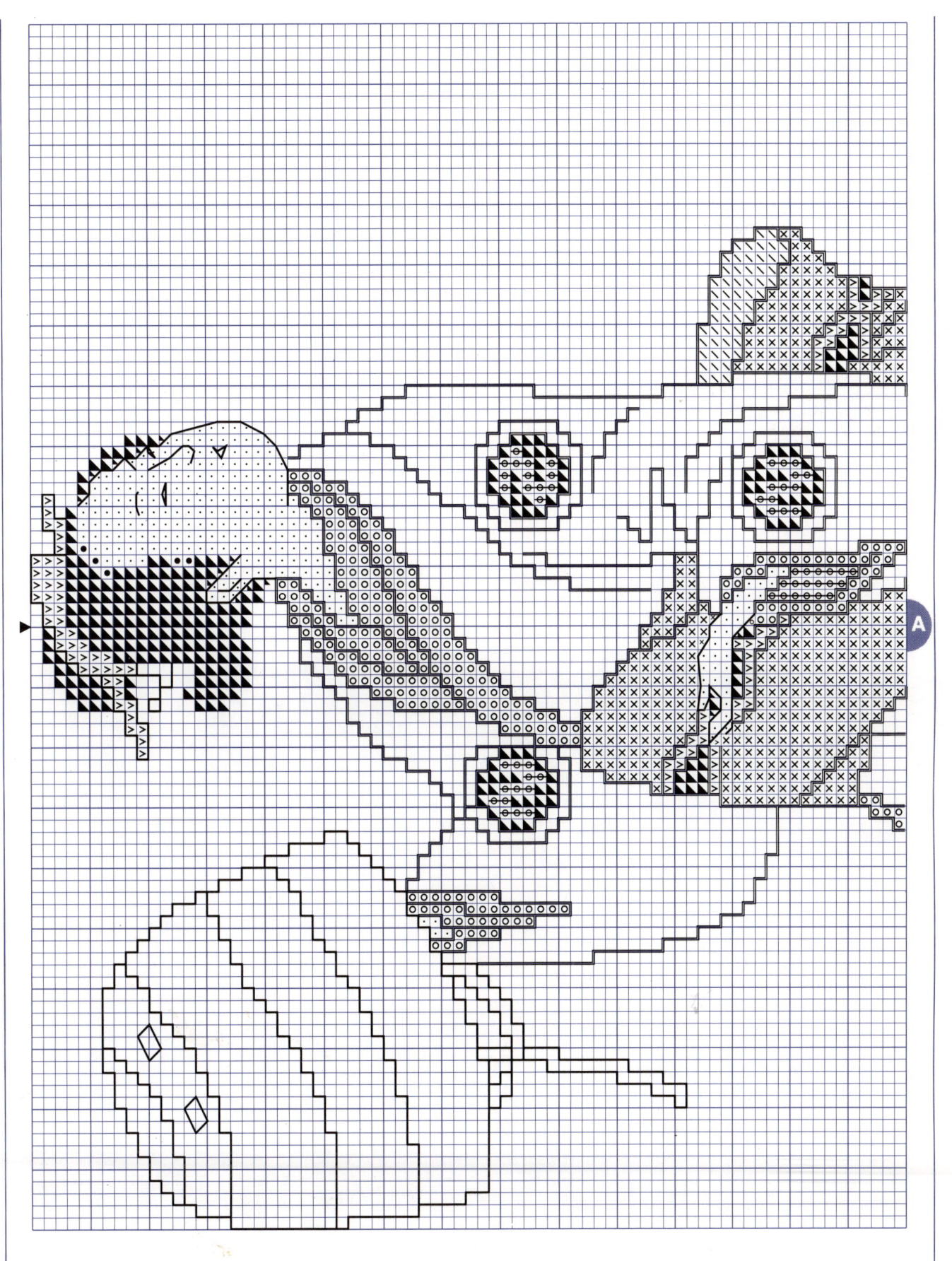

Backstitch mouth with 2 strands of 666.
Backstitch fan, mask, ribbons, head-dress, inside of ear, nose, face and foot
   with 1 strand of 414.
All other backstitching should be done with 1 strand of 310.

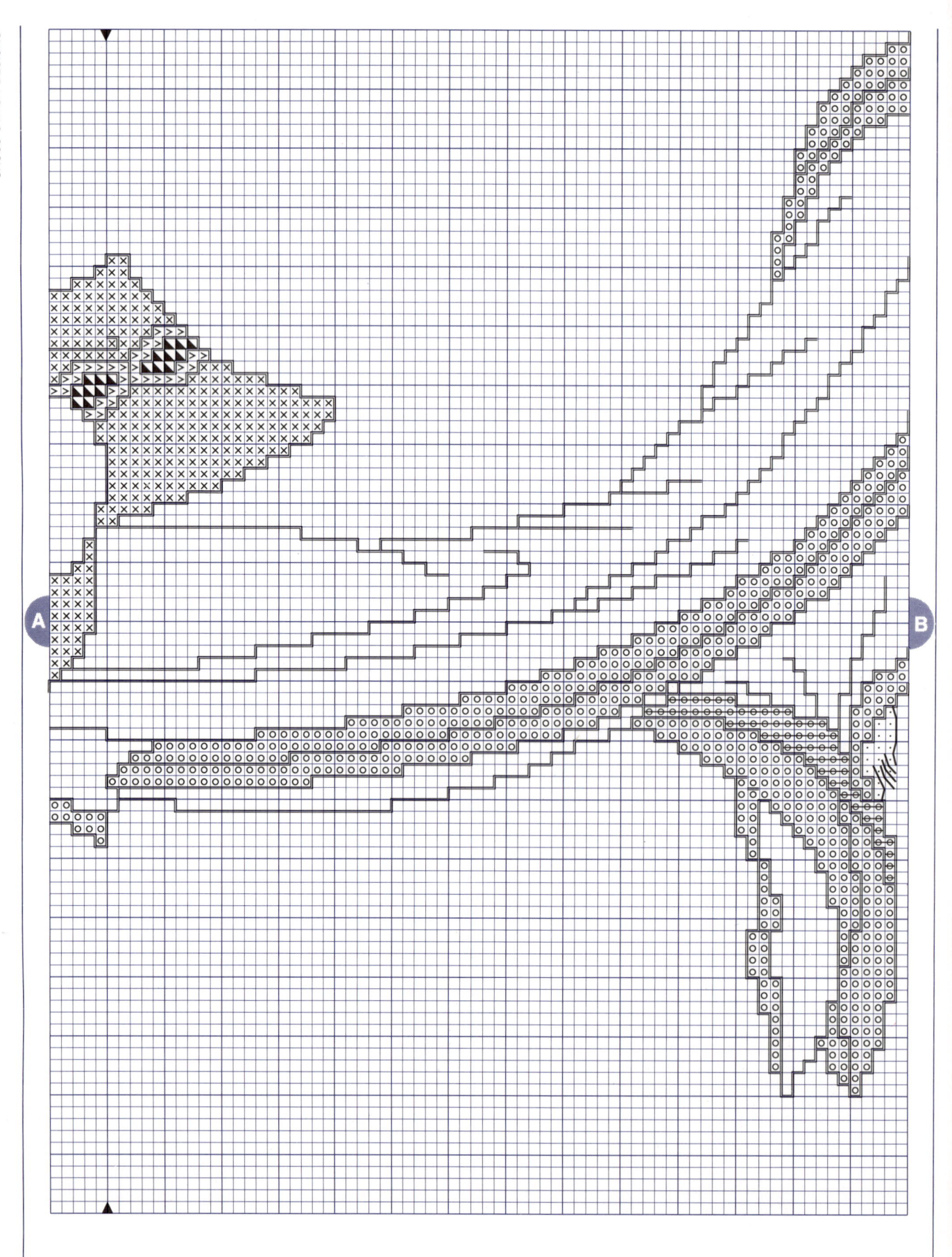

CROSS STITCH DESIGNS

A　　　　　　　　　　　　　　　　　　　　　　　　　　　　　　　　B

60　TORII

JAPANESE FASHIONS

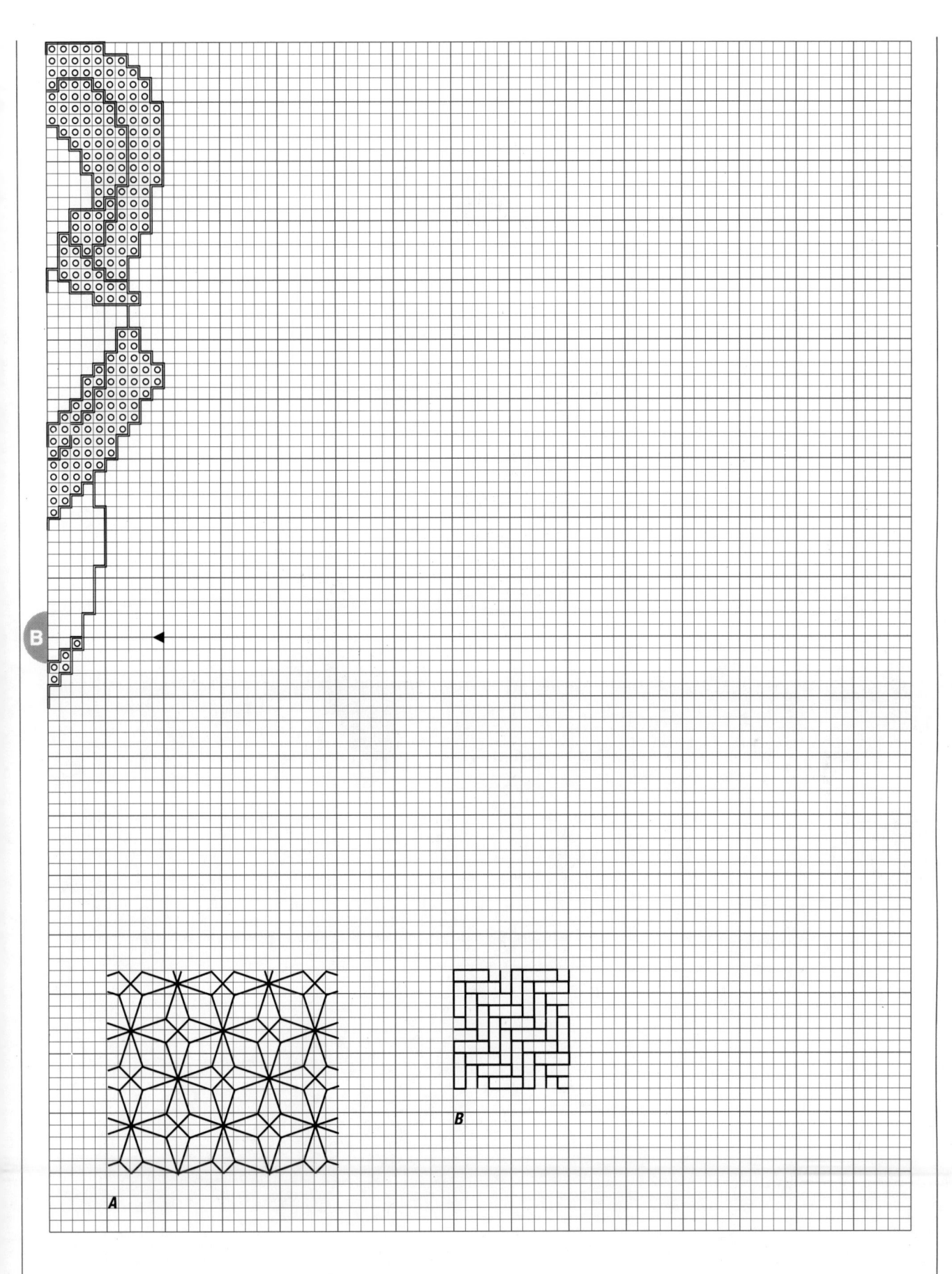

Fill the robe entirely with pattern **A** above using 1 strand of 414, but leaving a single row around the black circular designs blank. Also leave the bottom central area blank. After completing the backstitching on the fan and mask, completely fill the area with the basket-weave pattern **B** above using 1 strand of 729.

TORII

Kaigetsudo (1714)

Fabric

Count	Centimetres	Inches
10	58 × 35	23 × 14
14	45 × 30	18 × 12
18	40 × 26	16 × 11
22	34 × 25	14 × 10

This design is 166 stitches high by 81 stitches wide.

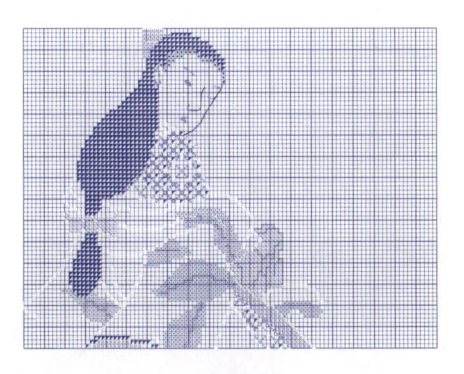

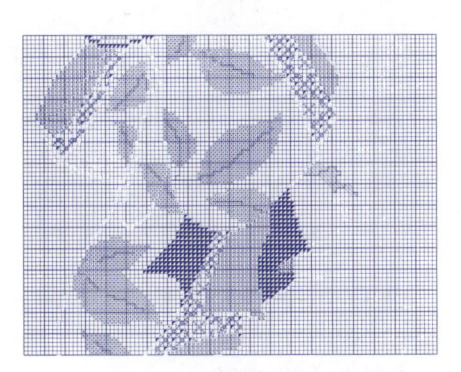

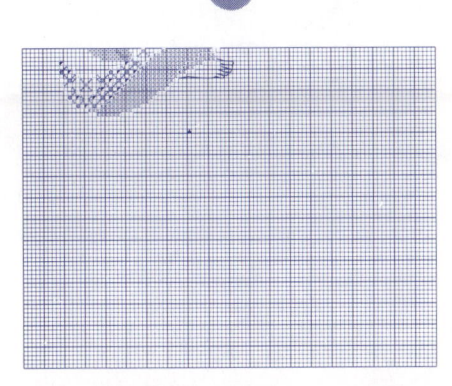

A

B

Thread

Use two strands throughout for cross stitch. For details of the backstitching see the instructions on the chart.

DMC Art 117   1 skein each of the following.

⌄	◤	310	(black)
⌄	×	414	(grey)
—	v	415	(light grey)
⌄	\	504	(very light green)
⌄	c	597	(turquoise)
—	o	608	(vermilion)
—		666	(red)
⌄	∧	725	(gold)
⌄	•	844	(very dark grey)
	·	948	(pink)

Backstitching

———	414	1 strand
═══	310	1 strand

JAPANESE FASHIONS

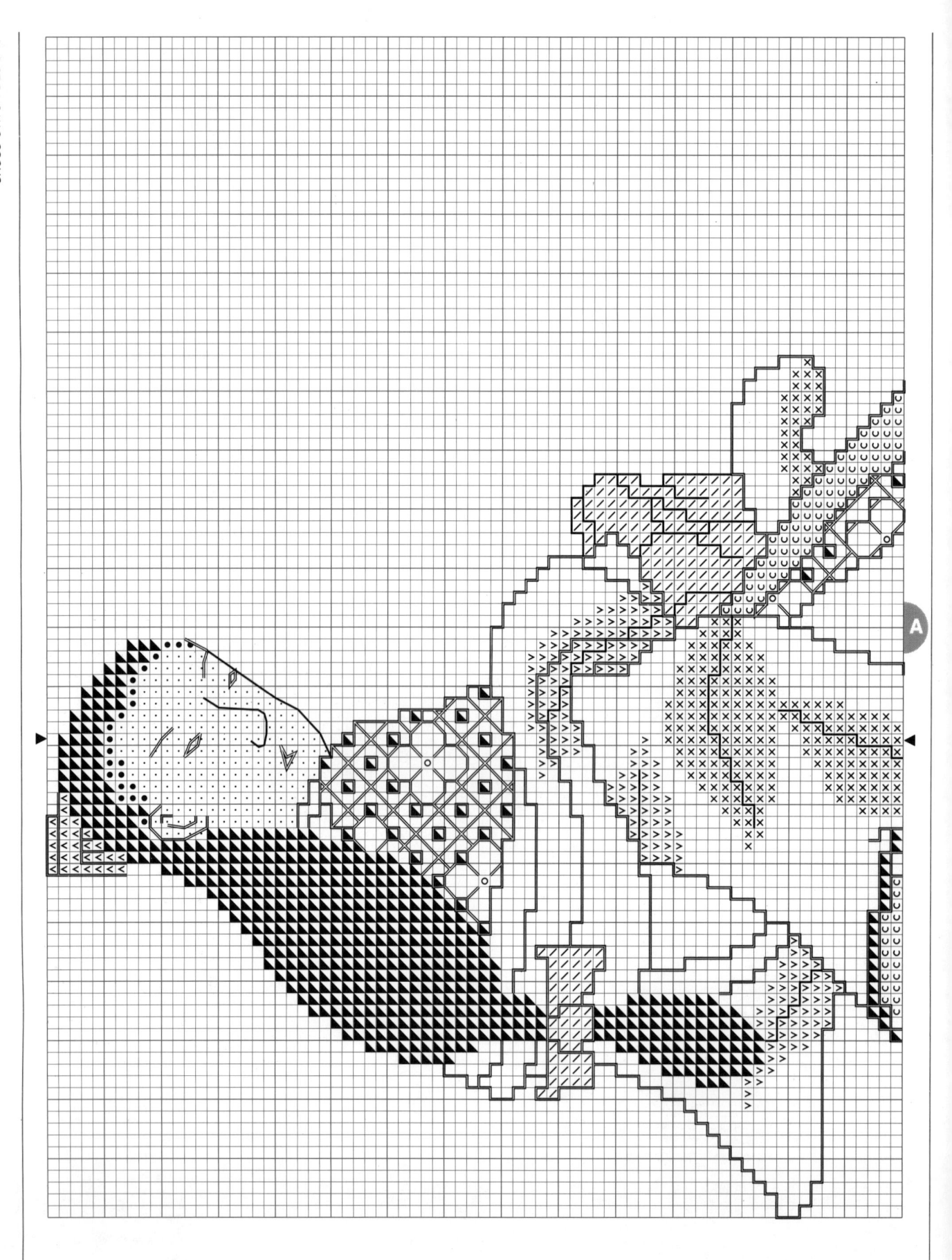

CROSS STITCH DESIGNS

64 KAIGETSUDO

JAPANESE FASHIONS

65

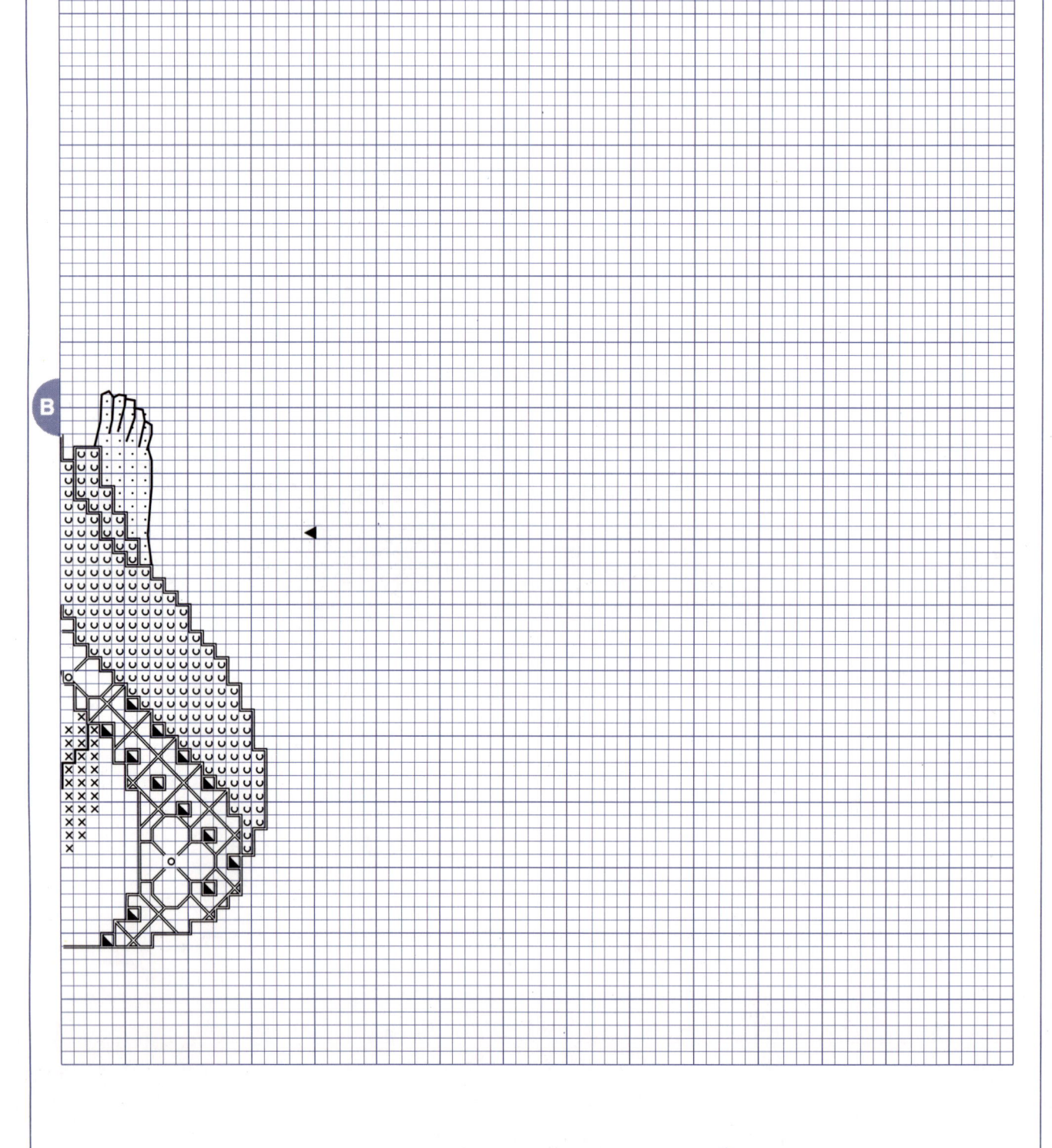

Backstitch mouth with 2 strands of 666 or any other red.
Backstitch ear, eyes and brows with 1 strand of 310.
Backstitch face outline, nose, foot and very light green area of robe with 1 strand of 414.

KAIGETSUDO

CROSS STITCH DESIGNS

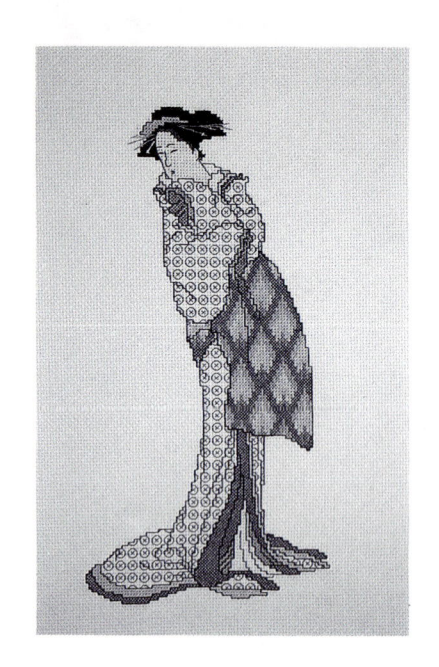

Kitao (1783)

Fabric

Count	Centimetres	Inches
10	55 × 34	22 × 14
14	44 × 29	18 × 12
18	38 × 25	15 × 10
22	34 × 24	14 × 10

This design is 160 stitches high by 74 stitches wide.

Thread

Use 2 strands throughout for cross stitch. For details of the backstitching see the instructions on the chart.

DMC Art 117   1 skein each of the following.

\		white	
▼		310	(black)
+		315	(dark rose)
•		414	(grey)
×		562	(teal)
—		666	(red)
○		704	(green)
v		729	(gold)
/		761	(light pink)
—		778	(rose)
·		948	(very light pink)
^		3041	(mauve)

Backstitching

—— 414   1 strand
—— 310   1 strand

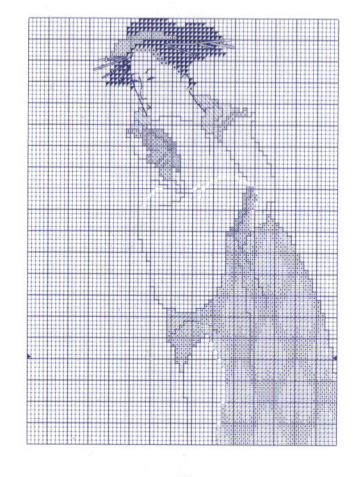

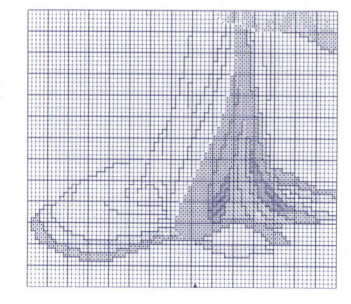

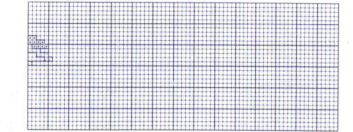

A

1

68

JAPANESE FASHIONS

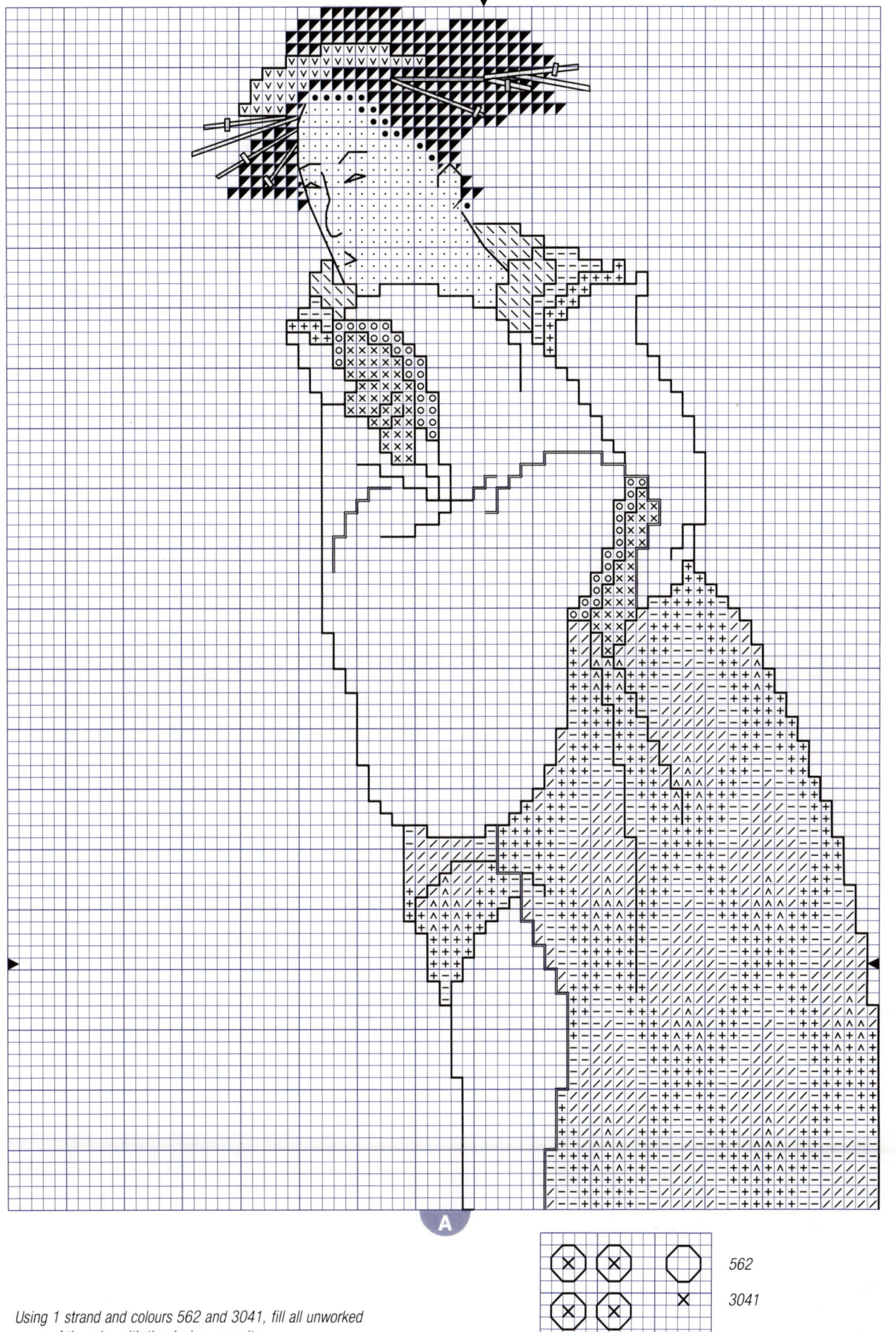

Using 1 strand and colours 562 and 3041, fill all unworked areas of the robe with the design opposite.

562
3041

69

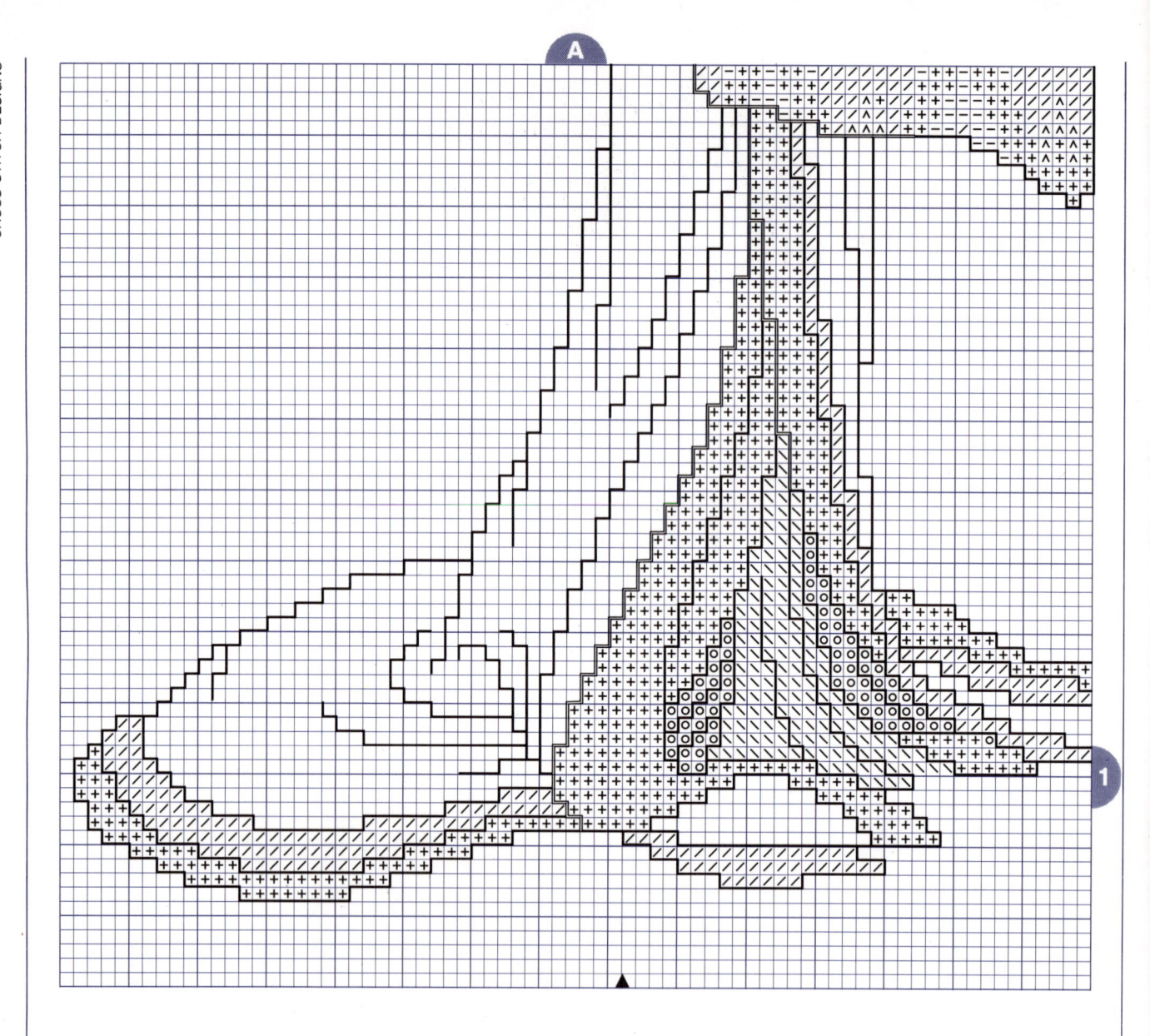

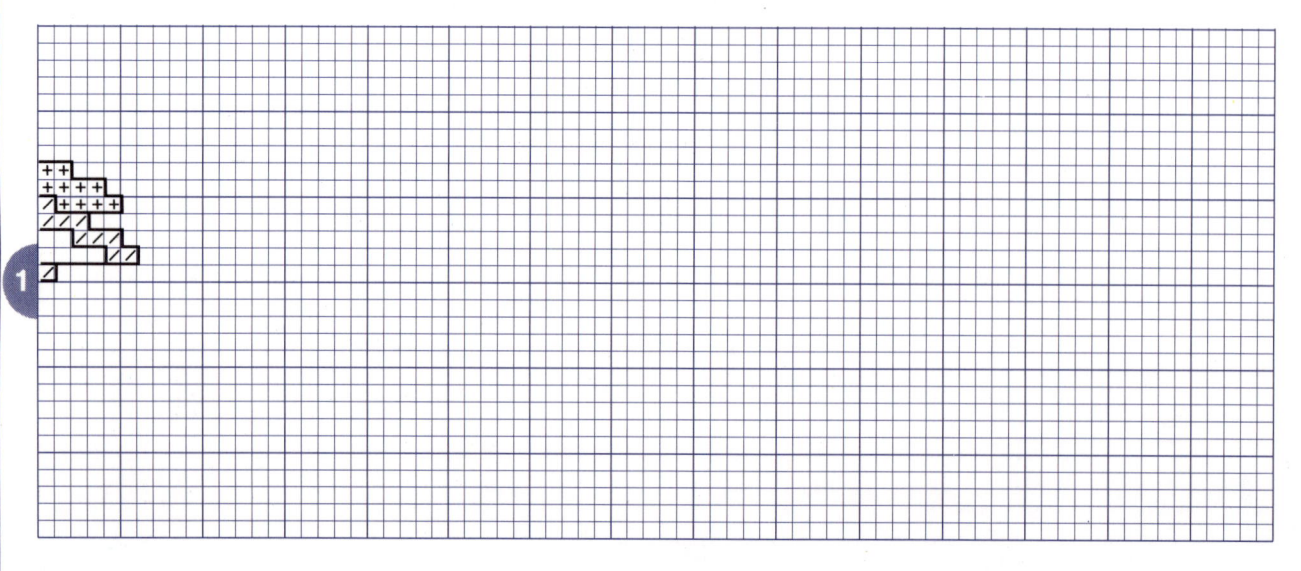

Backstitch the hairpins with 2 strands of 729.
Backstitch the mouth with 2 strands of 666.
Backstitch the eyes and brows with 1 strand of 310.
Backstitch the nose, lower face and nape of neck with 1 strand of 414.
Use 1 strand for all other backstitching.

KITAO

CROSS STITCH DESIGNS

FRENCH FASHIONS, 1913

On a recent visit to Paris I discovered a quaint little shop across the street from Notre Dame Cathedral. While sorting through the assorted tourist trash I came across a range of postcards featuring the fashions of 1913. Their appeal was immediate, and I bought several. Although they are fabulously French, I have chosen to name them after some of the women who have played a big part in my life.

Lucy Ellen

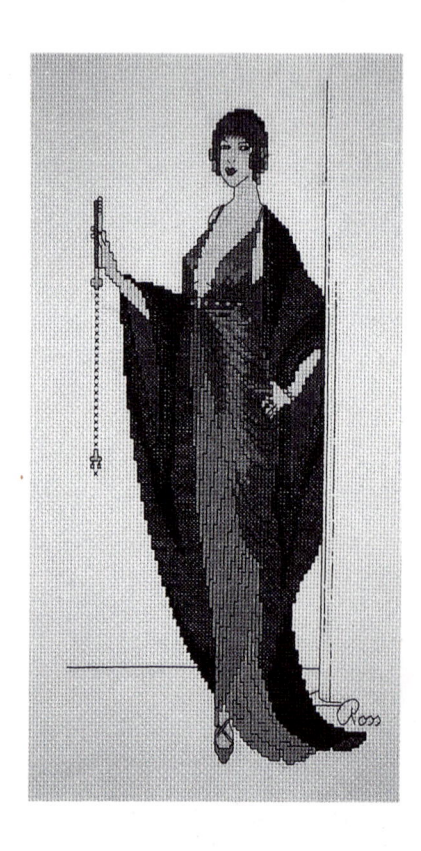

Fabric

Count	Centimetres	Inches
10	60 × 36	24 × 15
14	46 × 30	19 × 12
18	41 × 26	16 × 11
22	35 × 30	14 × 10

This design is 177 stitches high by 83 stitches wide.

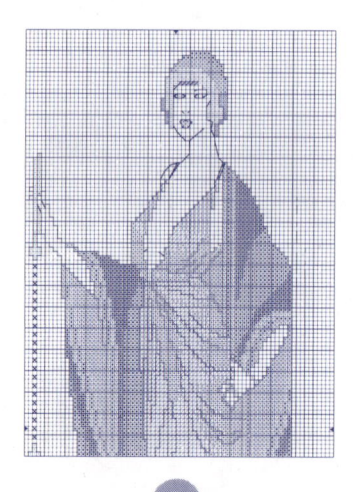

A

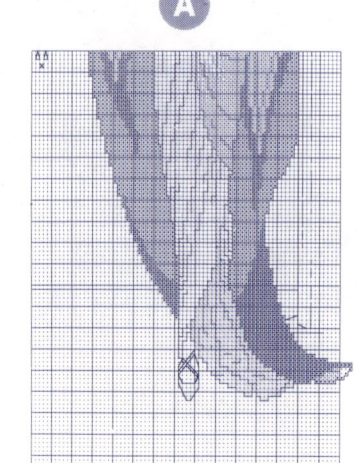

Thread

Use two strands throughout for cross stitch. For details of the backstitching see the instructions on the chart.

DMC Art 117   1 skein each of the following.

—	o	414	(grey)
—	—	434	(brown)
↙	\	471	(green)
—	×	498	(burgundy)
—	•	550	(purple)
—	ı	726	(yellow)
↙	+	732	(dark olive)
↙	c	733	(olive)
↙	/	734	(light olive)
↙		844	(dark pewter)
	•	948	(flesh)
	v	991	(teal)

Backstitching

——   844   1 strand

72

FRENCH FASHIONS

73

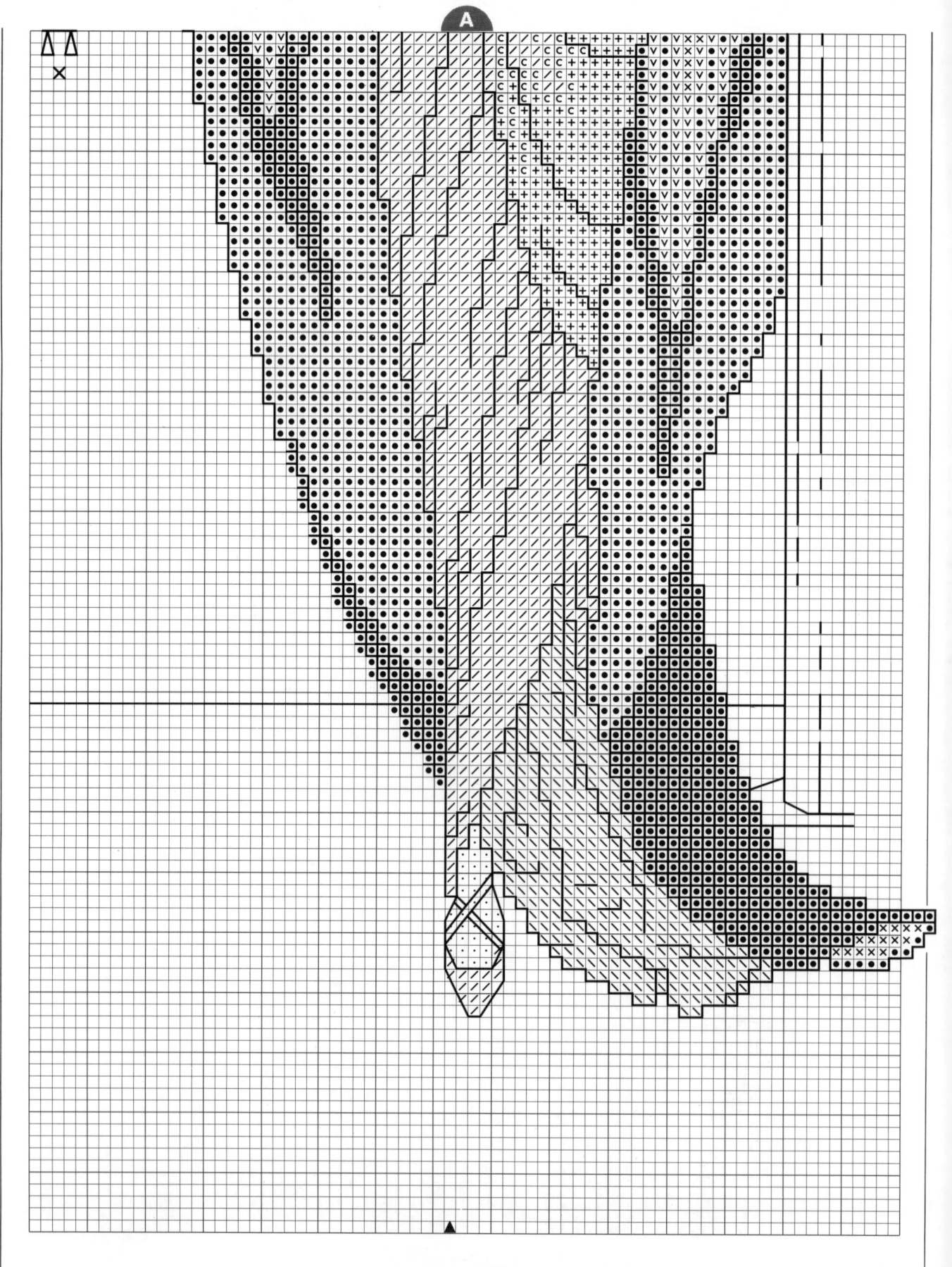

The areas shown ⊡ should be worked in cross stitch with 2 strands of 550, then backstitched around each individual cross stitch with 1 strand of 991.
Backstitch shoe straps with 2 strands of 734 and 1 strand of 844 on either side.
Backstitch fringe with 2 strands of 434 in the direction shown on the chart over the stitch in 948.

LUCY ELLEN

CROSS STITCH DESIGNS

Stella Adele

Fabric

Count	Centimetres	Inches
10	58 × 40	23 × 16
14	45 × 33	18 × 13
18	38 × 28	15 × 11
22	35 × 26	14 × 11

This design is 168 stitches high and 94 stitches wide.

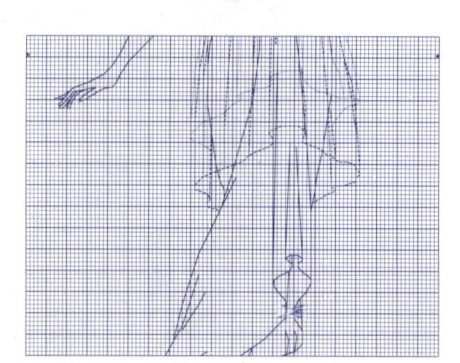

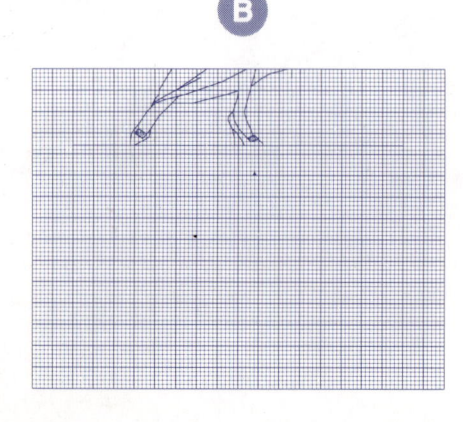

Thread

Use two strands throughout for cross stitch and one strand for backstitching other than the backstitching indicated by a double line, which should be worked with two strands.

DMC Art 117   1 skein each of the following.

	318	(light grey)
×	400	(brown)
	414	(grey)
T	444	(yellow)
•	844	(dark grey)
o	912	(green)
·	948	(flesh)

Backstitching

——	844	1 strand
═══	844	2 strands
– – –	414	1 strand
······	318	1 strand

A

B

STELLA ADELE

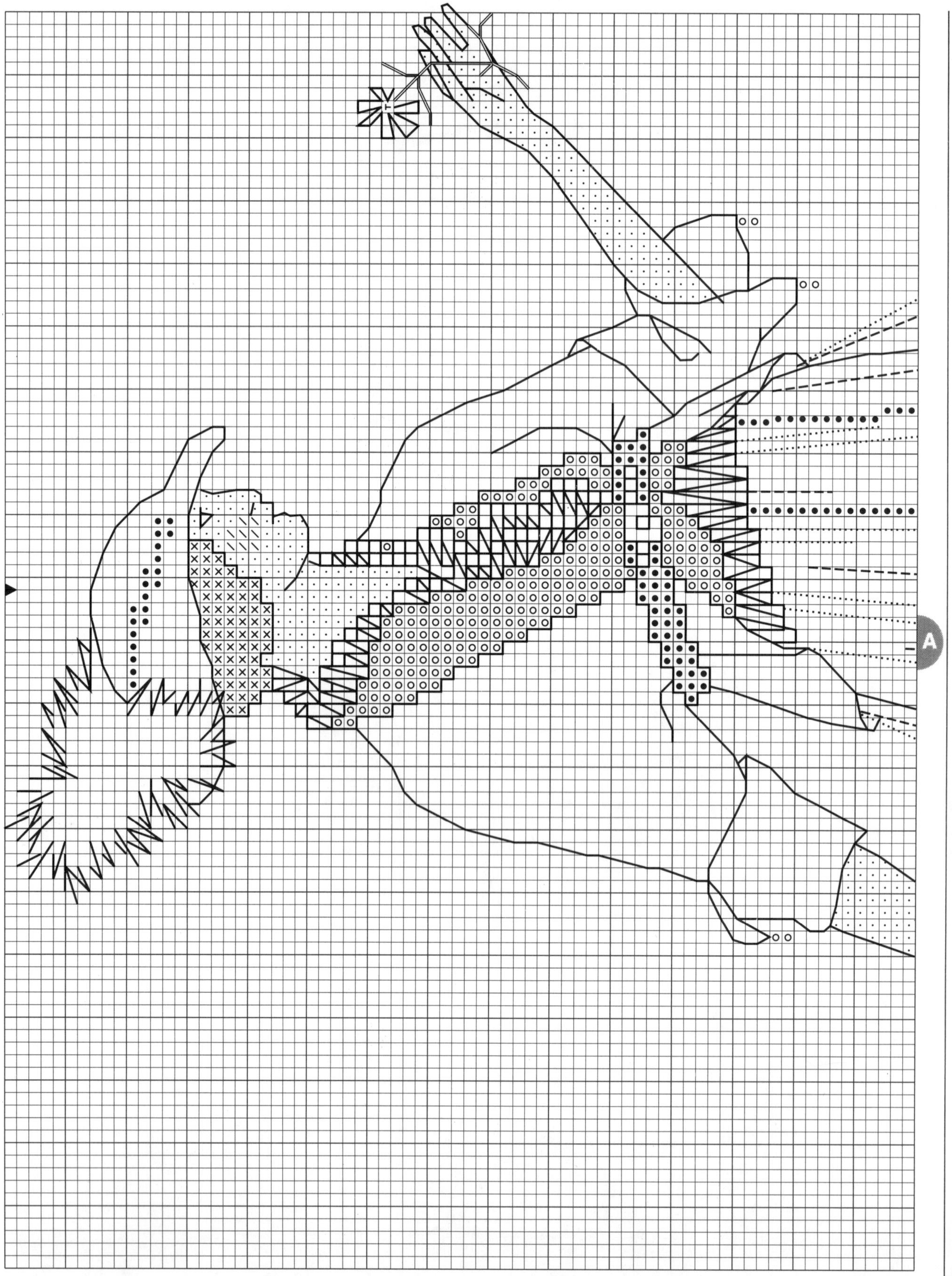
A

FRENCH FASHIONS

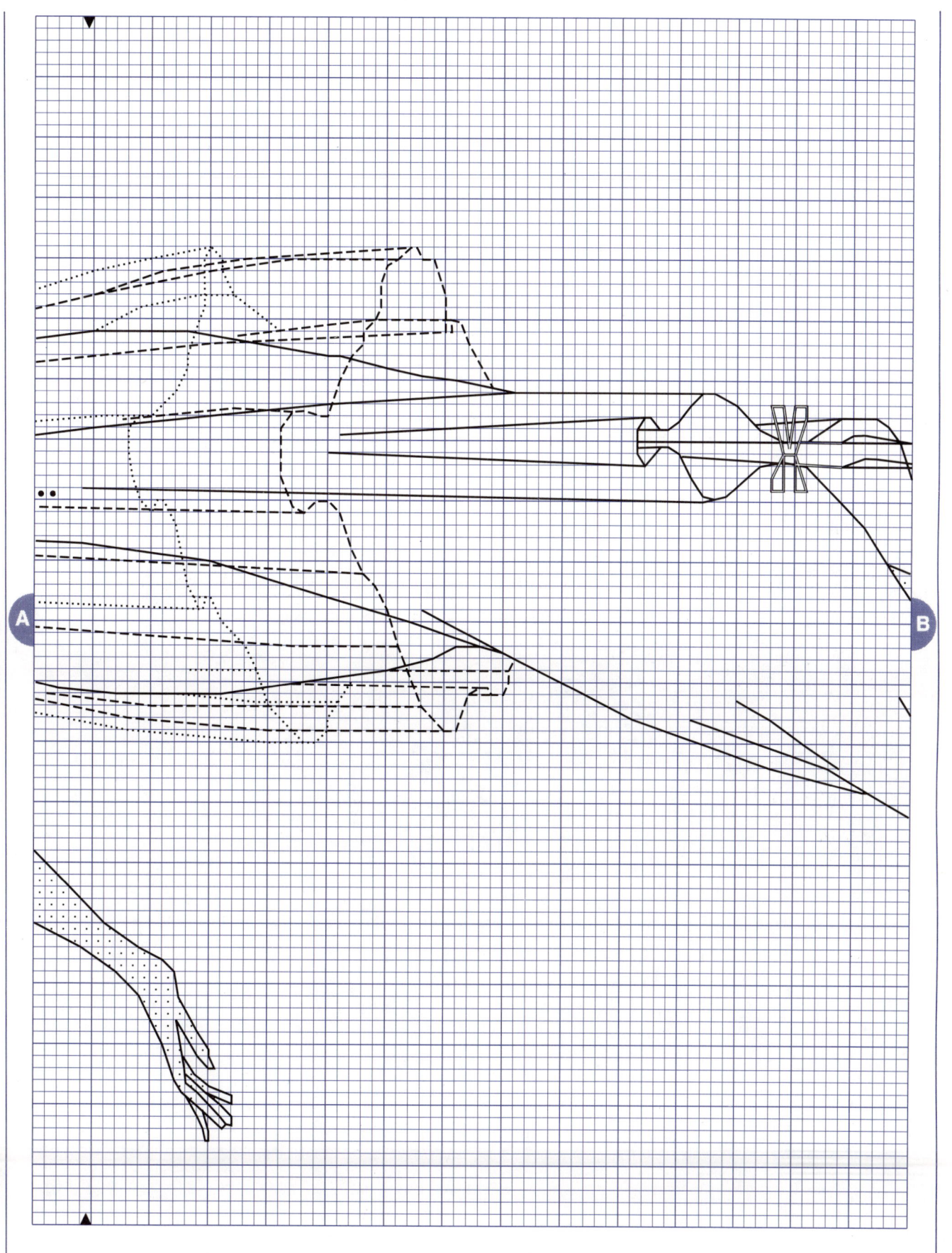

79

STELLA ADELE

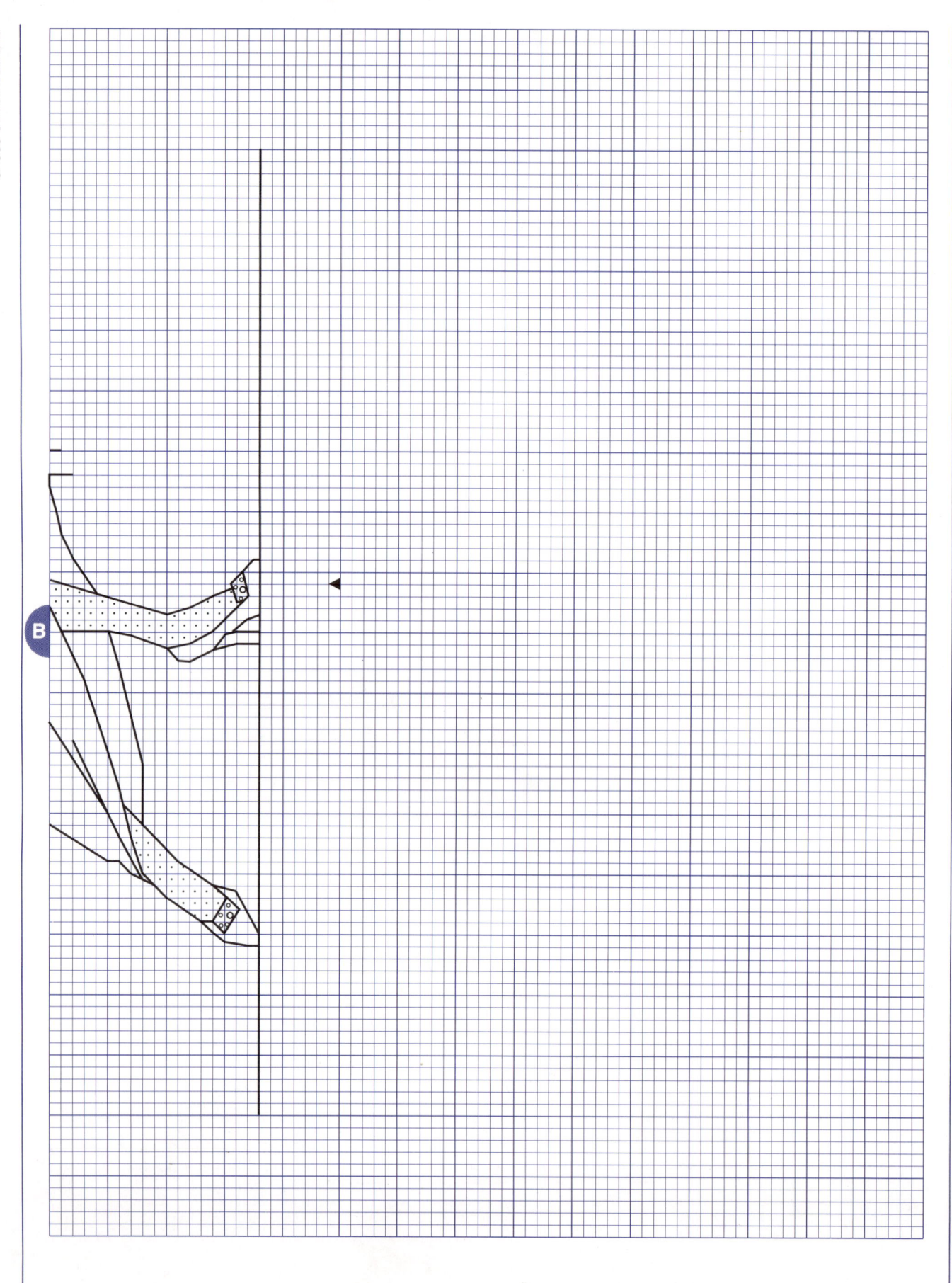

ALICE MAY

CROSS STITCH DESIGNS

Alice May

Fabric

Count	Centimetres	Inches
10	54 × 45	22 × 18
14	45 × 38	18 × 15
18	38 × 33	15 × 13
22	33 × 28	13 × 11

This design is 156 stitches high by 121 stitches wide.

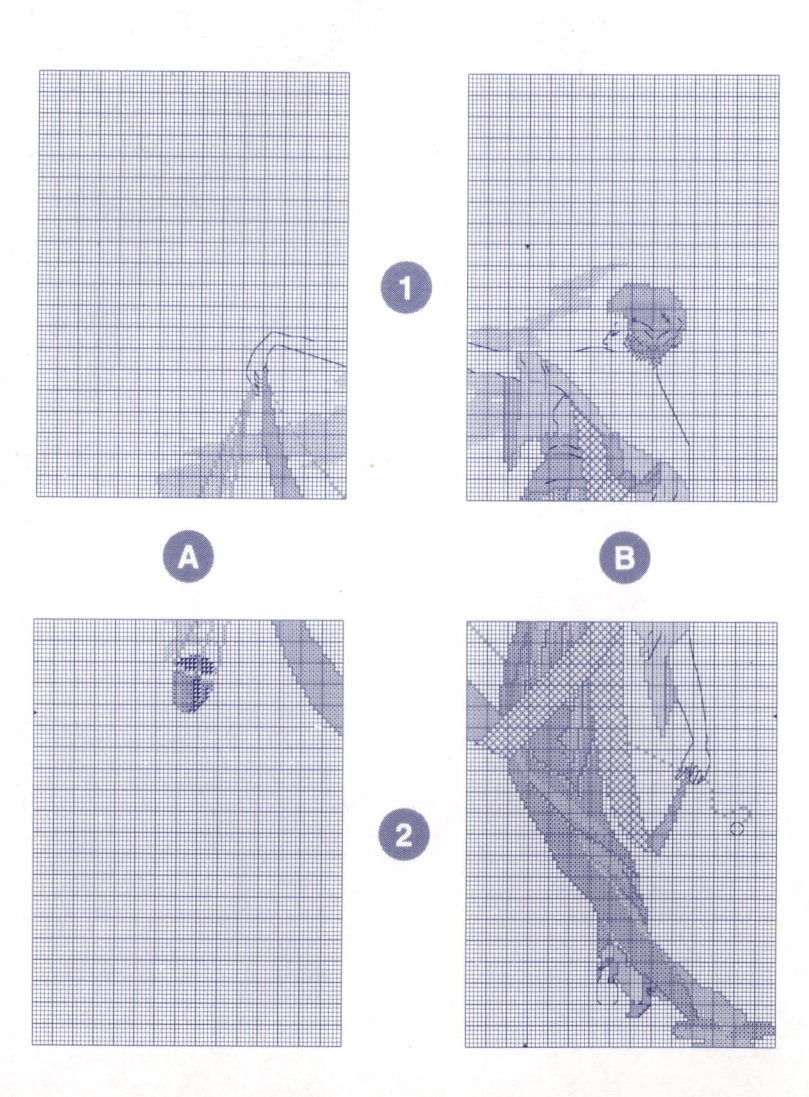

Thread

Use two strands throughout for cross stitch. For details of the backstitching see the instructions on the chart.

DMC Art 117   1 skein each of the following.

∽	–	224	(pink)
∽	.	225	(light pink)
—	c	452	(mushroom)
—	•	550	(dark purple)
—	v	552	(purple)
—	L	553	(light purple)
∽	x	608 355	(vermilion)
∽	o	725	(gold)
—	▼	780	(dark tan)
∽	*	781	(tan)
∽	^	782	(copper)
—	+	783	(dark gold)
∽	/	3072	(smoke)

Backstitching

∽	x	608	(French knot)
			2 strands
∽	/	781	2 strands
—		844	1 strand

82

FRENCH FASHIONS

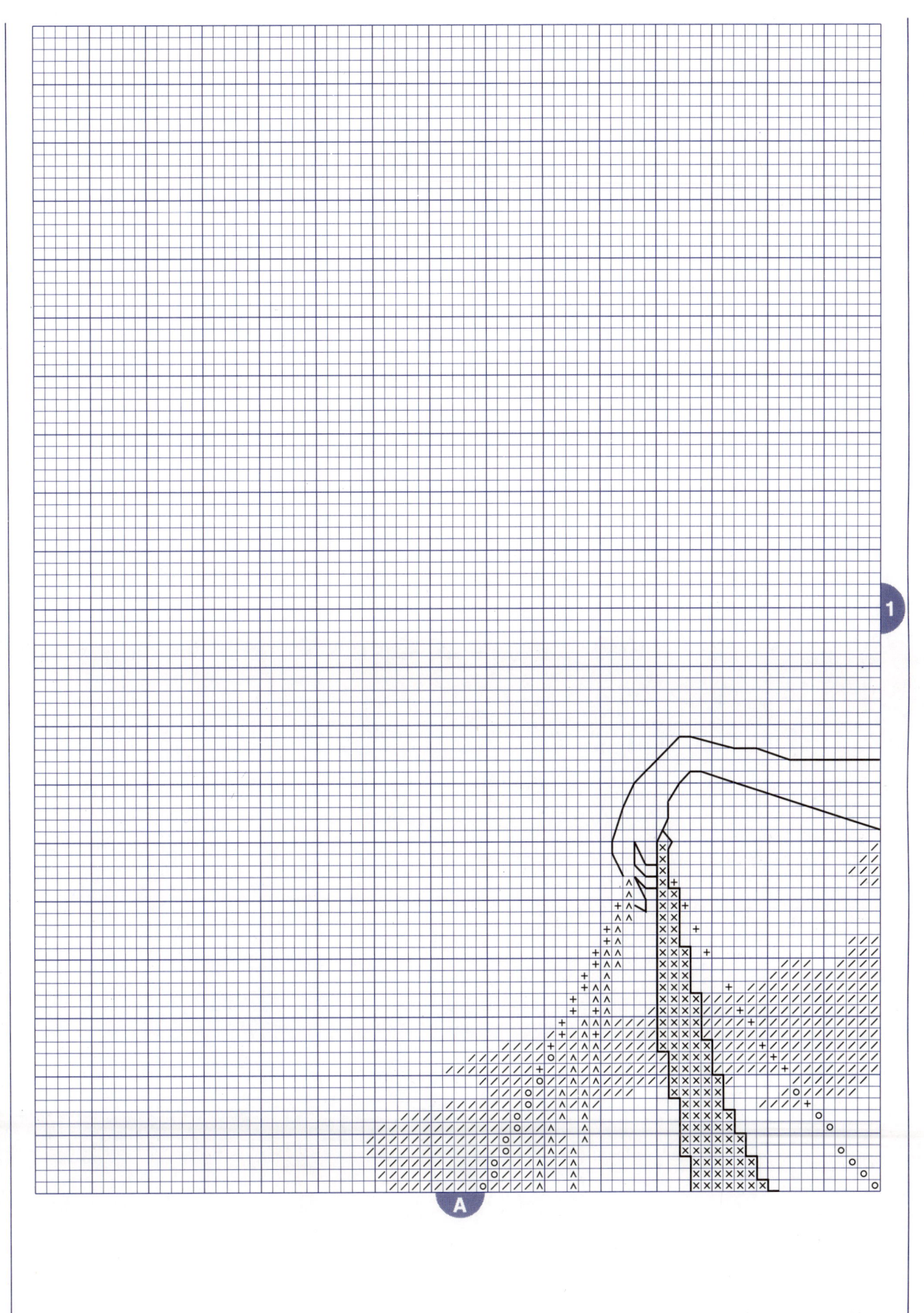

83

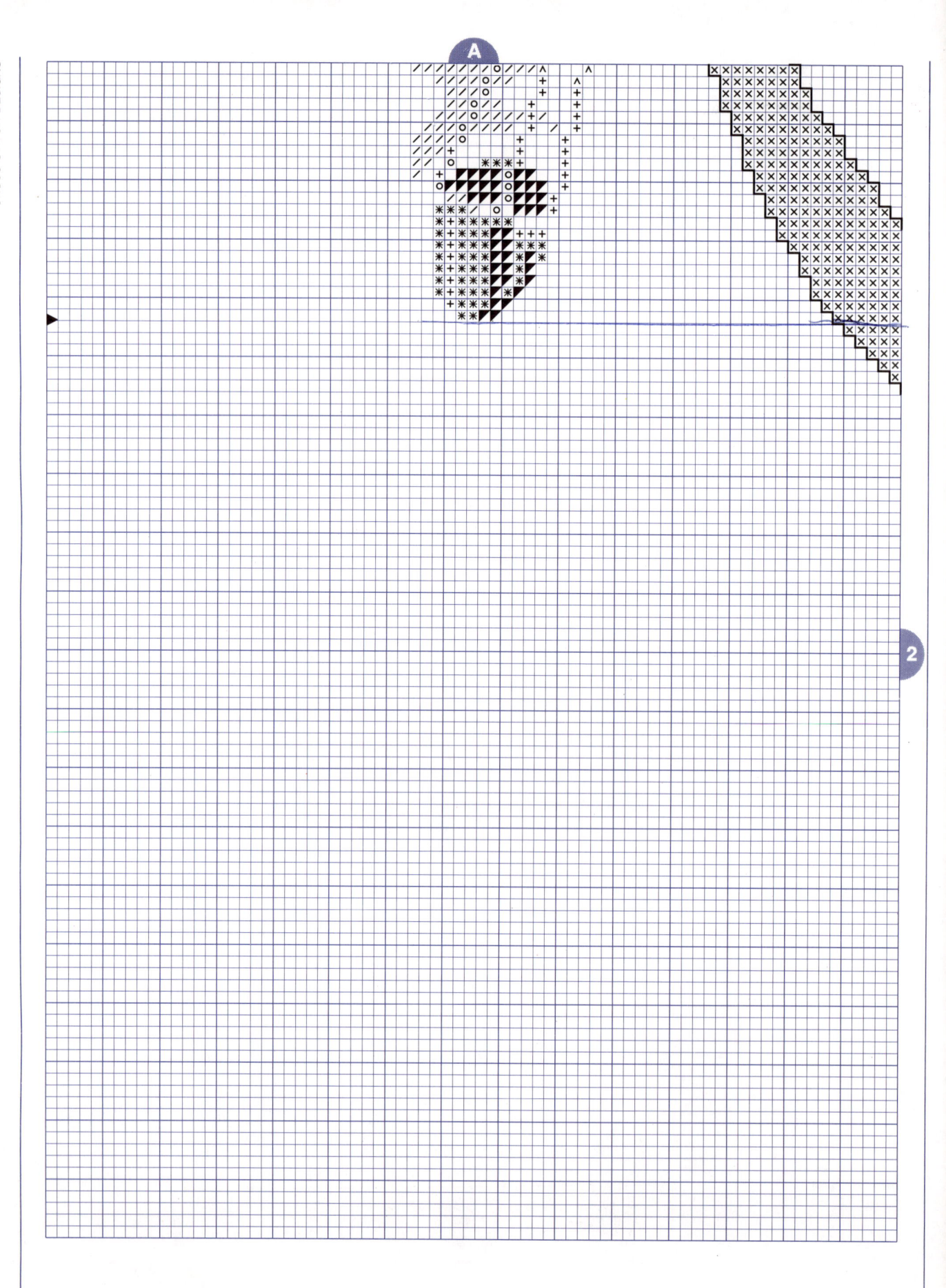

CROSS STITCH DESIGNS

ALICE MAY

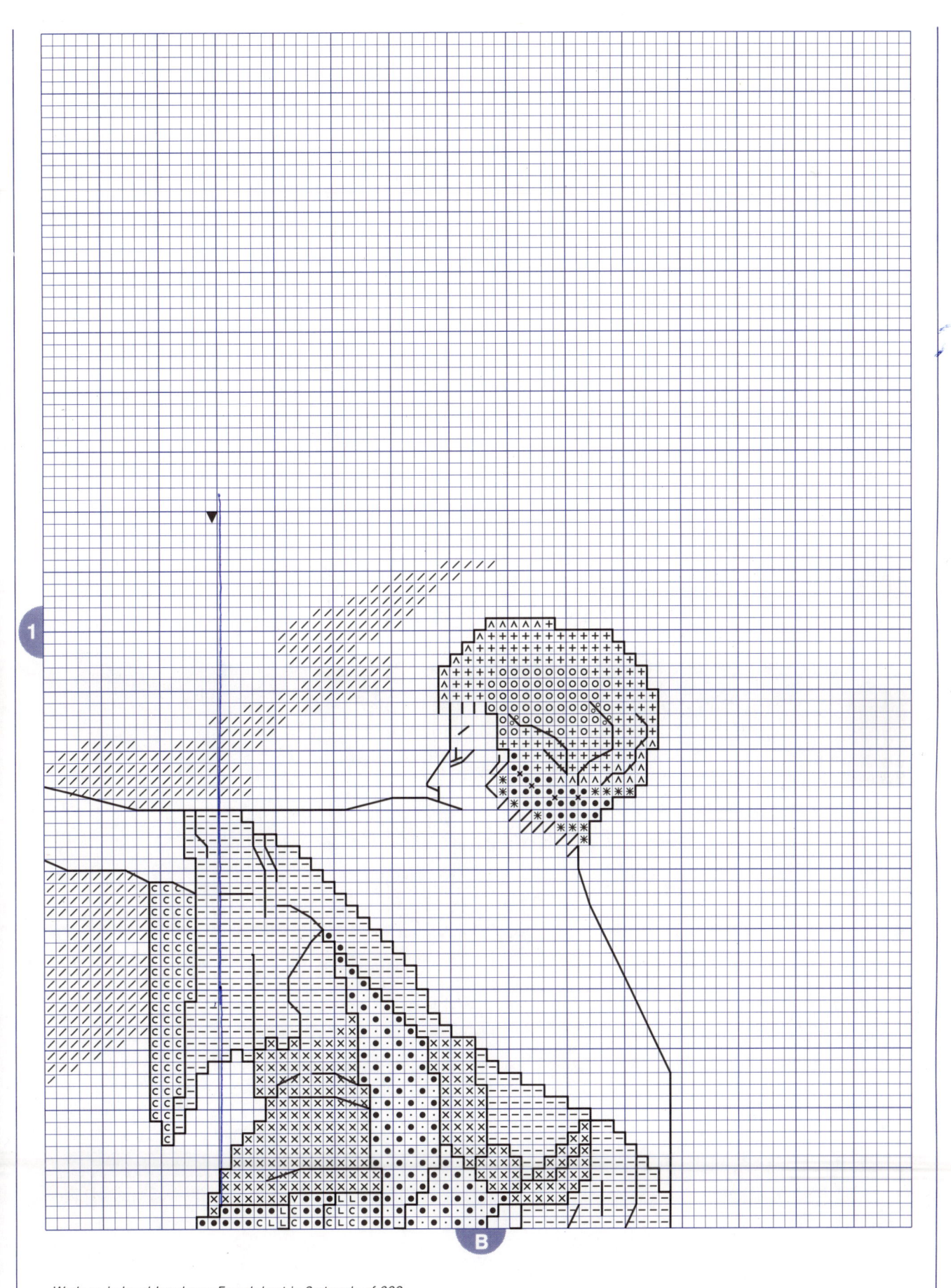

Work × in head-band as a French knot in 2 strands of 608.
Work / at nape of neck in 2 strands of 781.
Stitch ring with 2 strands of 725.
All other backstitching should be done with 1 strand of 844.

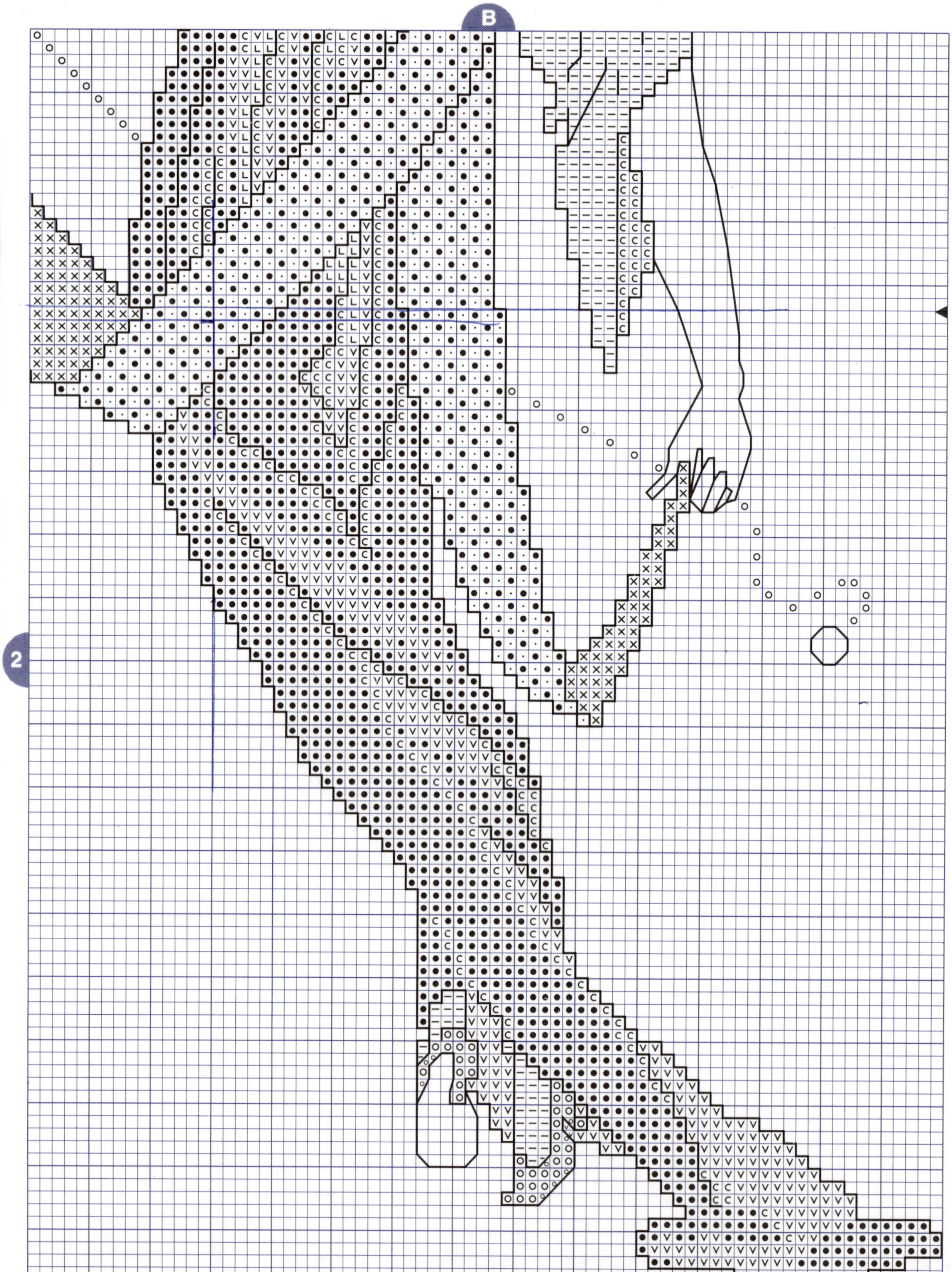
B
2

Lynly Elliott

Fabric

Count	Centimetres	Inches
10	51 × 41	20 × 16
14	41 × 33	16 × 13
18	35 × 29	14 × 12
22	30 × 26	12 × 11

This design is 138 stitches high by 99 stitches wide.

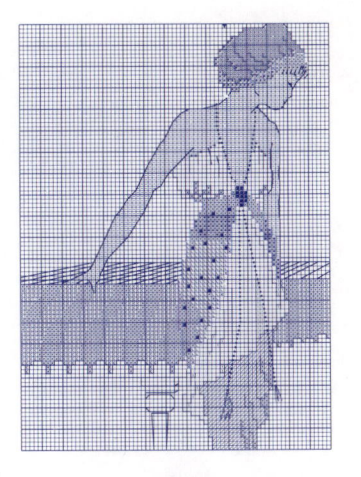

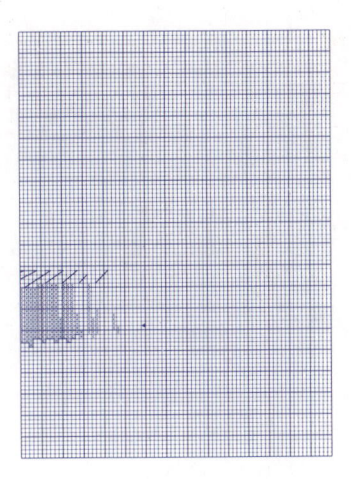

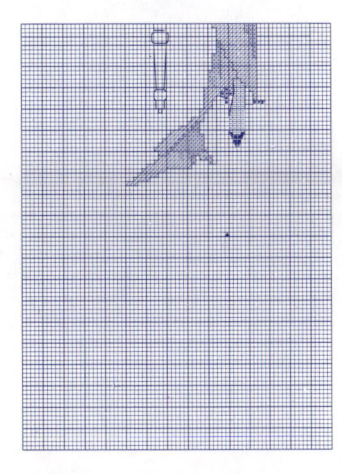

Thread

Use one strand throughout for cross stitch except for colour 413, for which you should use two strands. For details of the backstitching see the instructions on the chart.

DMC Art 117   1 skein each of the following.

·	white	
✱	317	(dark grey)
×	318	(grey)
■	413	(grey)
L	415	(light grey)
c	472	(light green)
o	722	(light tangerine)
I	762	(very light grey)
ĸ	922	(rust)
–	951	(very light pink)
╱	964	(aqua)

Backstitching

——	318	1 strand
══	310	1 strand

FRENCH FASHIONS

LYNLY ELLIOTT

Backstitch the fringe with 2 strands of 922.
Work the French knots on the bodice and shoulders in 415.
Work the French knots on the skirt in 310.

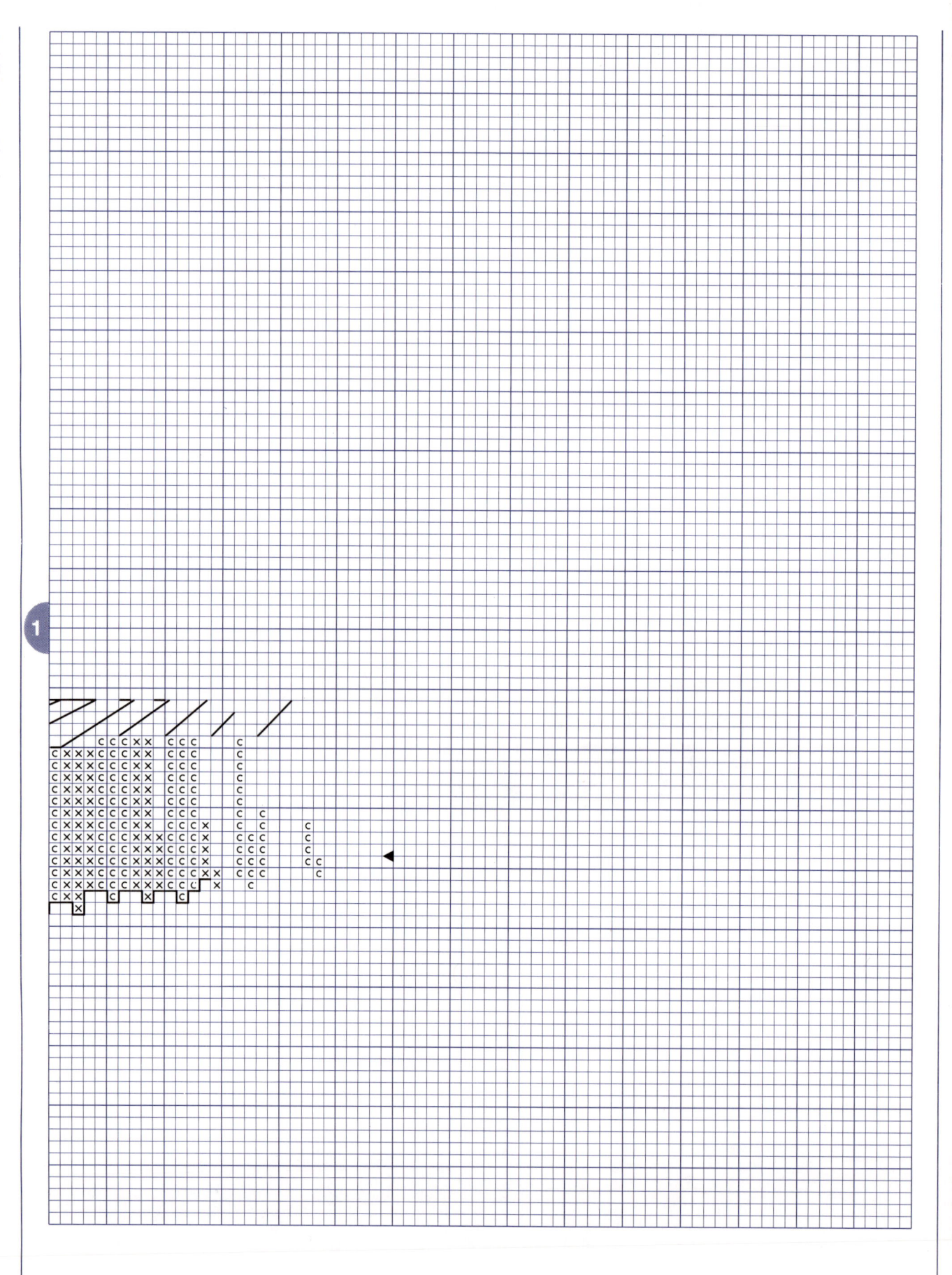

FRENCH FASHIONS

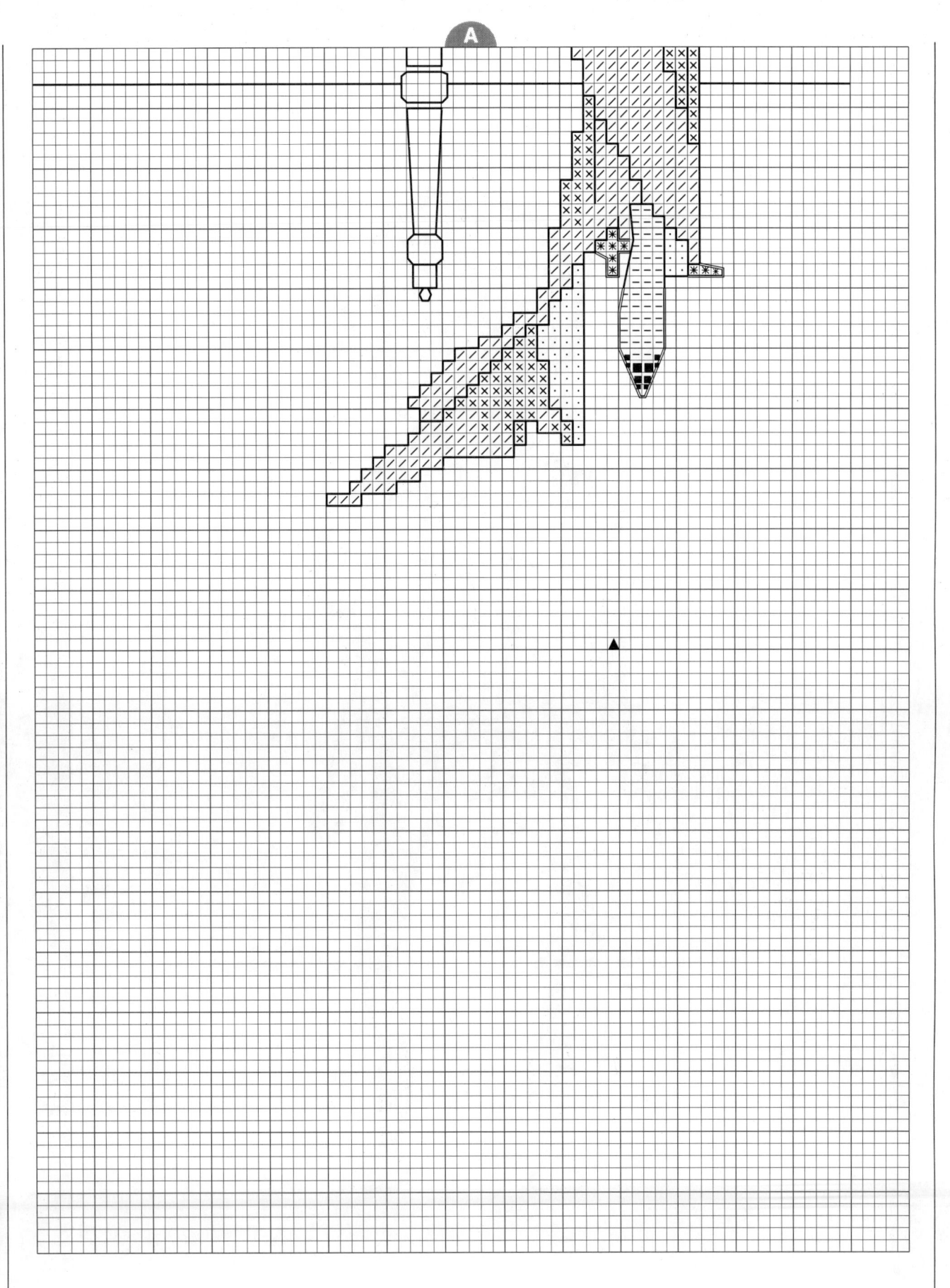

91

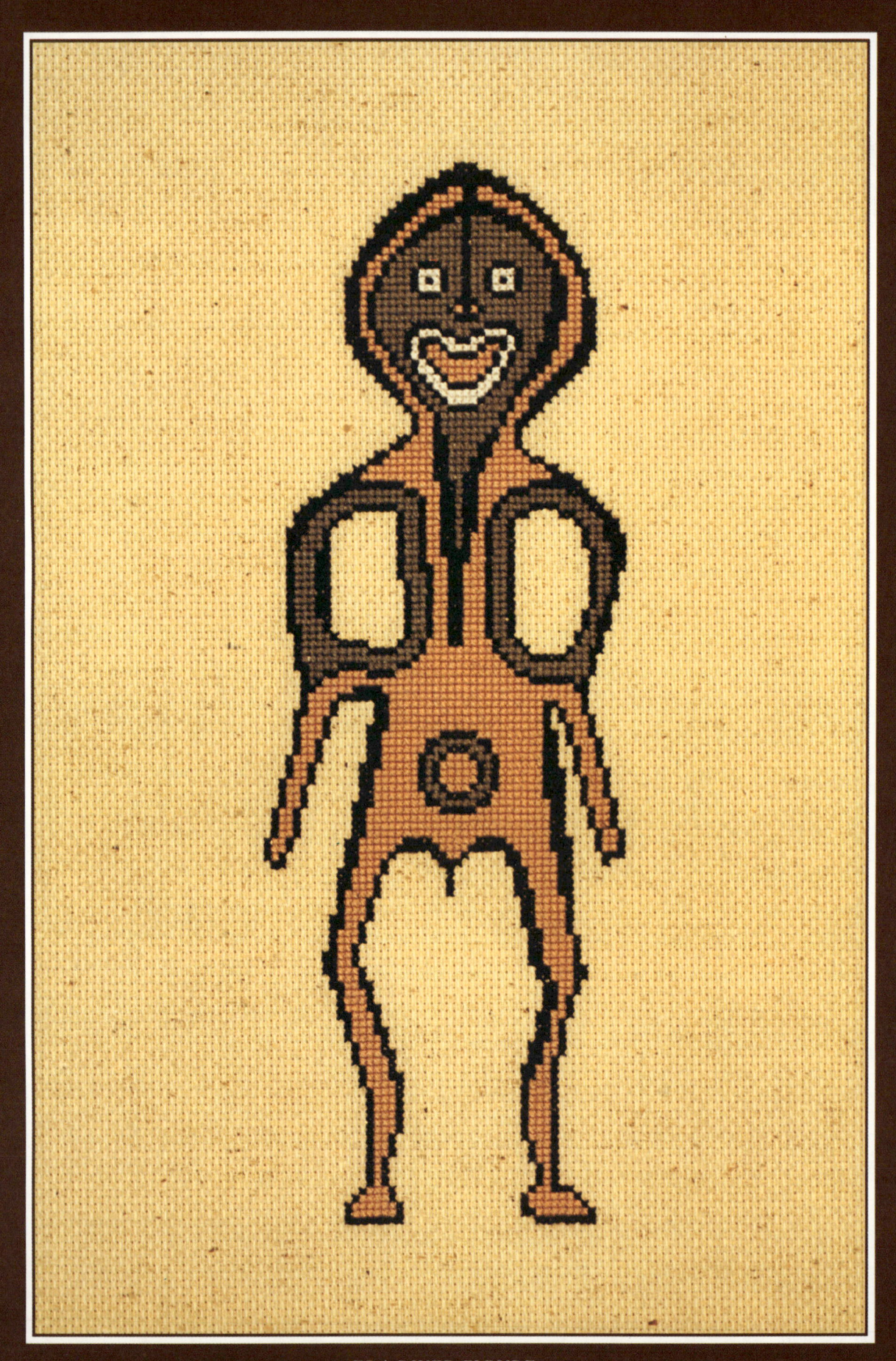

ERA RIVER FIGURE

PAPUA NEW GUINEA COLLECTION

Papua New Guinea is a country rich in primitive art. It is also a country culturally torn apart by having some 712 individual languages, each with its own dialects. It is unique in that the native population saw their first wheel on an aircraft. There are no trains: not even a road linking the north and south coastal areas. I lived there for twenty-seven years, during which time I was fortunate in being able to travel extensively: from the West Sepik, with its seemingly unlimited and diverse art, to the beautiful islands of the Milne Bay province and Bougainville.

For this series I have chosen two figures and three masks that lend themselves well to adaption to cross stitch. The colours I recommend are traditional, however I would strongly urge you to experiment and use the colours that suit your own decor – just remember to keep the darker shades dark and the lighter ones light. Although these designs look great on white, they are superb on Rustica or a similar fabric. And I let you use a little imagination in working out your own fabric sizes. Remember that cross stitch is very versatile!

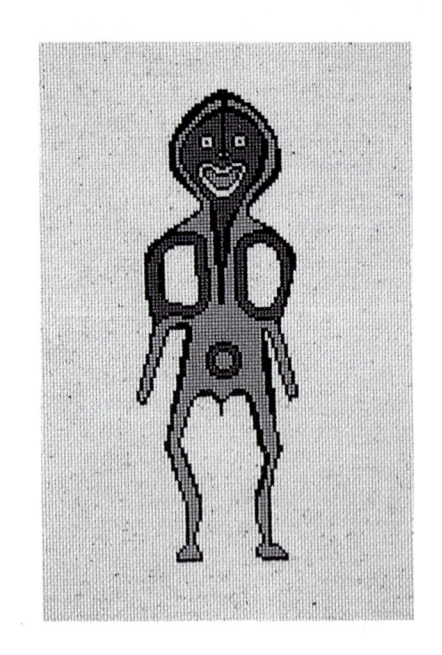

Era River Figure

This design is 140 stitches high by 49 stitches wide.

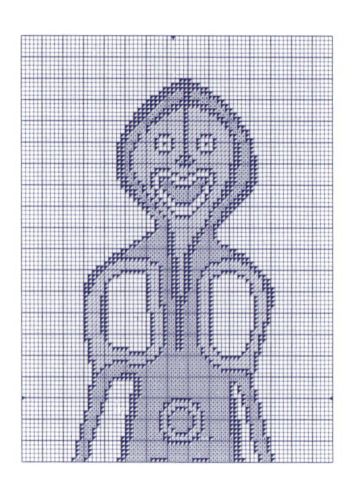

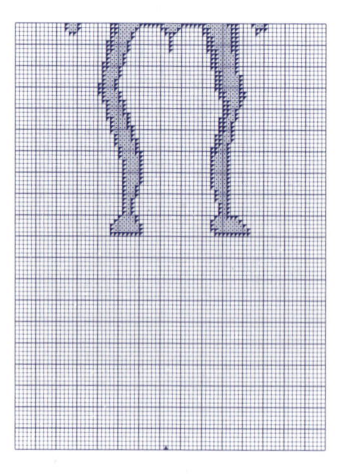

Ⓐ

Thread

Use two strands throughout for cross stitch.

DMC Art 117   1 skein each of the following.

- ·   white
- ▶   310   (black)
- ×   349   (red)
- ∕   783   (gold)

CROSS STITCH DESIGNS

94

PAPUA NEW GUINEA COLLECTION

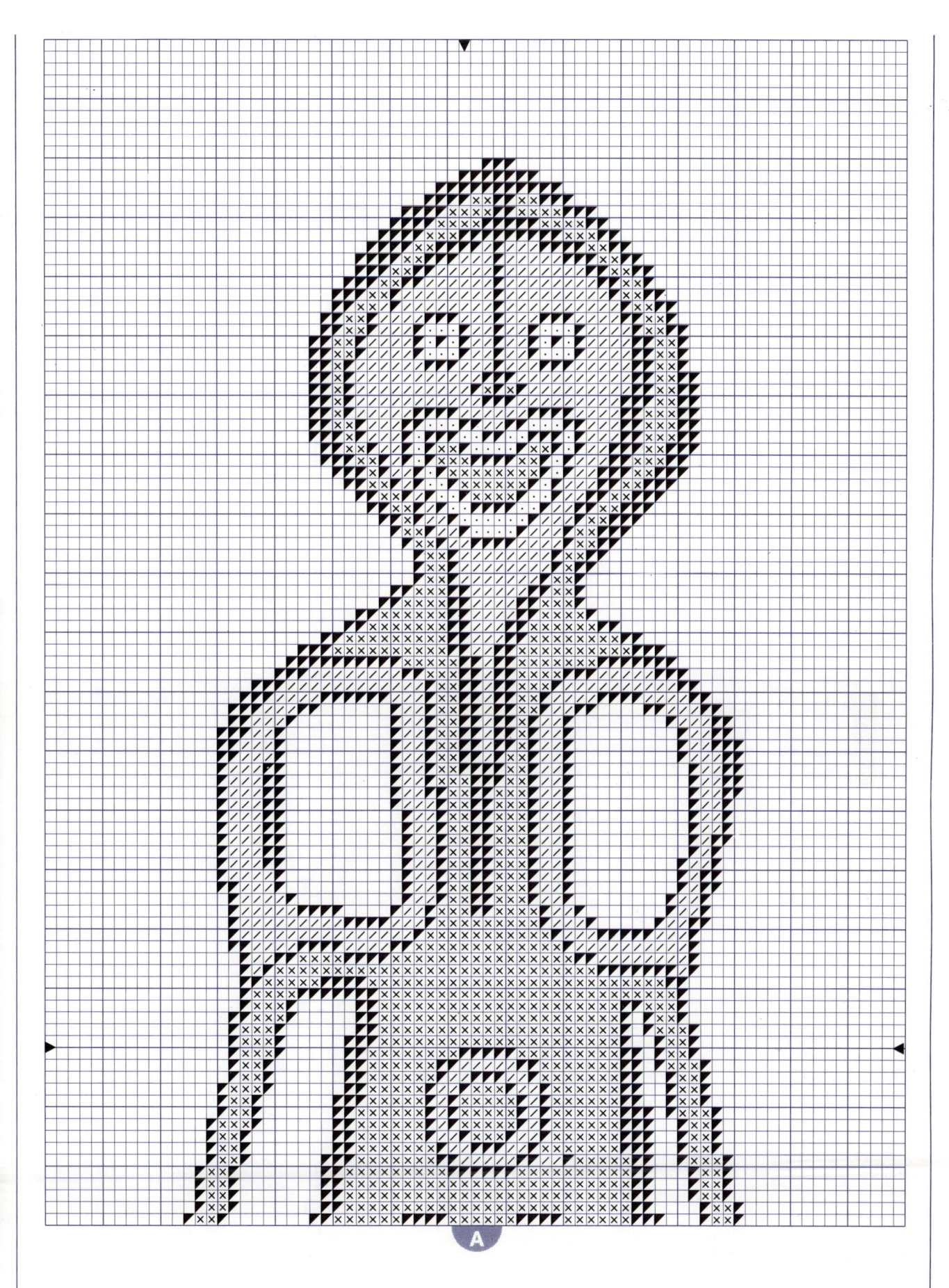

A

95

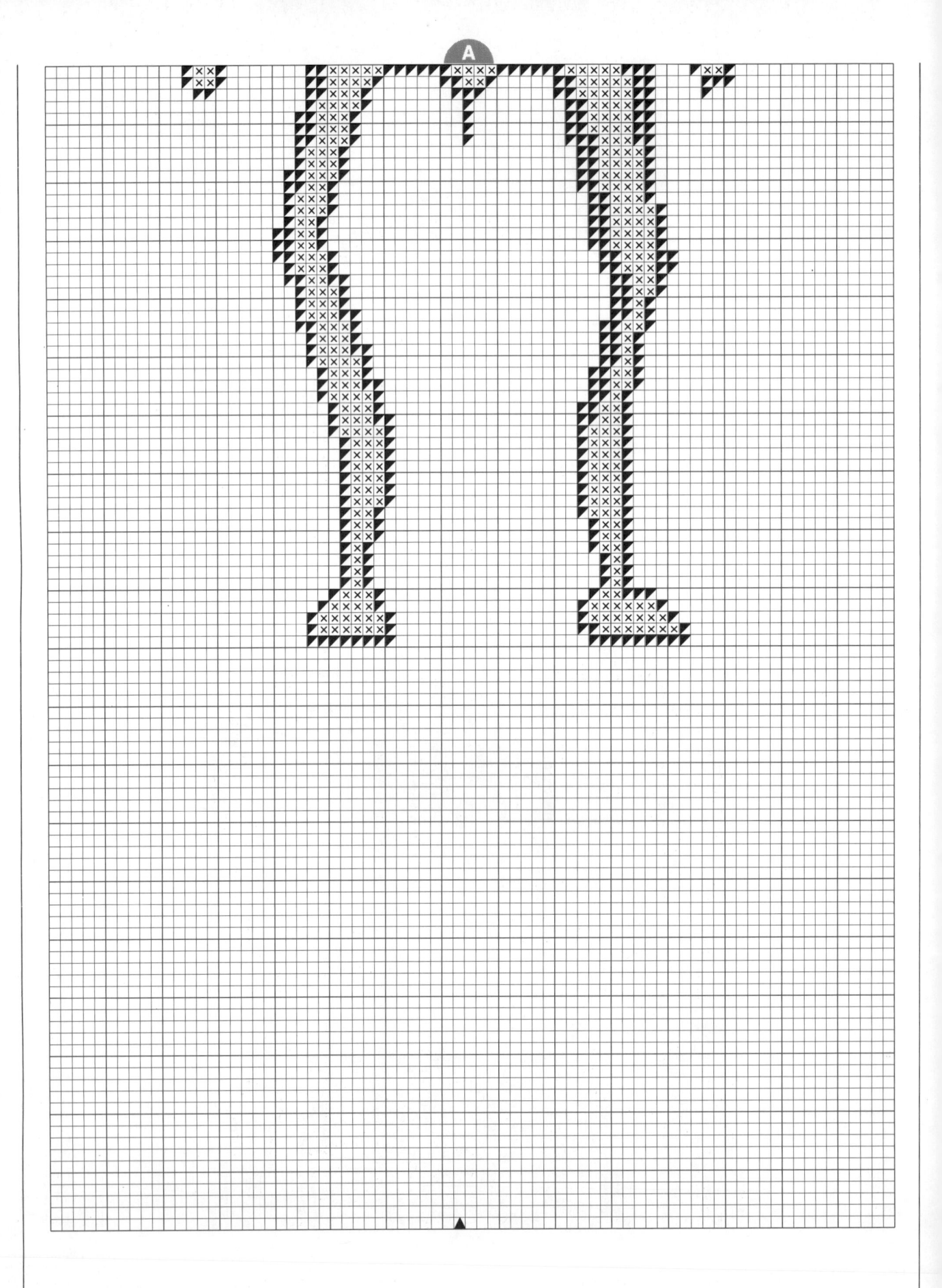

CROSS STITCH DESIGNS

96 ERA RIVER FIGURE

GULF PROVINCE FIGURE

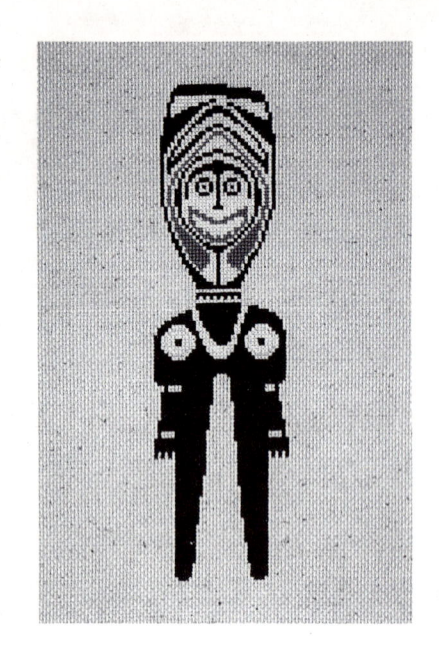

CROSS STITCH DESIGNS

Gulf Province Figure

This design is 140 stitches high by 39 stitches wide.

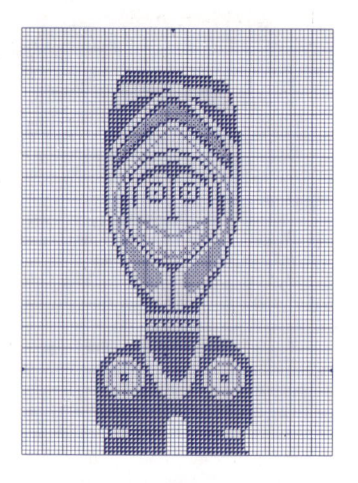

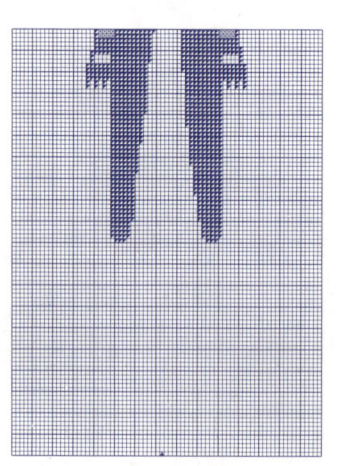

A

Thread
Use two strands throughout for cross stitch.

DMC Art 117   1 skein each of the following.

- ·   white
- ▼ 310   (black)
- × 349   (red)

PAPUA NEW GUINEA COLLECTION

A

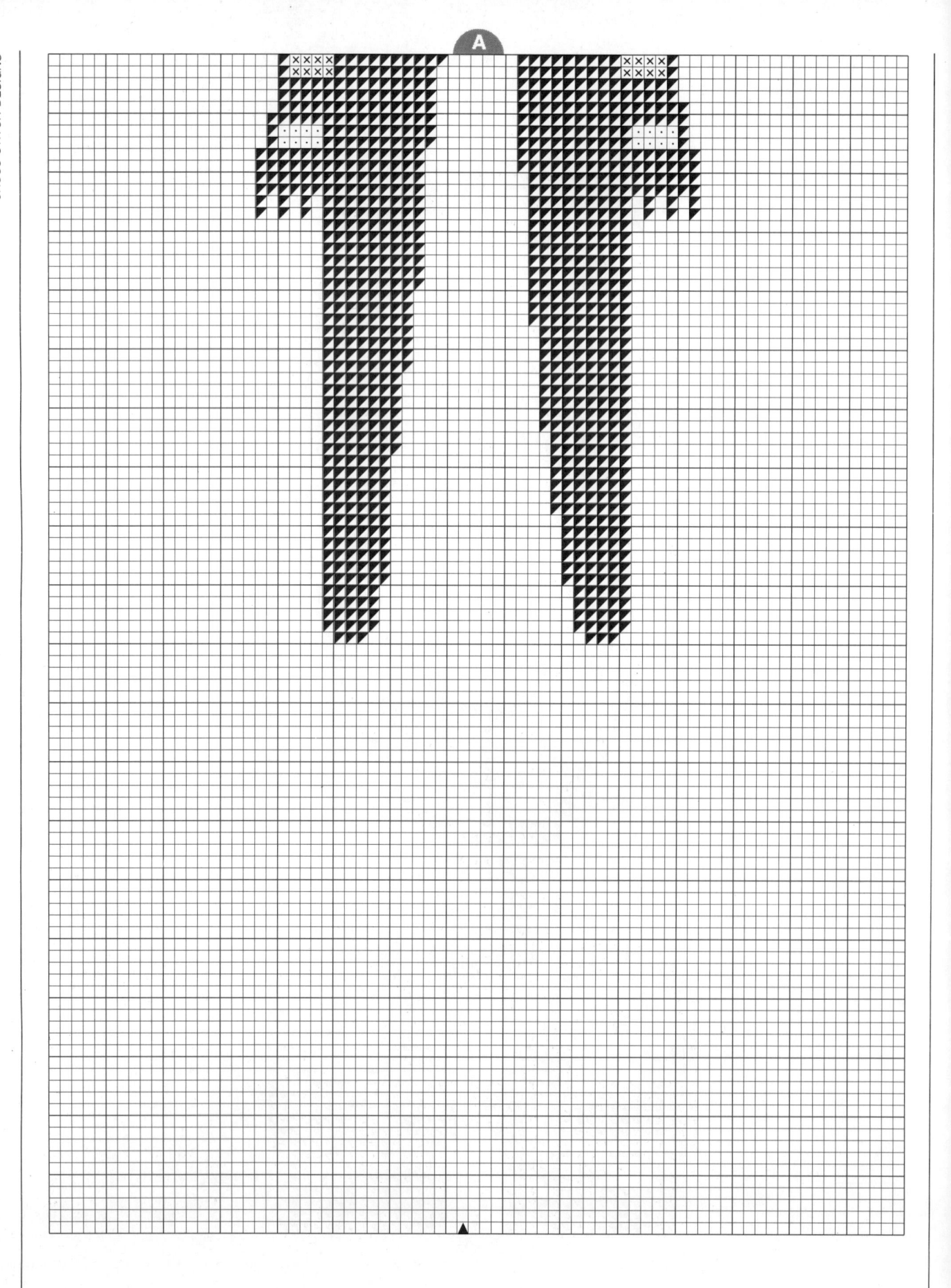

CROSS STITCH DESIGNS

100 GULF PROVINCE FIGURE

TAMI ISLAND MASK

CROSS STITCH DESIGNS

Tami Island Mask

This design is 140 stitches high by 67 stitches wide.

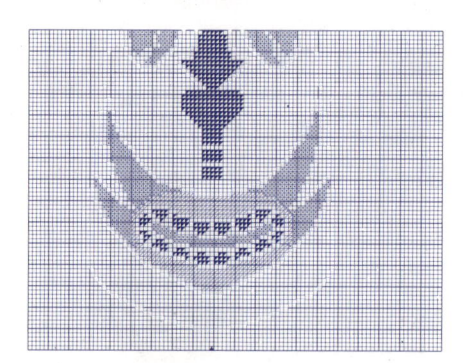

A

Thread

Use two strands throughout for cross stitch and one strand for backstitching.

DMC Art 117   1 skein each of the following.

·	white	
▼	310	(black)
×	349	(red)
∕	783	(gold)

Backstitching

——— 310   1 strand

102

103

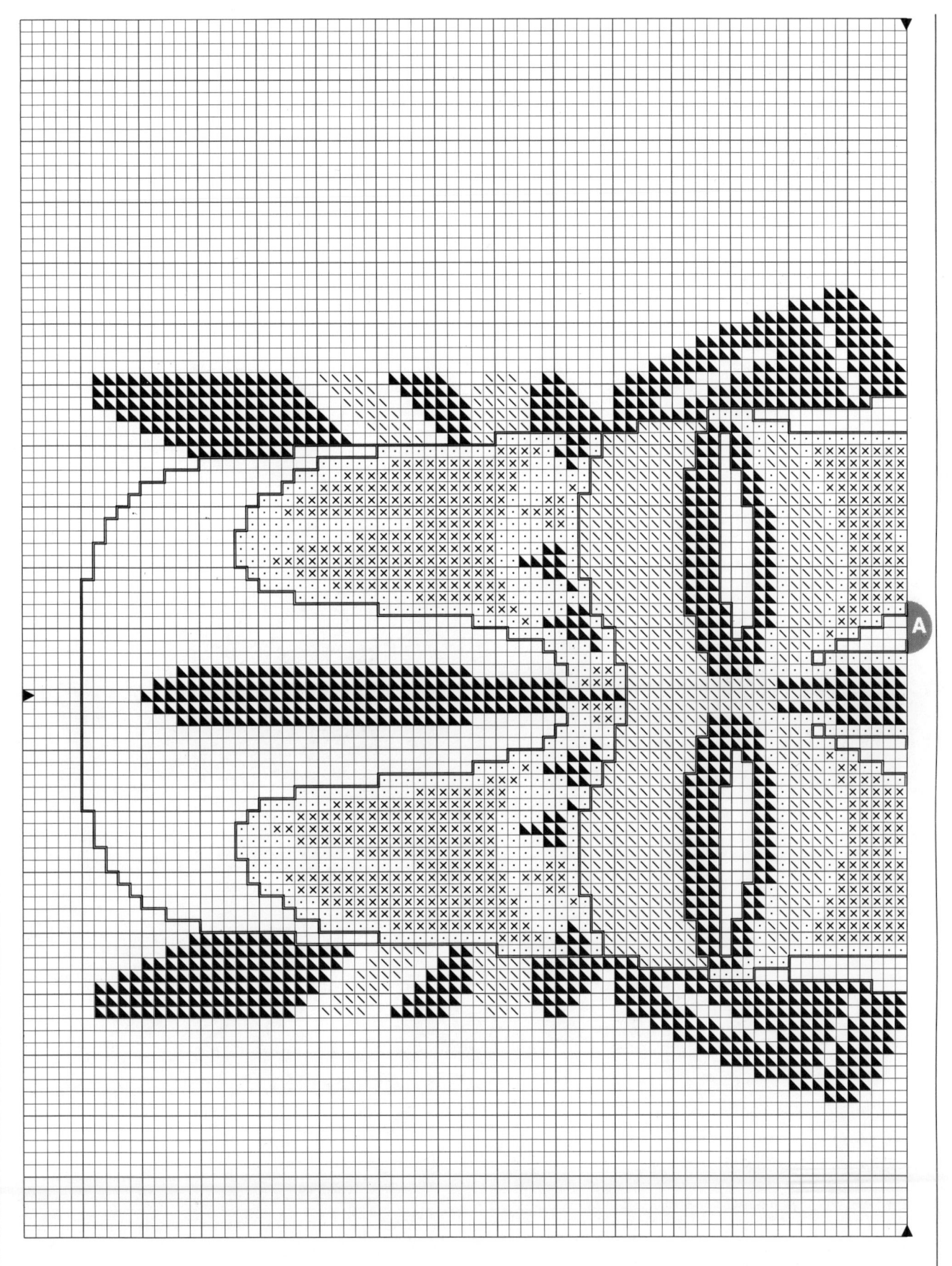

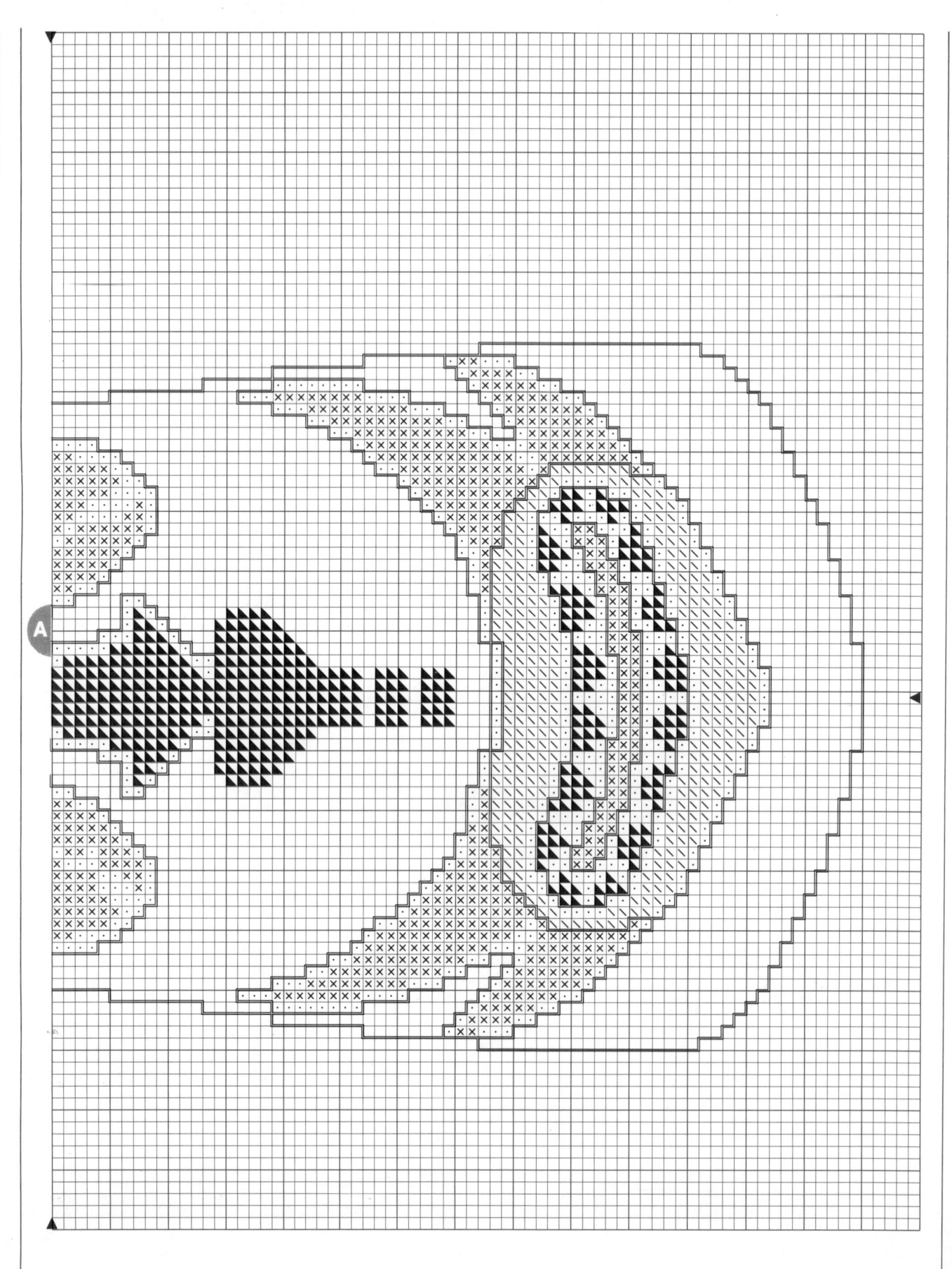

CROSS STITCH DESIGNS

104 TAMI ISLAND MASK

ABELAM MASK

Abelam Mask

This design is 140 stitches high by 90 stitches wide.

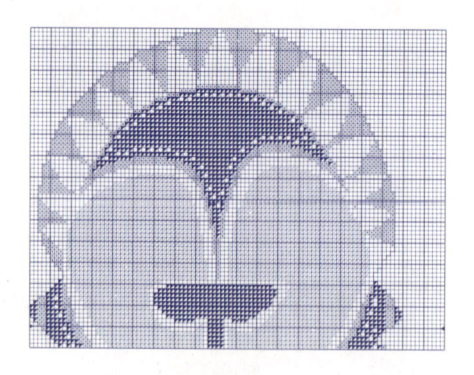

A

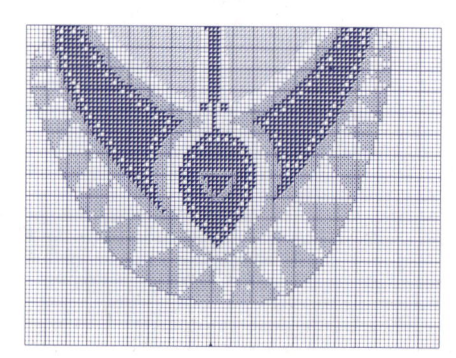

Thread

Use two strands throughout for cross stitch and one strand for backstitching.

DMC Art 117 1 skein each of the following.

	white	
▼	310	(black)
×	349	(red)
∕	783	(gold)

Backstitching

——— 310   1 strand

PAPUA NEW GUINEA COLLECTION

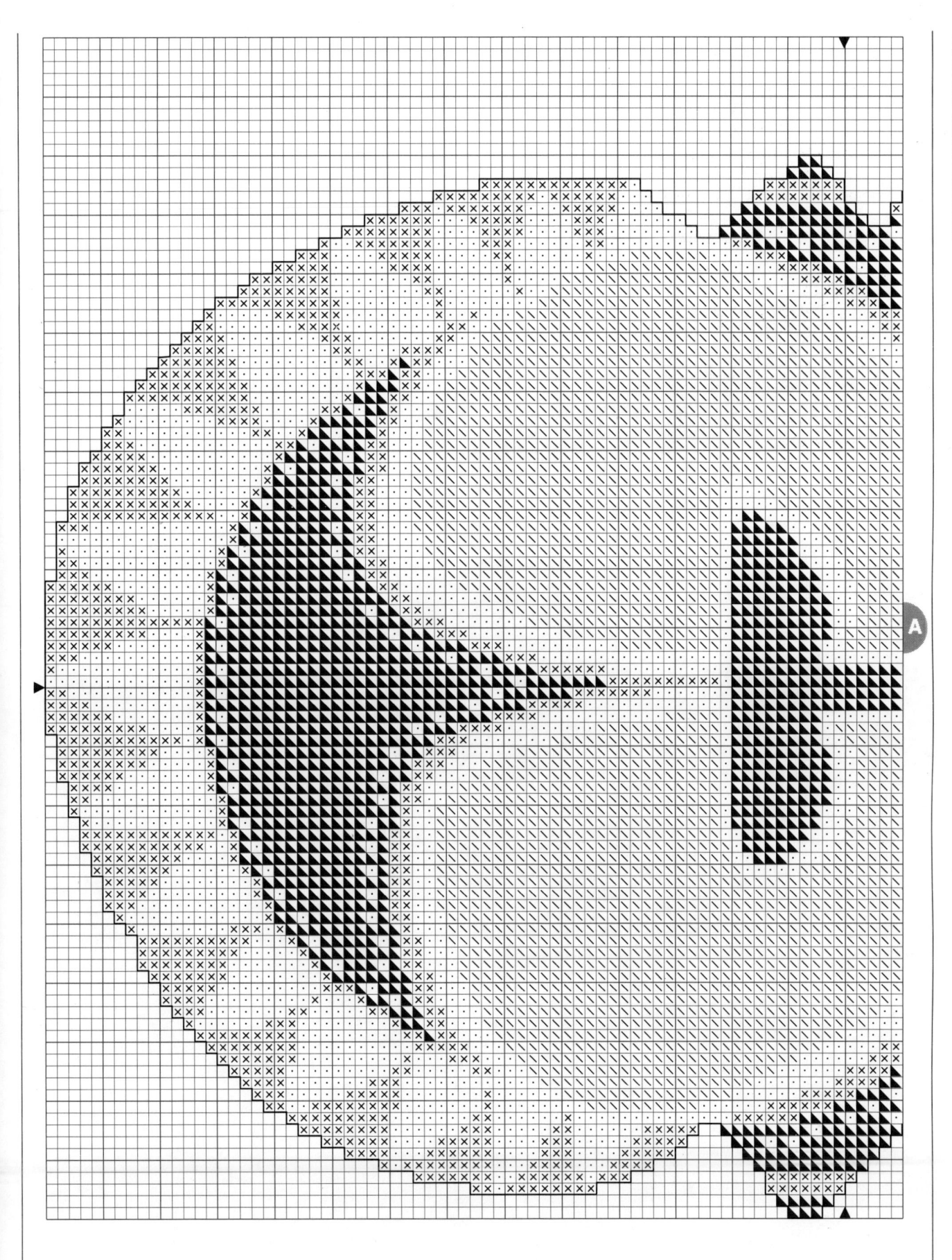

108 | ABELAM MASK

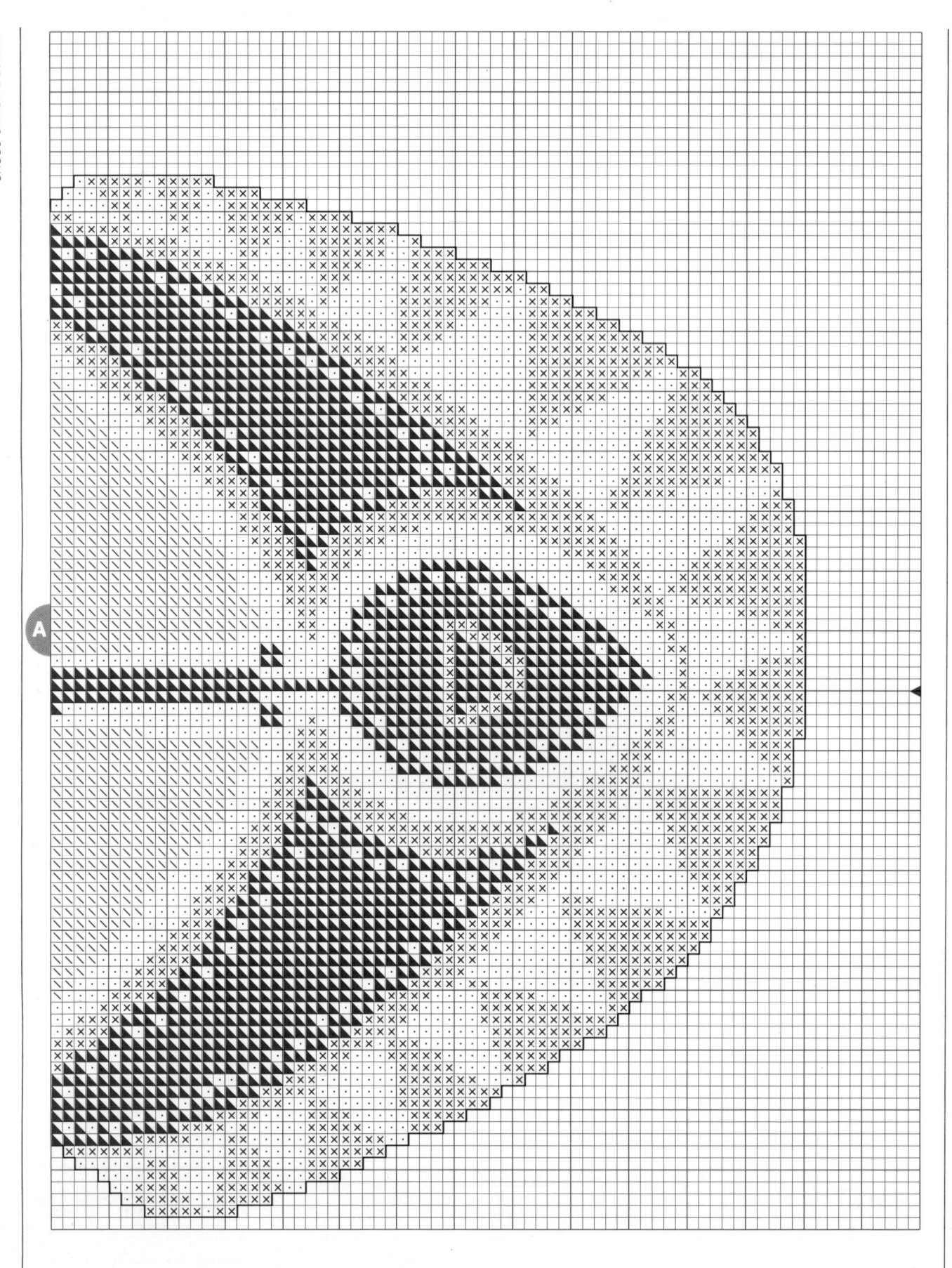

WEST SEPIK MASK

CROSS STITCH DESIGNS

West Sepik Mask

This design is 138 stitches high by 70 stitches wide.

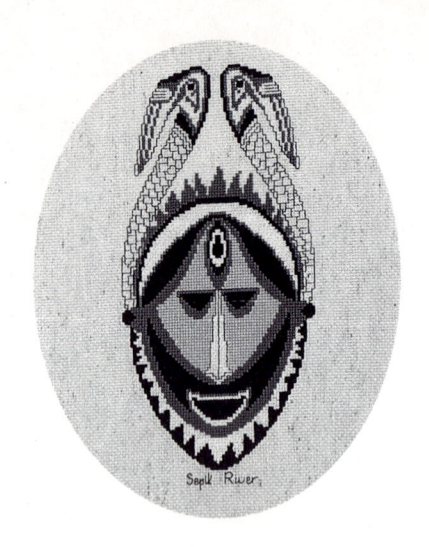

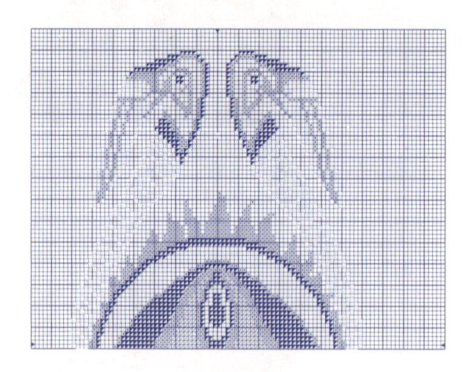

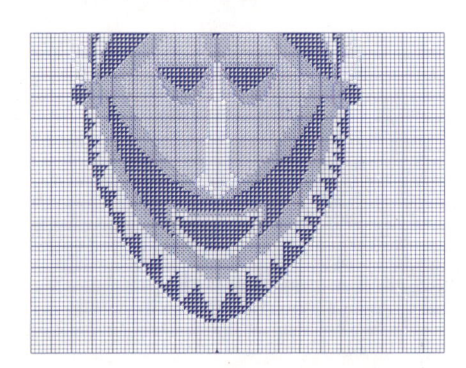

A

Thread

Use two strands throughout for cross stitch and one strand for backstitching.

DMC Art 117   1 skein each of the following.

·	white	
▼	310	(black)
×	349	(red)
∕	783	(gold)

Backstitching

══ 310   1 strand

110

PAPUA NEW GUINEA COLLECTION

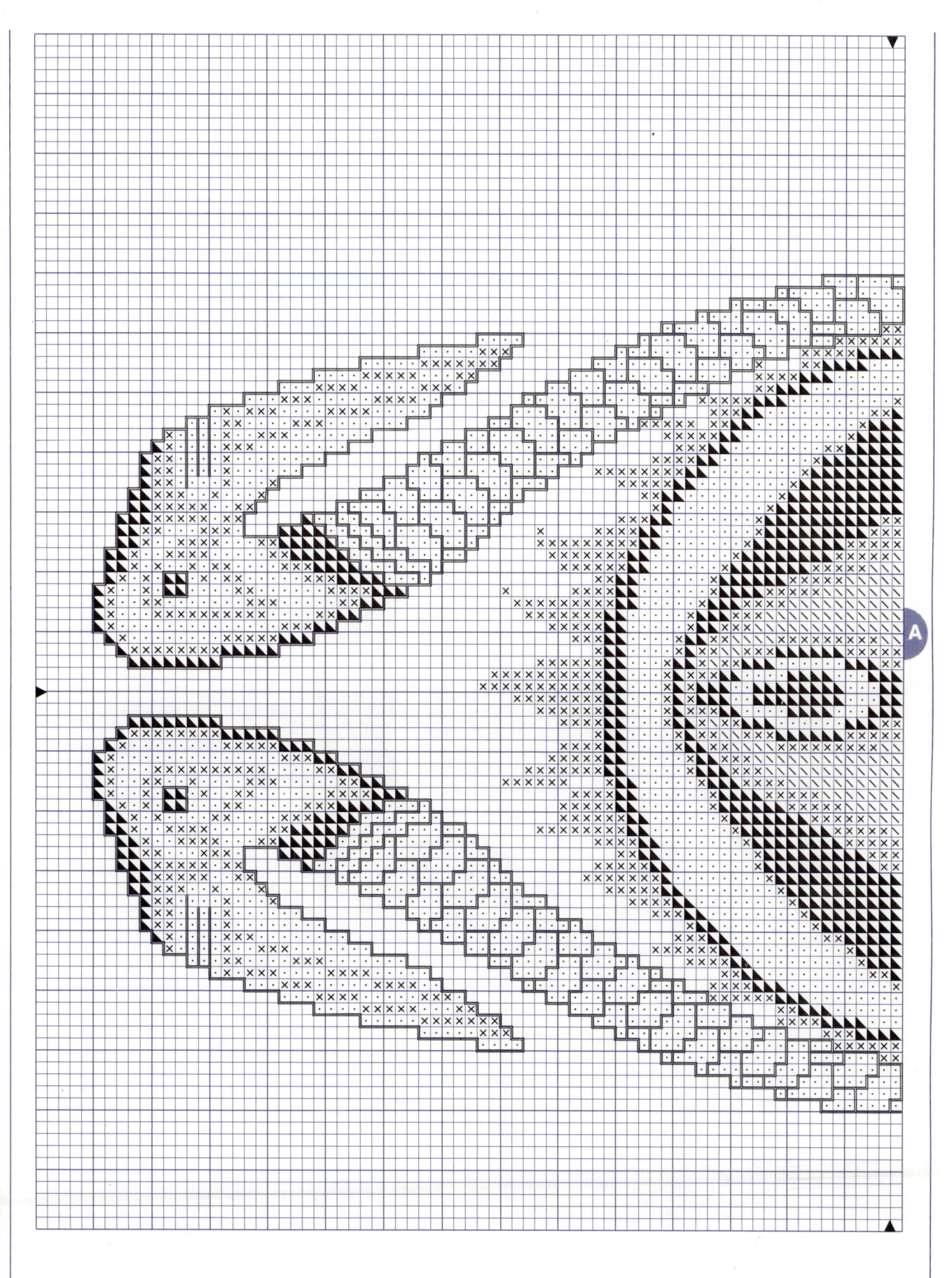

A

111

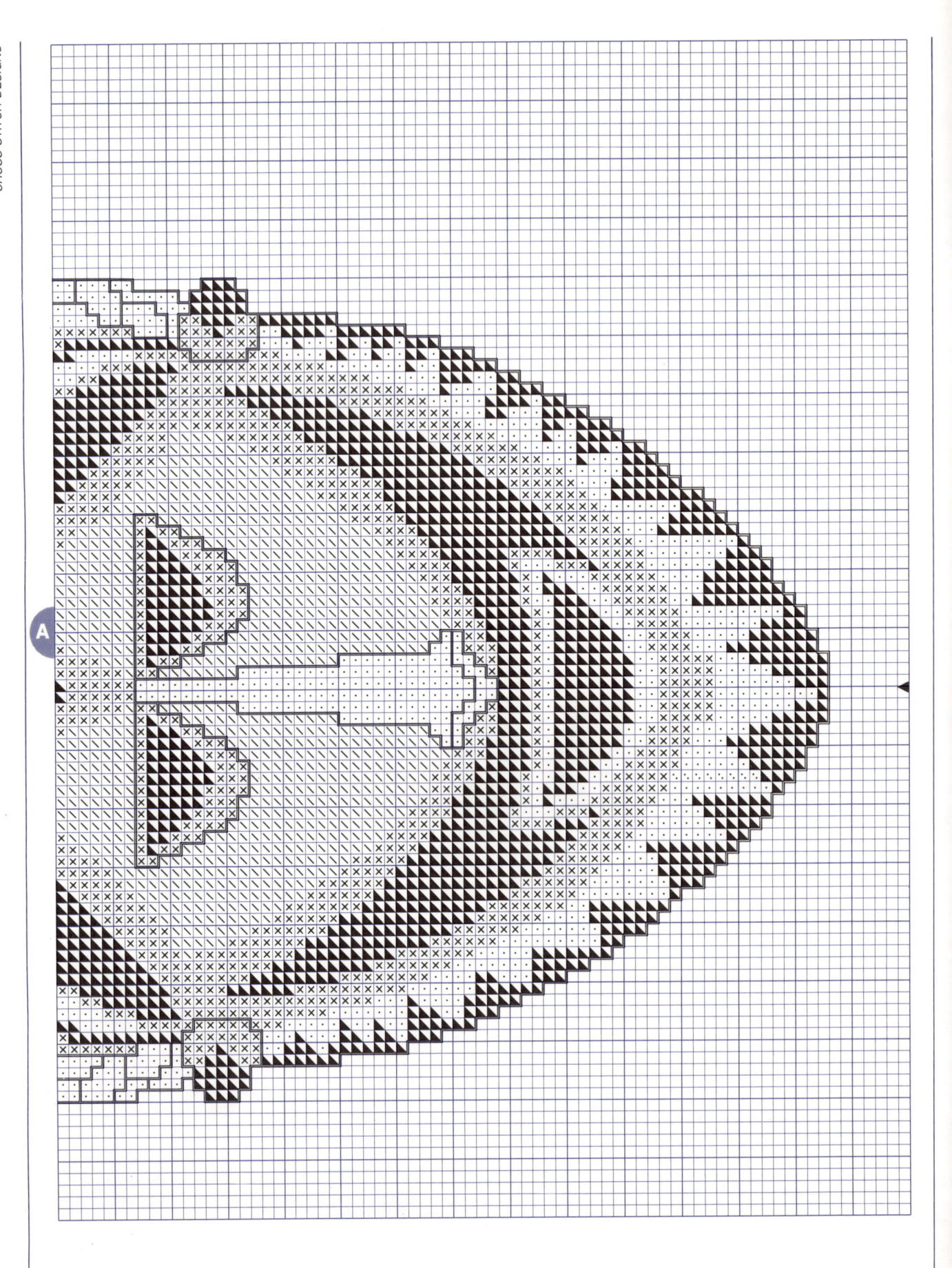

CROSS STITCH DESIGNS

A

112 WEST SEPIK MASK

MARILYN

CROSS STITCH DESIGNS

FACES

Marilyn

Marilyn Monroe, who was born Norma Jean Baker, lived from 1926 to 1962. She was *the* Hollywood sex goddess of her day, and an extremely talented actress. Her mysterious death was attributed to an overdose of sleeping pills. But then, I guess if you've stopped at this page, you probably know as much about her as I do.

At the time of Marilyn's death I was a teacher on Manus Island, the largest of the Admiralty Islands, which are the northernmost part of what was then the Territory of Papua New Guinea. I was so distressed at the news that I flew the school flag at half-mast, not realising that the children (who had never seen a movie) didn't know who Marilyn was. But then, so remote was the area that most of them had never even seen a car.

Fabric

For the cross stitch design only

Count	Centimetres	Inches
10	41 × 41	17 × 16
14	35 × 33	13 × 13
18	30 × 30	12 × 12
22	26 × 26	11 × 11

For the design with backstitch profile

Count	Centimetres	Inches
10	55 × 41	24 × 16
14	45 × 33	19 × 13
18	40 × 30	16 × 12
22	35 × 26	14 × 11

The cross stitch design is 102 stitches high and 96 stitches wide. With the backstitch profile the design is 173 stitches high by 104 stitches wide.

For chart layout see page 118.

Thread

Use two strands throughout for cross stitch and one strand for backstitching.

DMC Art 117   1 skein each of the following.

·	white	
×	304	(dark red)
c	666	(red)
^	961	(pink)
/	3032	(fawn)
▼	3371	(black/brown)
+	3790	(brown)

Backstitching

—   3032   1 strand (optional)

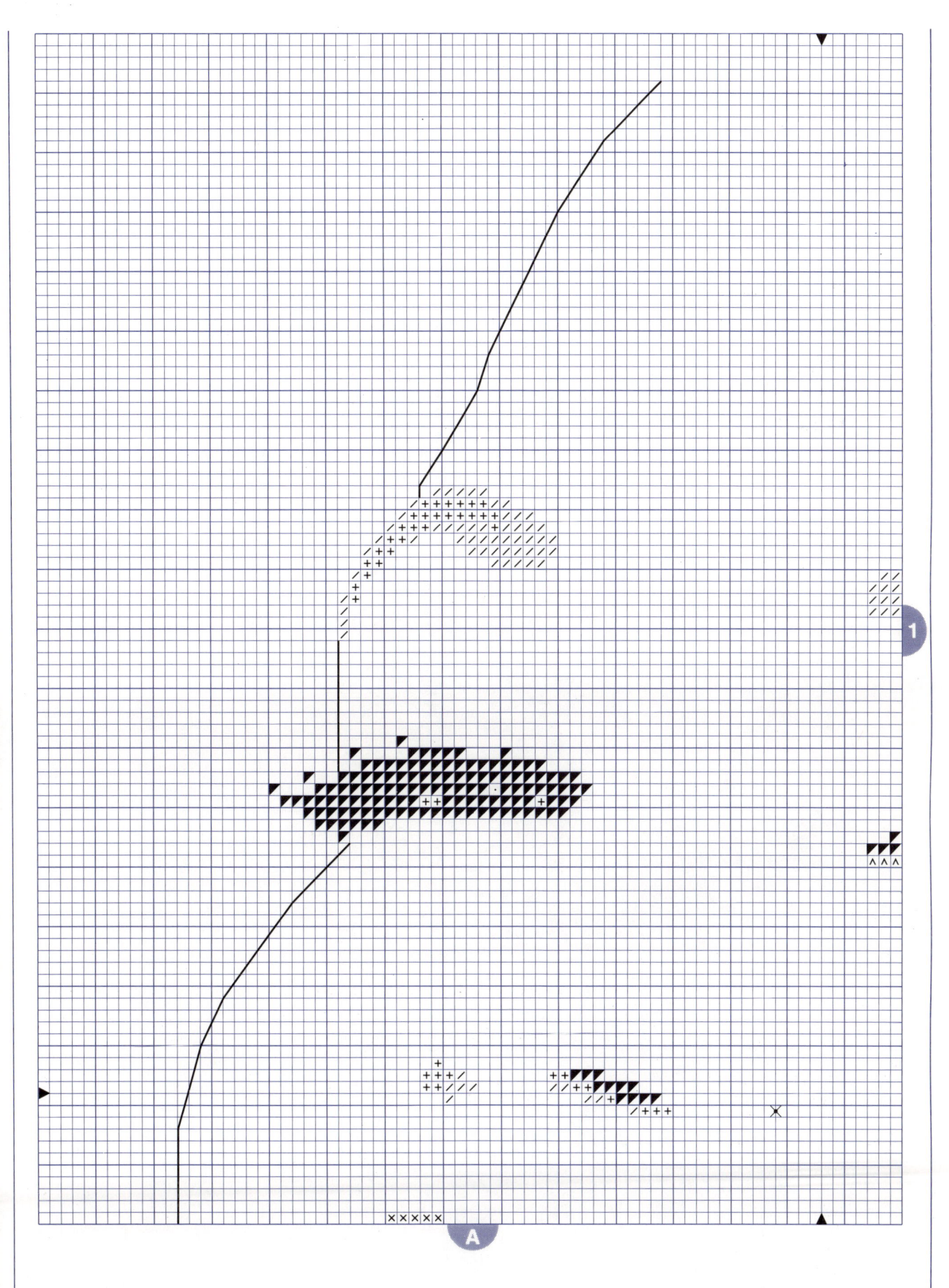

Centre of cross stitch design only indicated by four triangles.

Centre of design with backstitched profile indicated by cross.

FACES

115

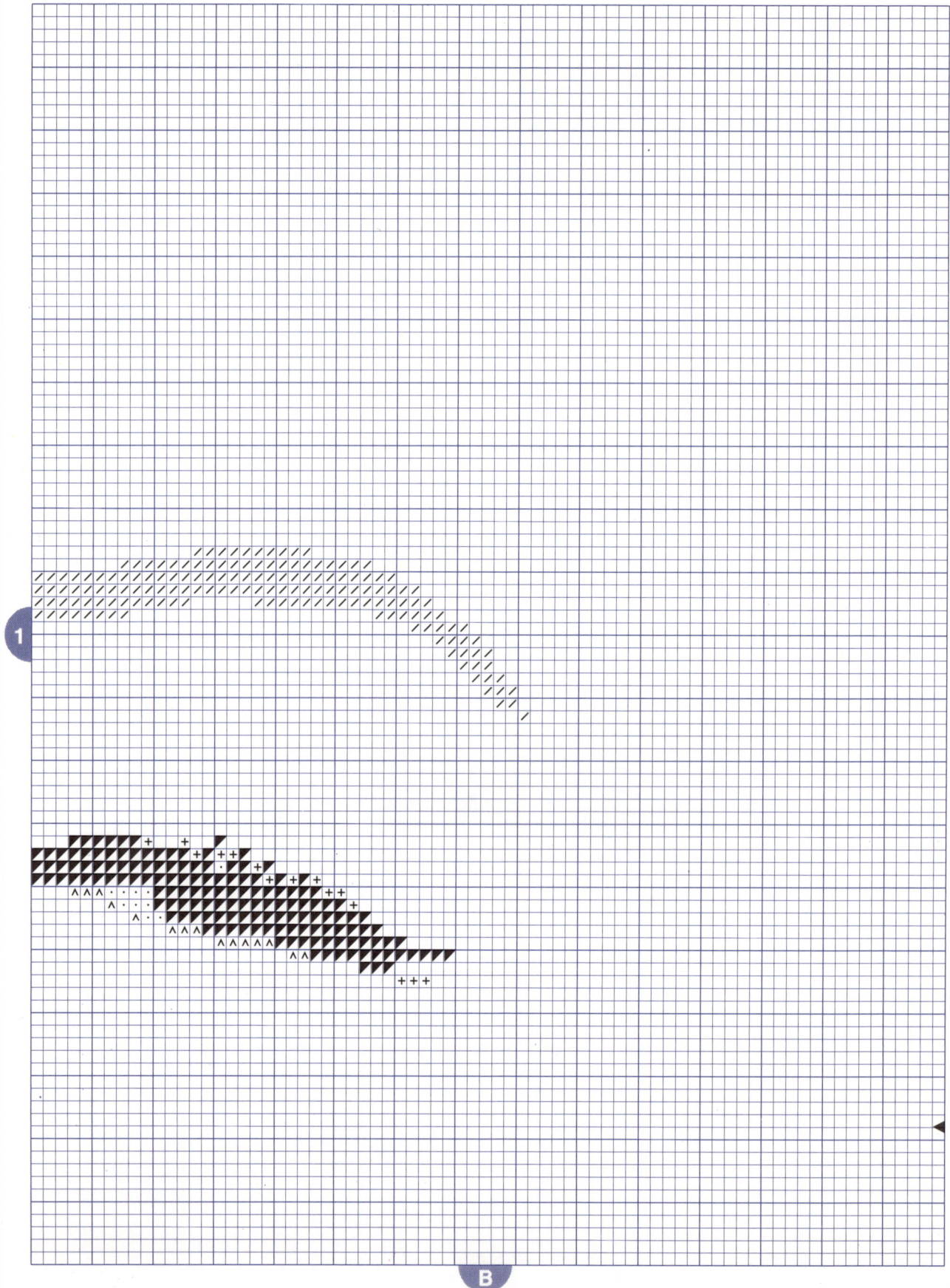

CROSS STITCH DESIGNS

116 MARILYN

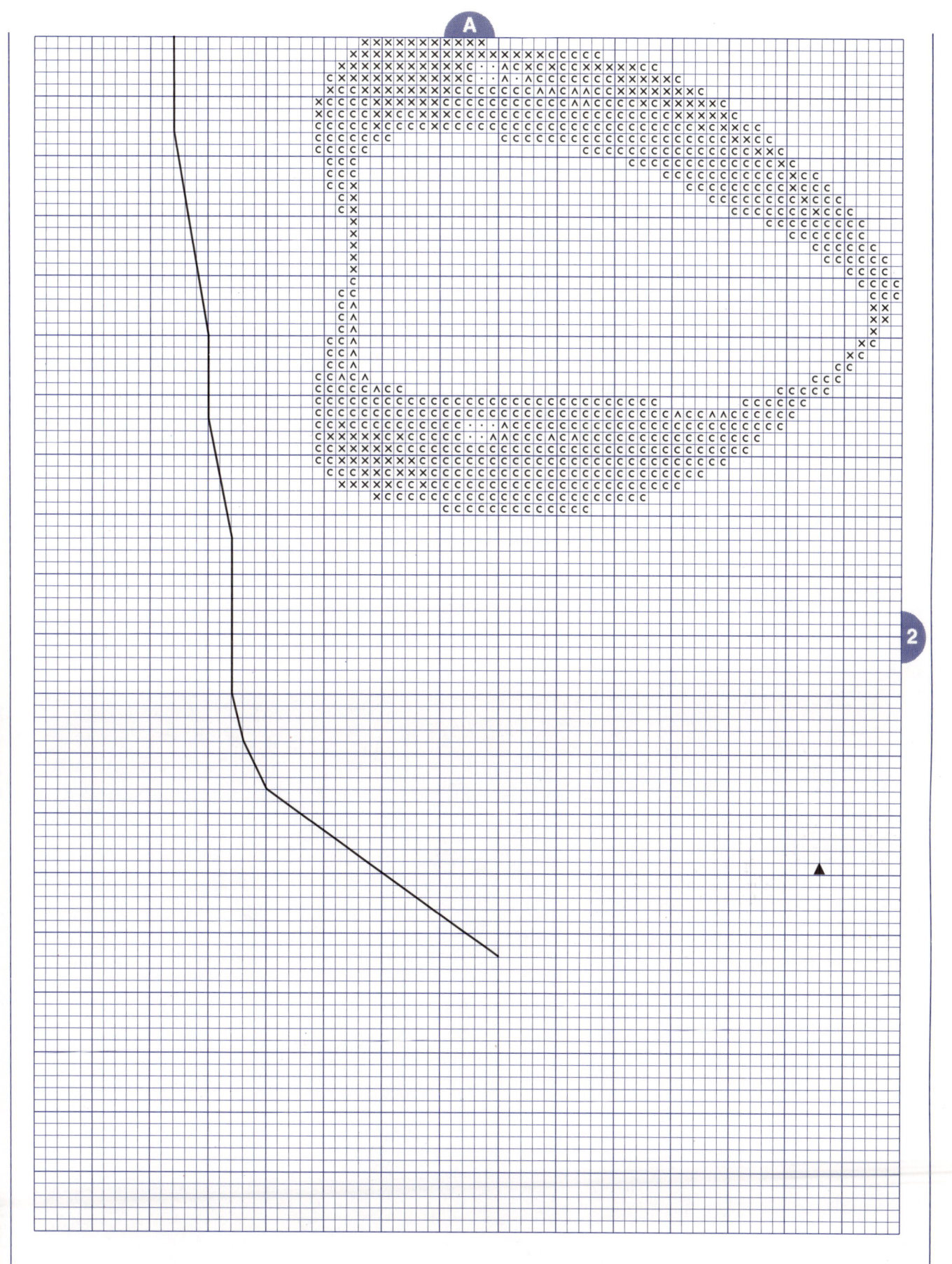

FACES

117

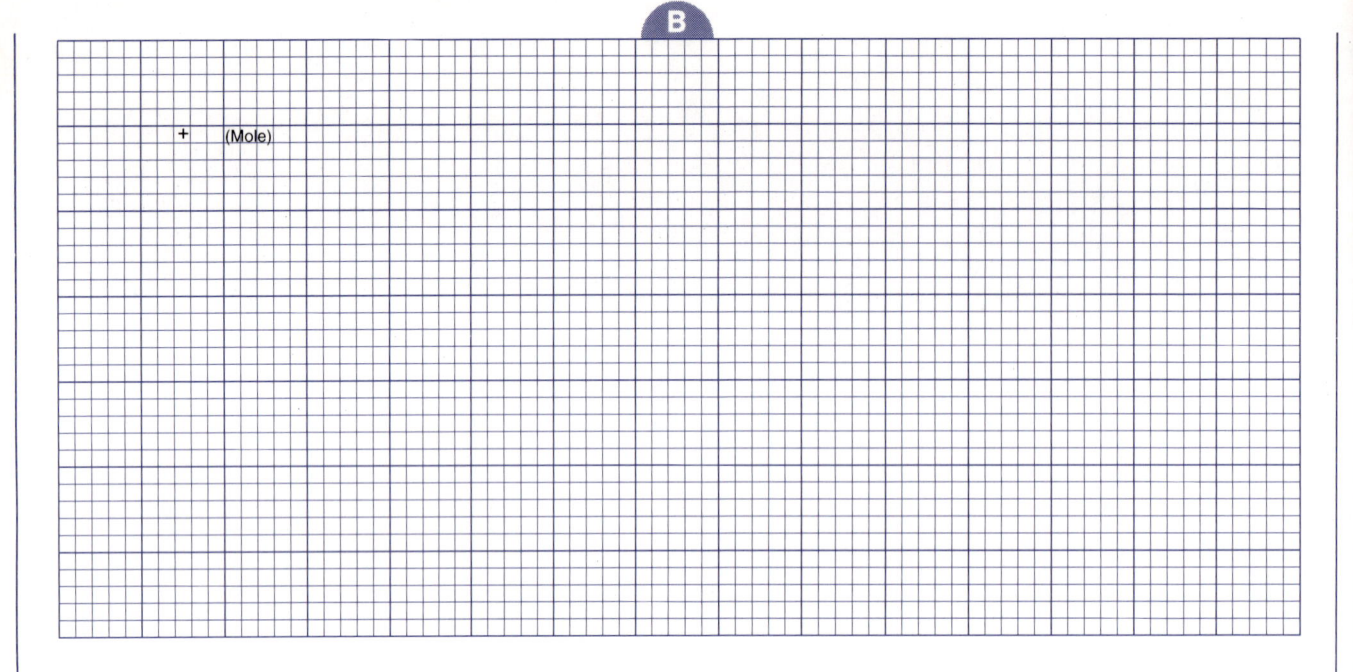

CROSS STITCH DESIGNS

+ (Mole)

MARILYN

118

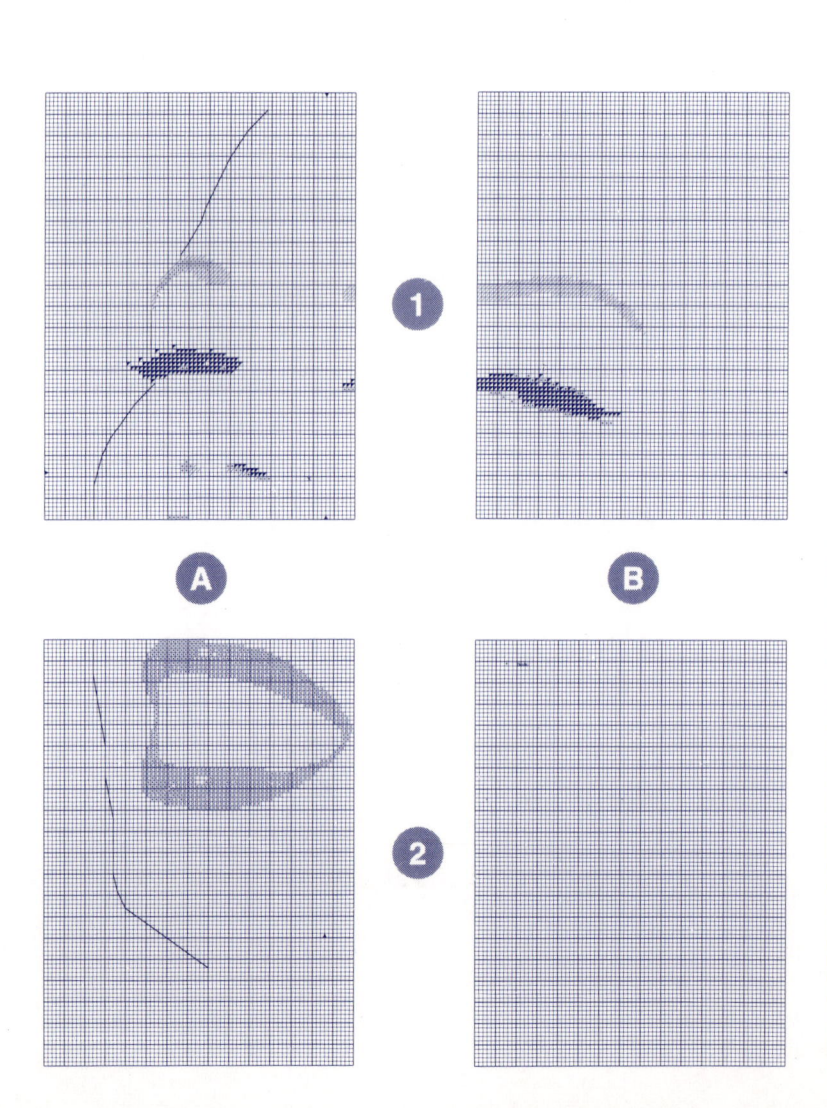

Sarah

French actress Sarah Bernhardt (1844–1923) thrilled the theatre-goers of her generation and became famous throughout the world. The film of her life, *The Incredible Sarah*, starred Glenda Jackson in the title role. Many of the posters for her performances were designed by Czechoslovakian-born artist Alfons Maria Mucha. This design is a detail from one of his posters, which I have reproduced in full under the title 'Gismonda'.

Fabric

Count	Centimetres	Inches
10	45 × 45	20 × 20
14	40 × 40	16 × 16
18	34 × 34	14 × 14
22	30 × 30	12 × 12

This design is 134 stitches high by 129 stitches wide.

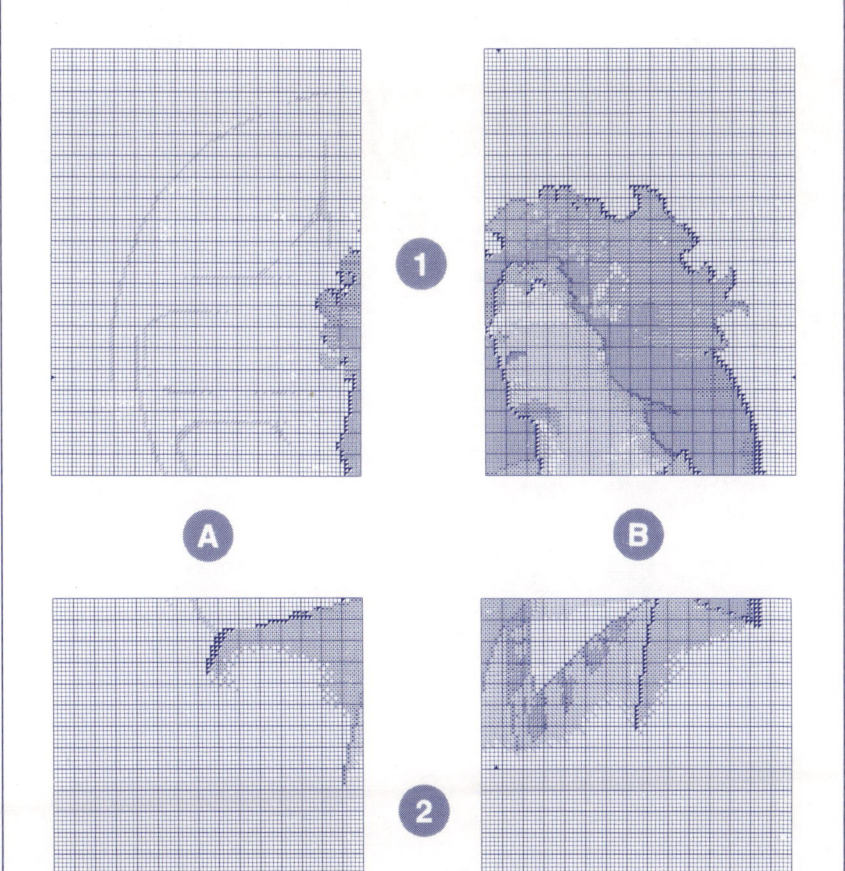

Thread

Use two strands throughout for cross stitch. For details of the backstitching see the instructions on the chart.

DMC Art 117   1 skein each of the following.

−	ecru	
▼	310	(black)
✴	317	(dark grey)
×	318	(grey)
⊼	503	(green)
ı	504	(light green)
⊙	666	(red)
·	712	(cream)
•	720	(dark tangerine)
○	721	(tangerine)
7	722	(light tangerine)
∕	729	(gold or use a metallic thread)
L	739	(light gold)
∧	743	(yellow)
z	744	(light yellow)
+	931	(grey blue)
v	962	(pink)
\	3072	(pearl)

Backstitching

═══	310	1 strand
───	317	1 strand
----	666	1 strand

FACES

SARAH

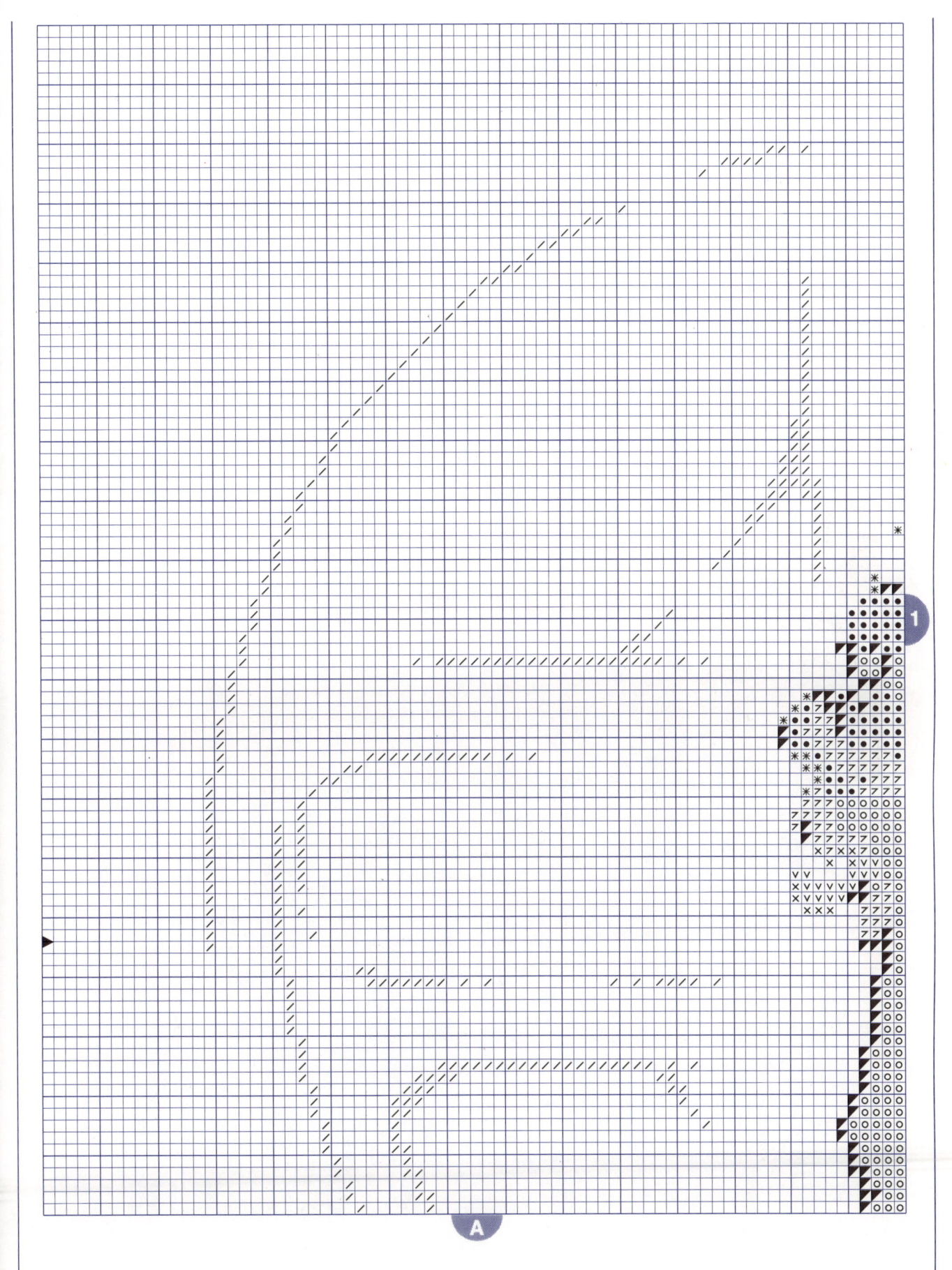

FACES

121

122 SARAH

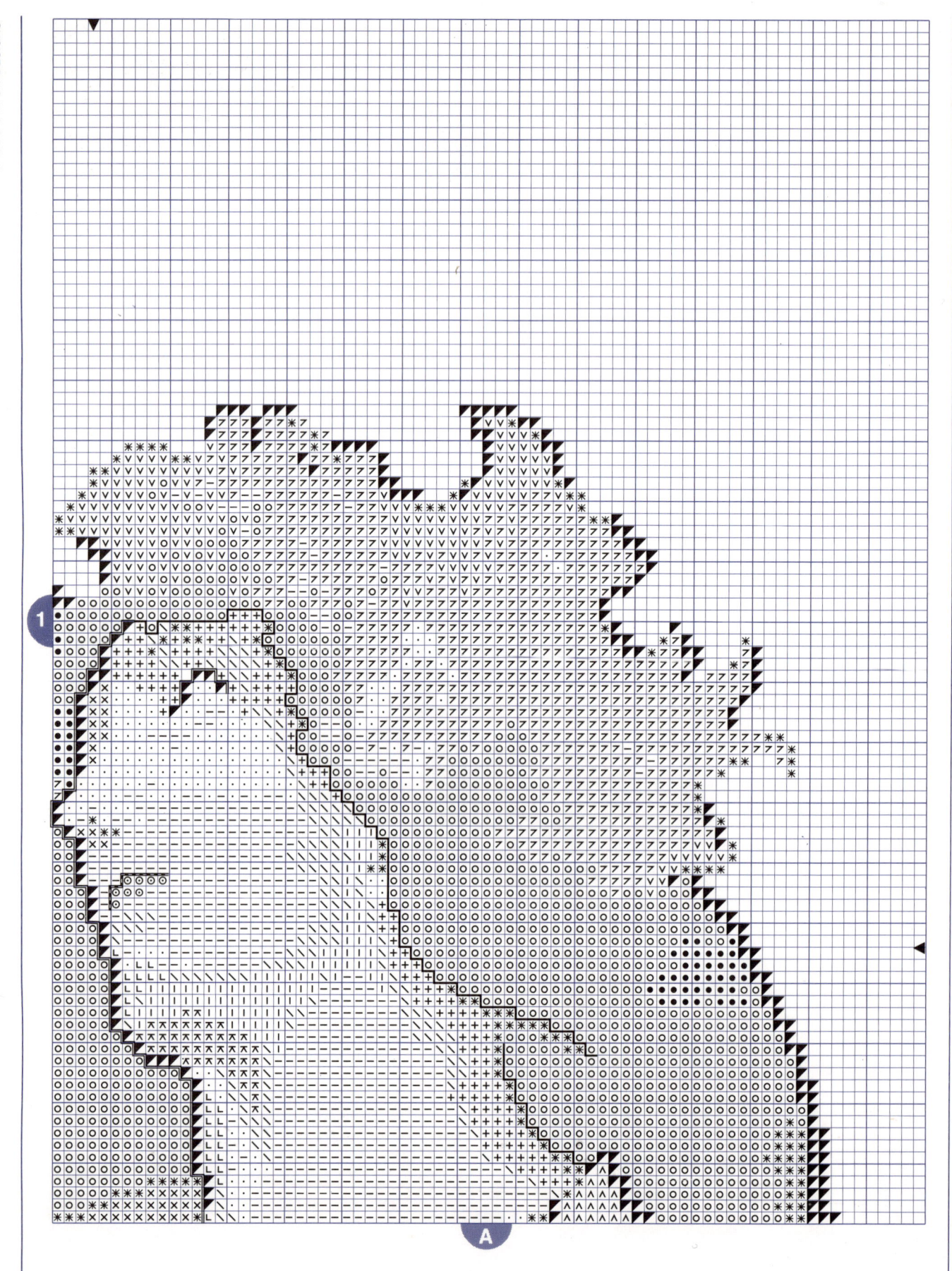

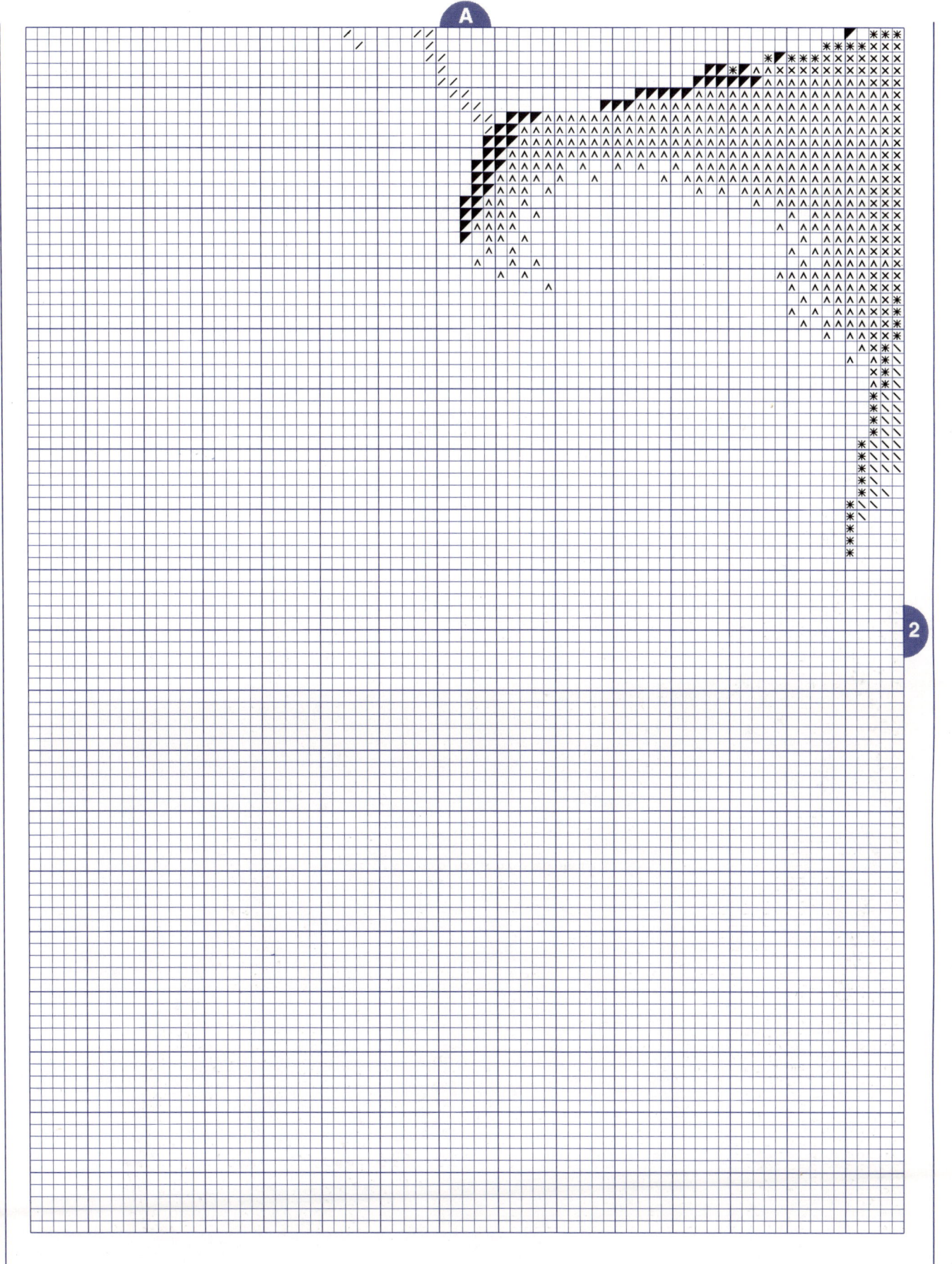

FACES

A

2

123

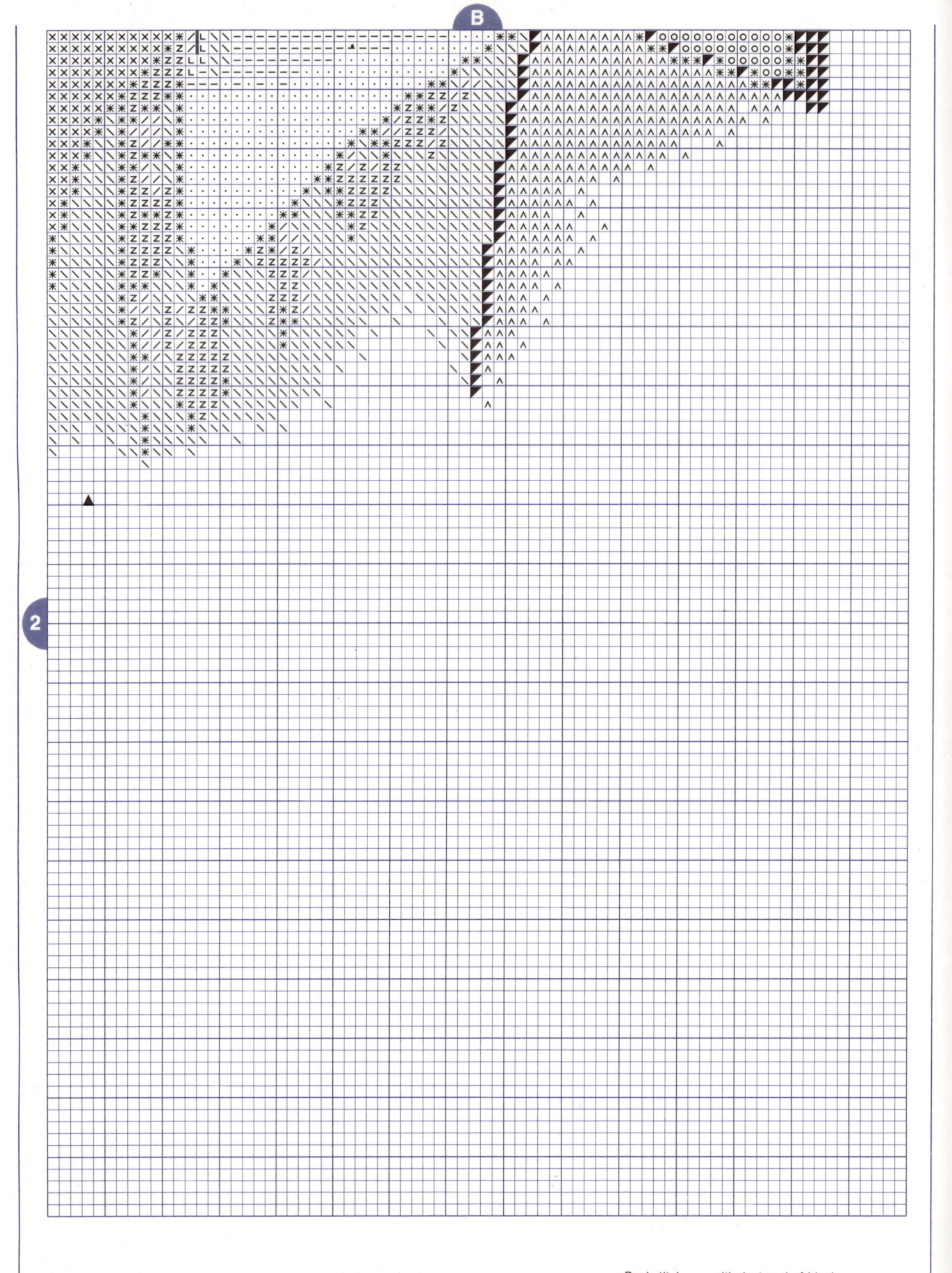

Backstitch eye with 1 strand of black.
Backstitch profile of face with 1 strand of black.
Backstitch hair with 1 strand of 317.
Backstitch mouth with 1 strand of 666.

WOMAN WEEPING

Woman Weeping

The destruction of the Basque capital, Guernica, by the forces of General Franco angered Picasso to such an extent that he painted the magnificent mural *Guernica*, which vividly expresses the anguish and horror of the disaster. In 1937 he followed *Guernica* with the painting *Woman Weeping* – the original of this now hangs in the National Gallery of Victoria, Melbourne, Australia.

The following nine pages are my interpretation of this dramatic piece. I have stitched it in needlepoint on 16 count canvas, but have charted it for either needlepoint or cross stitch.

Fabric

For cross stitch, allowing an outer edge of 7.5 cm or 3 inches

Count	Centimetres	Inches
10	83 × 68	33 × 27
14	80 × 53	32 × 21
18	53 × 46	21 × 18
22	47 × 40	19 × 16

For needlepoint, allowing an outer edge of 12.5 cm or 5 inches

Count	Centimetres	Inches
10	93 × 78	37 × 31
16	68 × 58	23 × 19

This design is 270 stitches high by 210 stitches wide.

Thread

Use two strands throughout for cross stitch.

DMC Art 117   1 skein each of the following.

Symbol	Number	Colour
·	white	
α	211	(dark rose)
▼	310	(black)
●	312	(dark blue)
∷	318	(grey)
∣	320	(leaf green)
+	322	(blue)
∕	445	(lemon)
⁊	472	(light green)
⁒	500	(very dark green)
⊙	502	(sage)
×	550	(dark purple)
к	553	(purple)
∴	554	(lilac)
ℓ	642	(straw)
o	666	(red)
−	704	(green)
c	827	(light blue)
×	839	(brown)
∧	841	(light brown)
∥	844	(dark pewter)
=	926	(steel)
s	958	(dark aqua)
v	959	(aqua)
'	991	(dark teal)
⋊	3371	(black/brown)
N	3778	(coral)

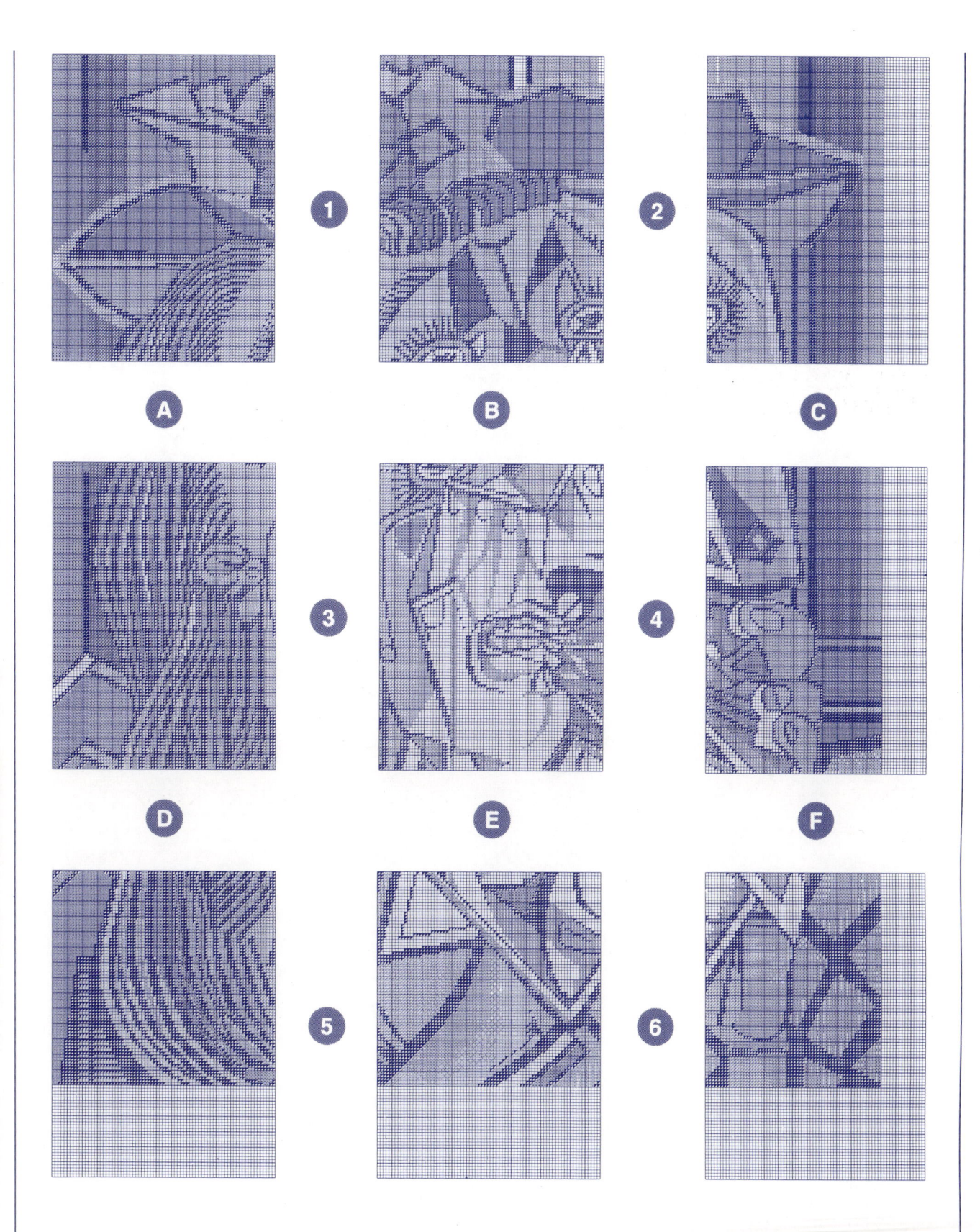

FACES

127

128 WOMAN WEEPING

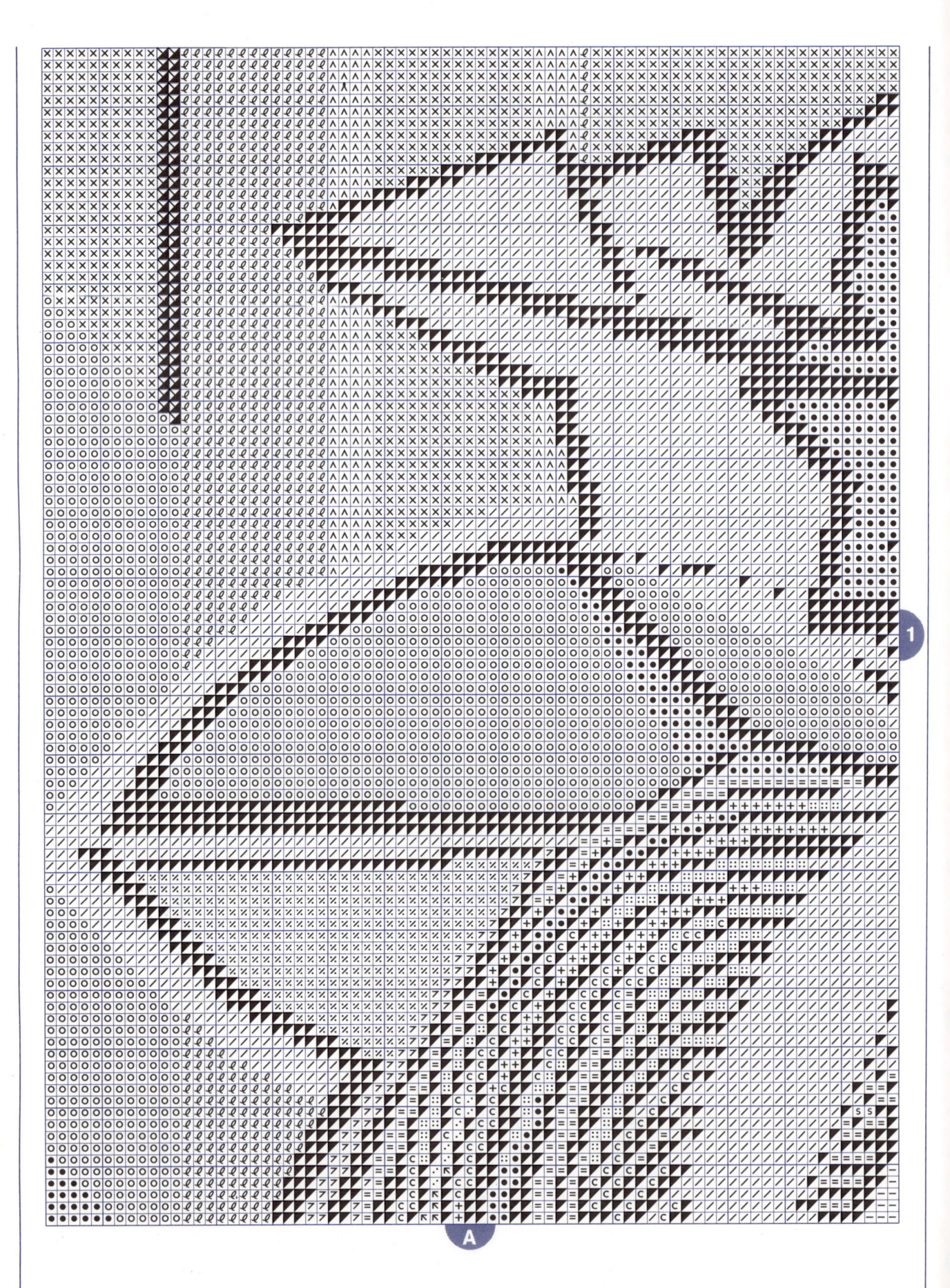

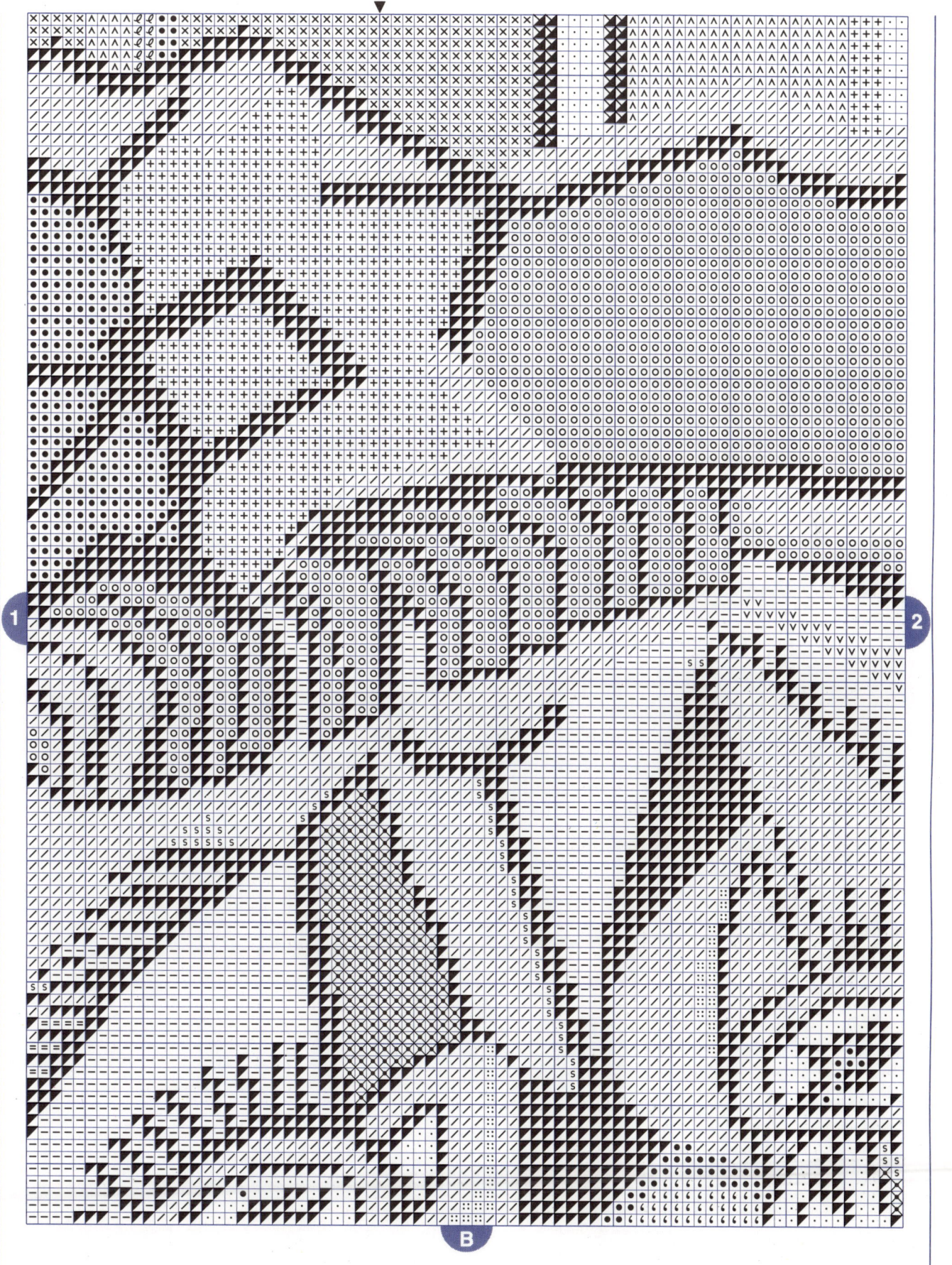

FACES

129

WOMAN WEEPING

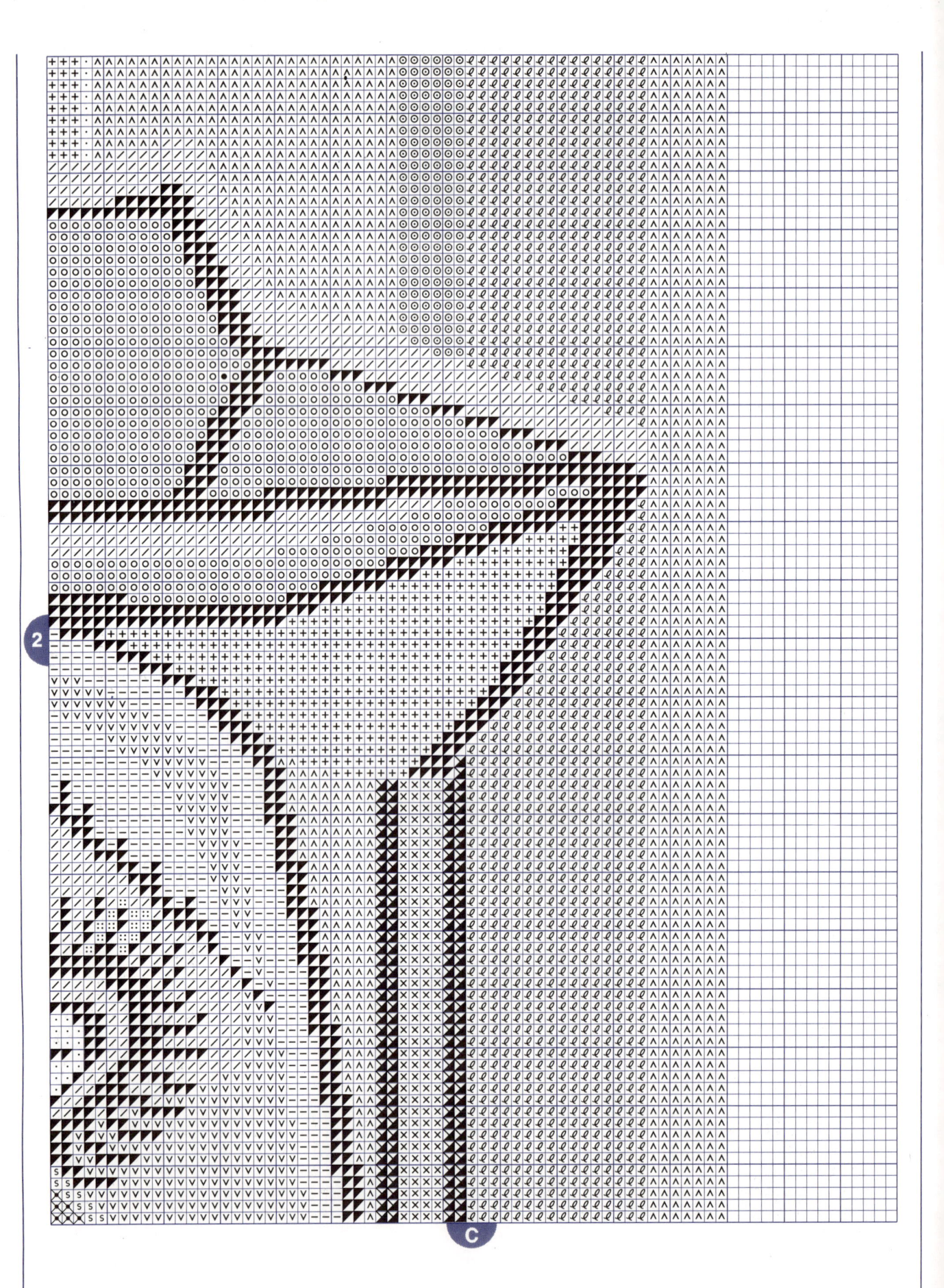

131

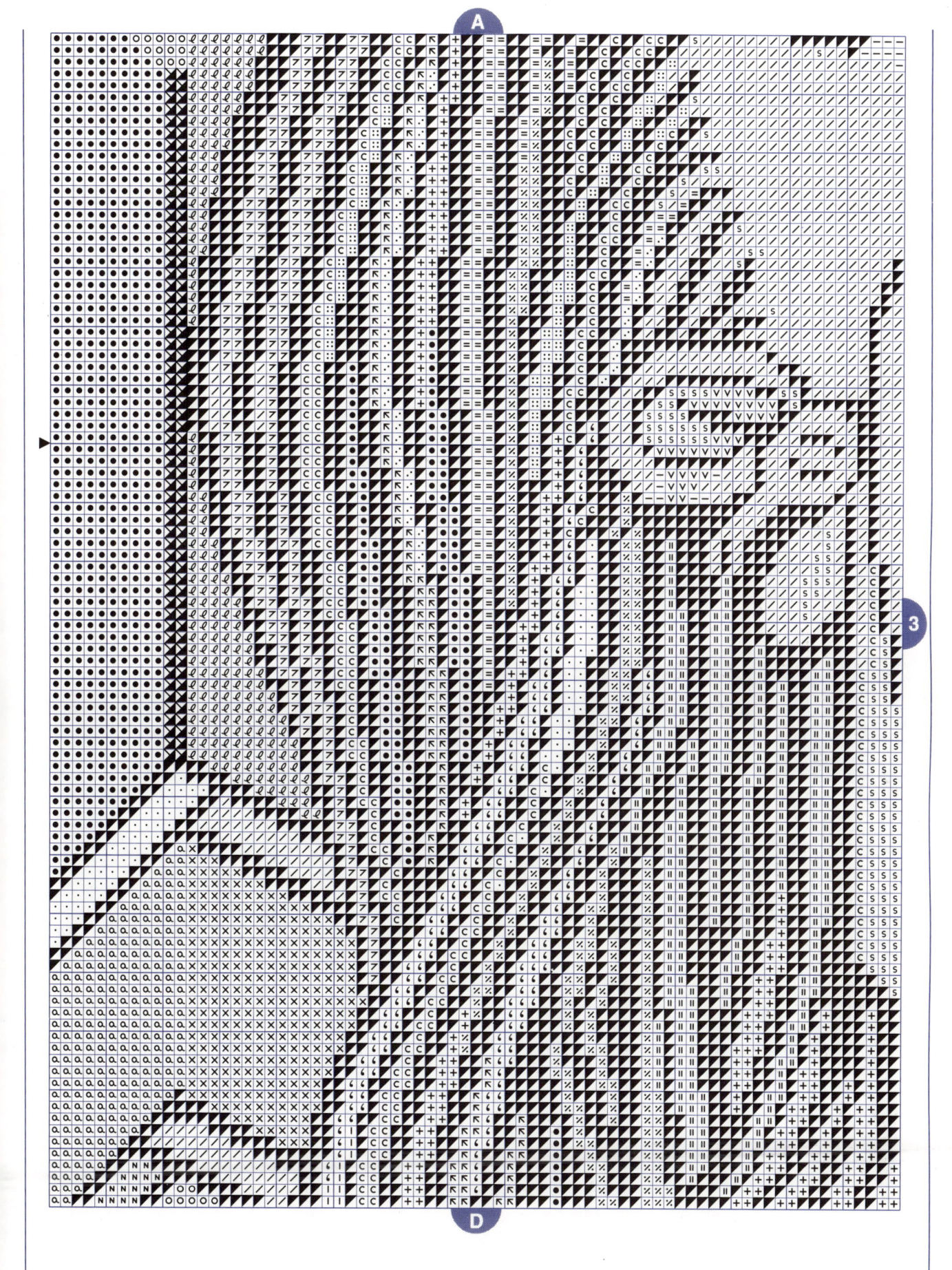

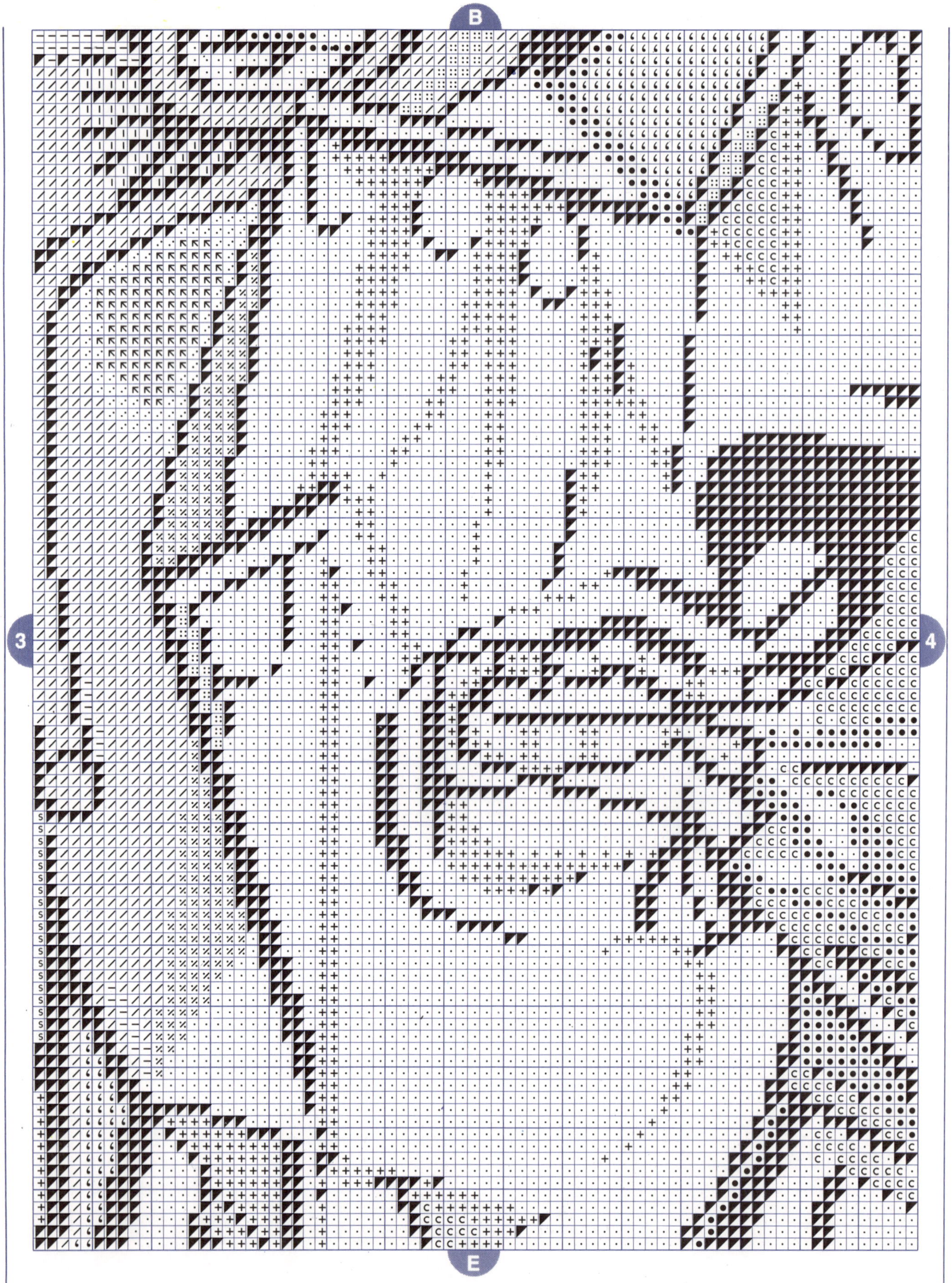
B
3
4
E

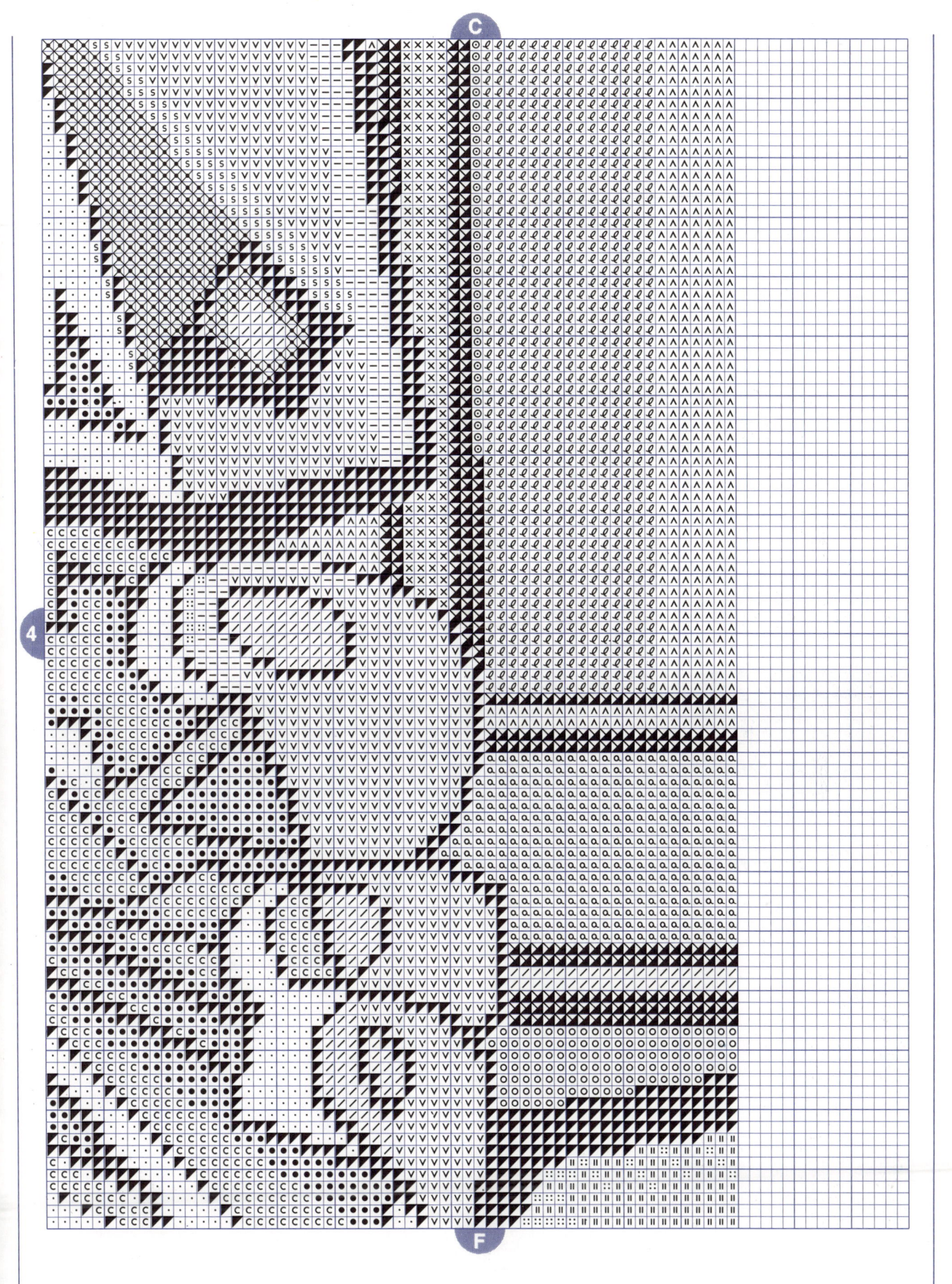

FACES

WOMAN WEEPING

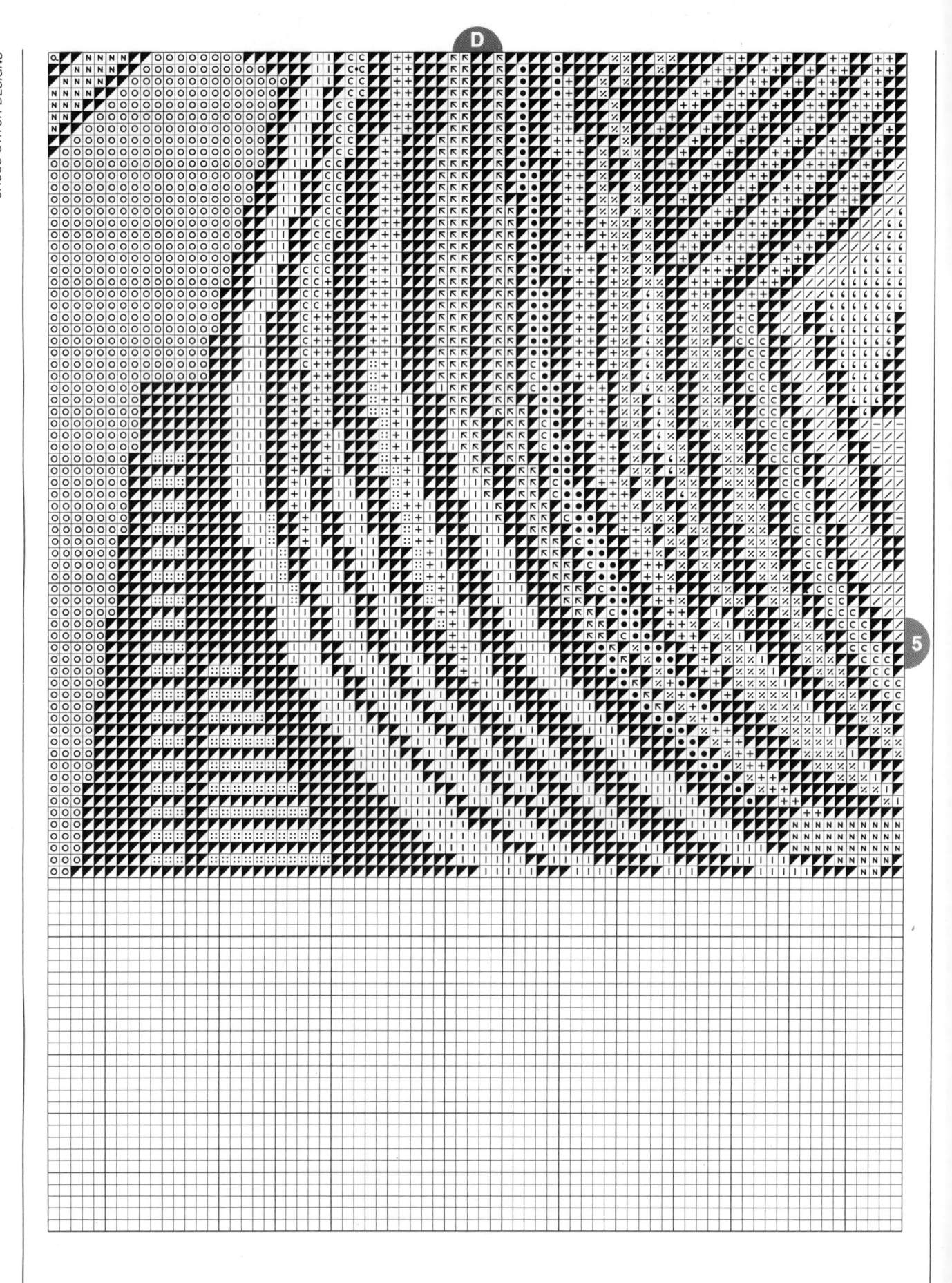

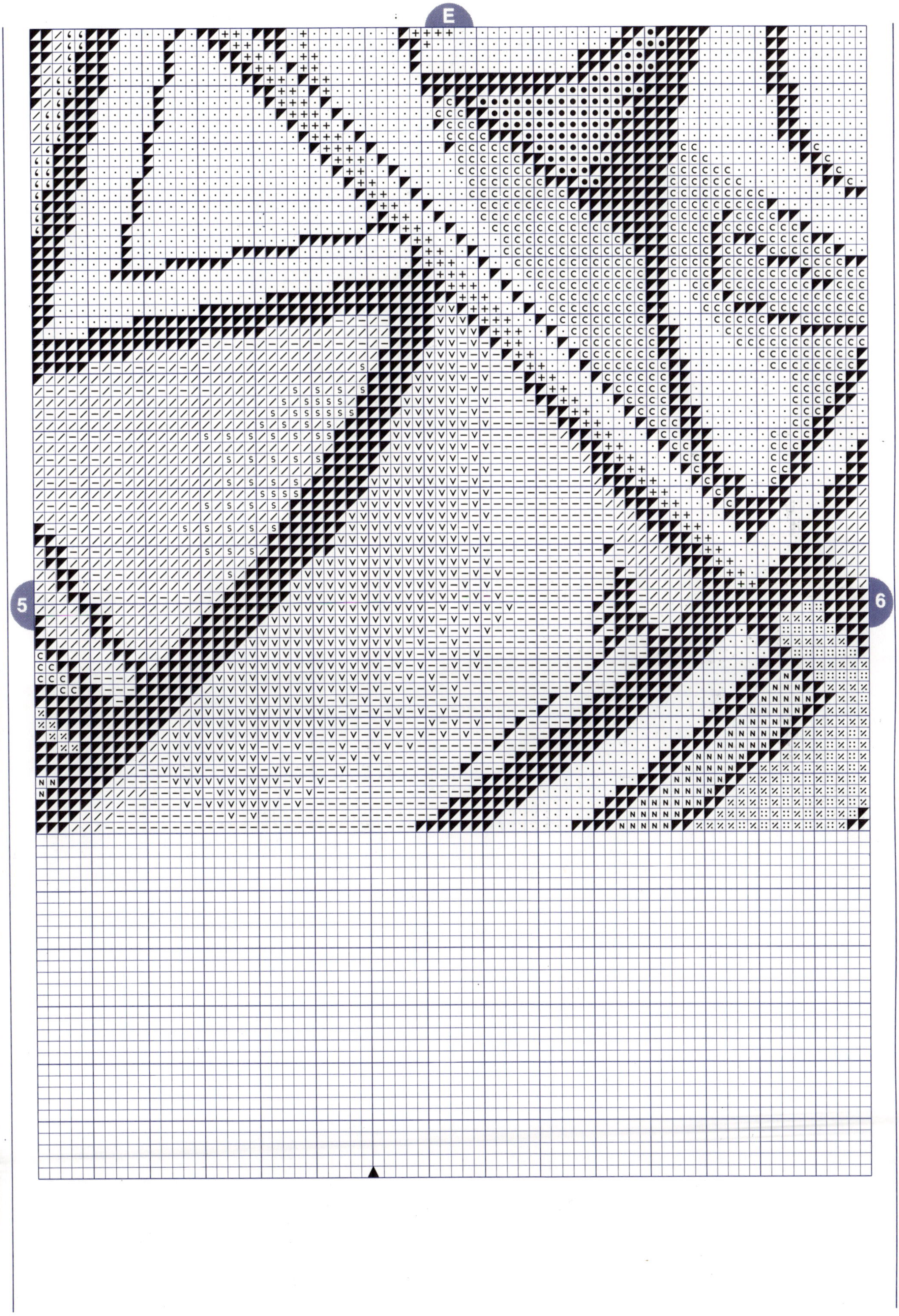
E
5
6

136 | WOMAN WEEPING

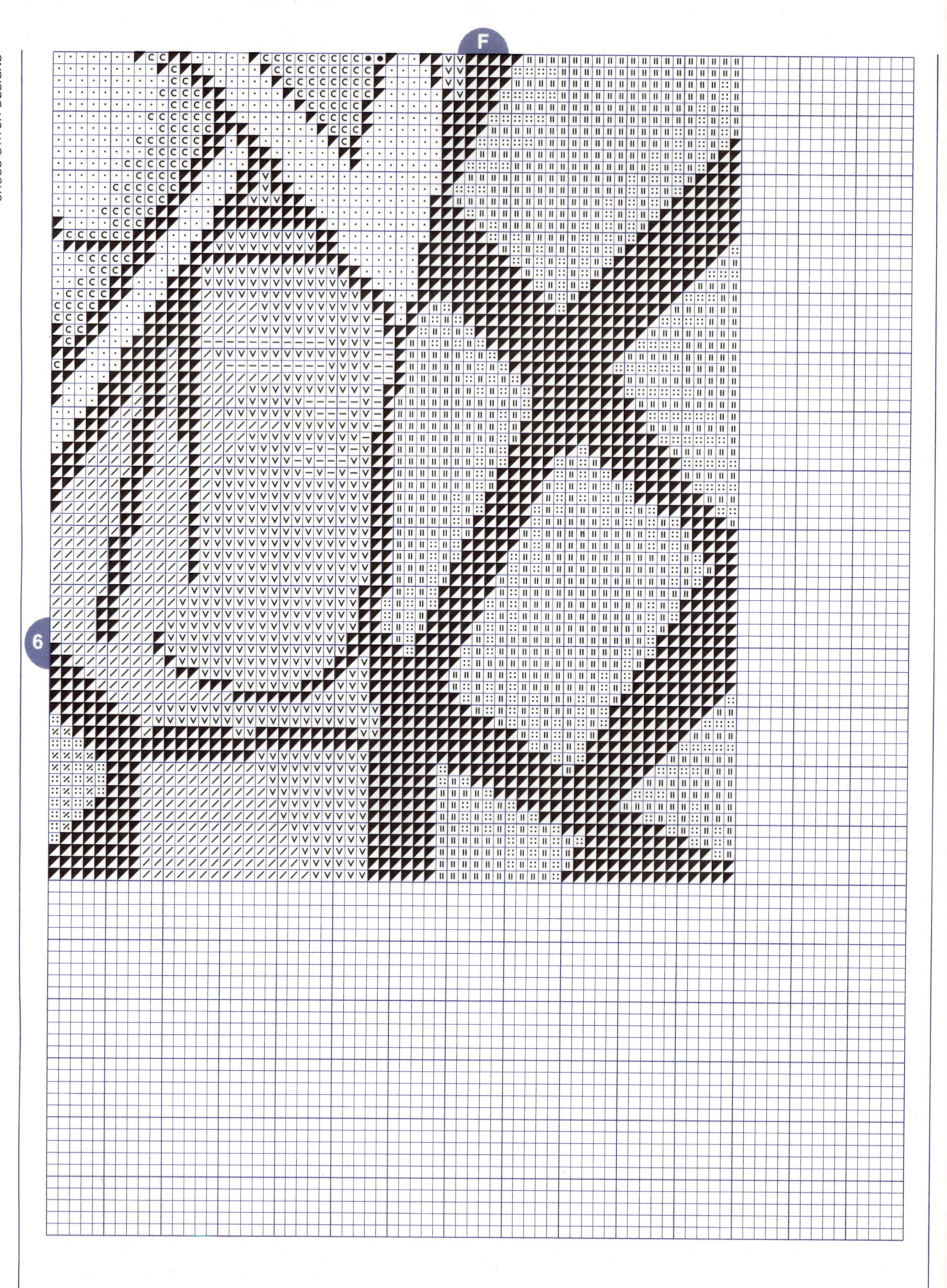

TUTANKHAMEN

Tutankhamen

The funerary mask of the Pharoah Tutankhamen, discovered when his tomb was opened in 1922, was superbly crafted from wood, blackened with bitumen and decorated with beaten gold.

My original of this piece was worked as a needlepoint on 16 count canvas. The design is 324 stitches by 270 stitches. My recommended fabric size below is for cross stitch. If working it as needlepoint, please allow additional material for the surround. Either work on black fabric or stitch all the surrounding areas black.

Fabric

Count	Centimetres	Inches
10	100 × 83	39 × 33
14	73 × 64	29 × 26
18	61 × 53	24 × 21
22	53 × 47	21 × 19

This design is 324 stitches high by 270 stitches wide.

Thread

Use two strands throughout for cross stitch.

DMC Art 117

·	white	
⊙	208	(purple)
▼	310	(black)
ı	318	(grey)
×	420	(brown)
+	422	(fawn)
•	501	(teal)
∕	727	(light yellow)
L	809	(light blue)
∴	818	(light pink)
−	993	(aqua)
✽	996	(blue)
v	3045	(dark gold)
к	3363	(green)
o	3609	(pink)

139

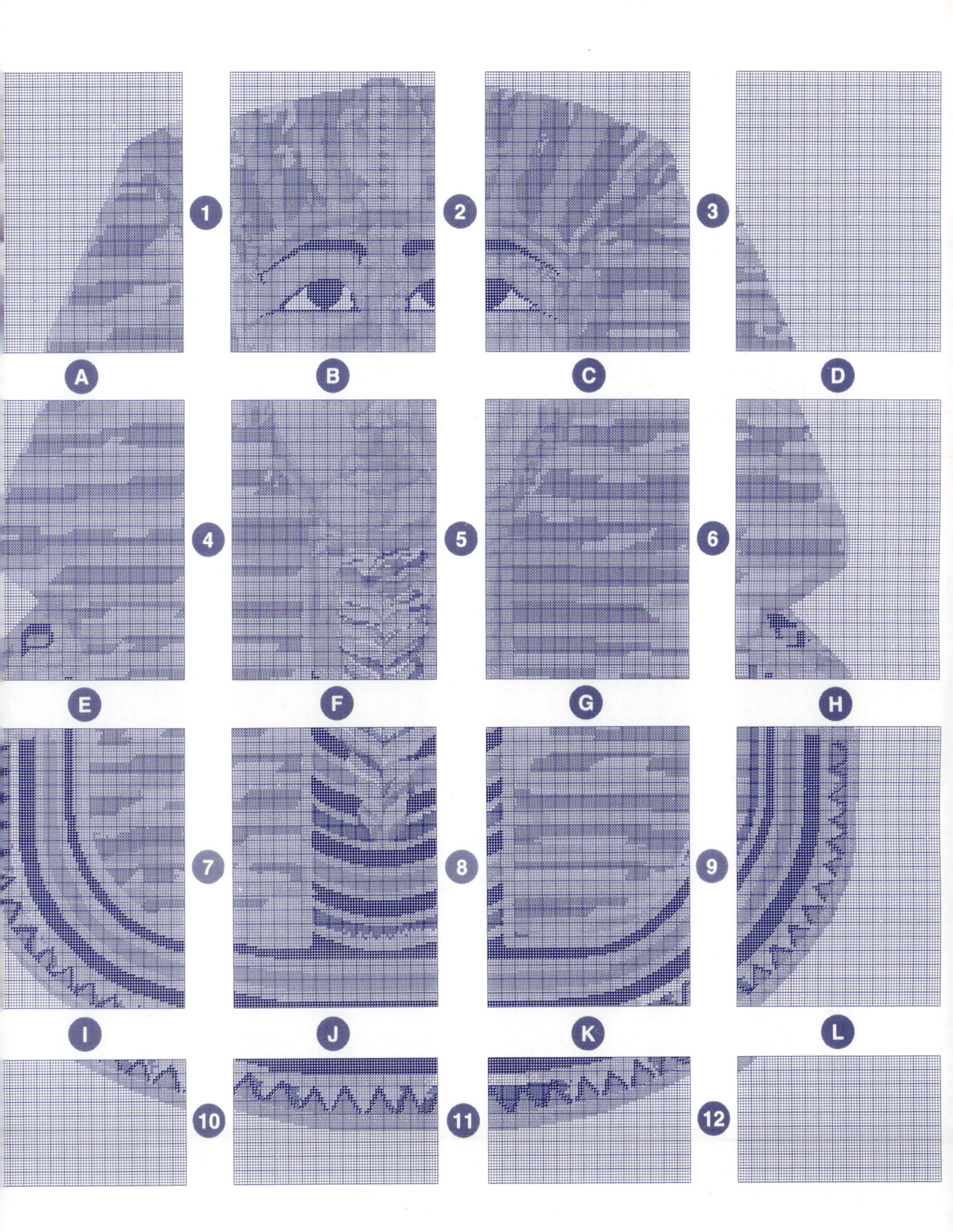

TUTANKHAMEN

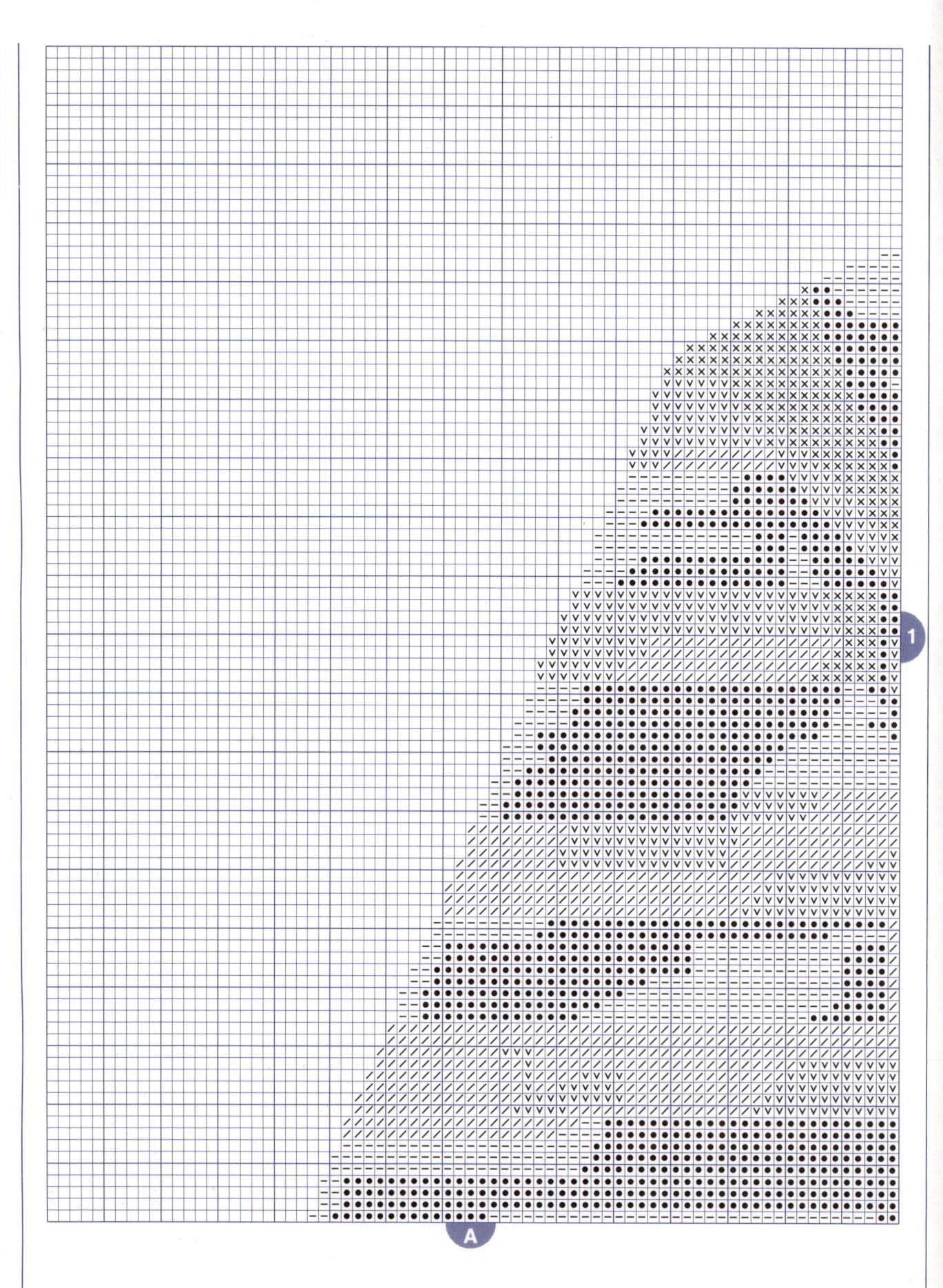

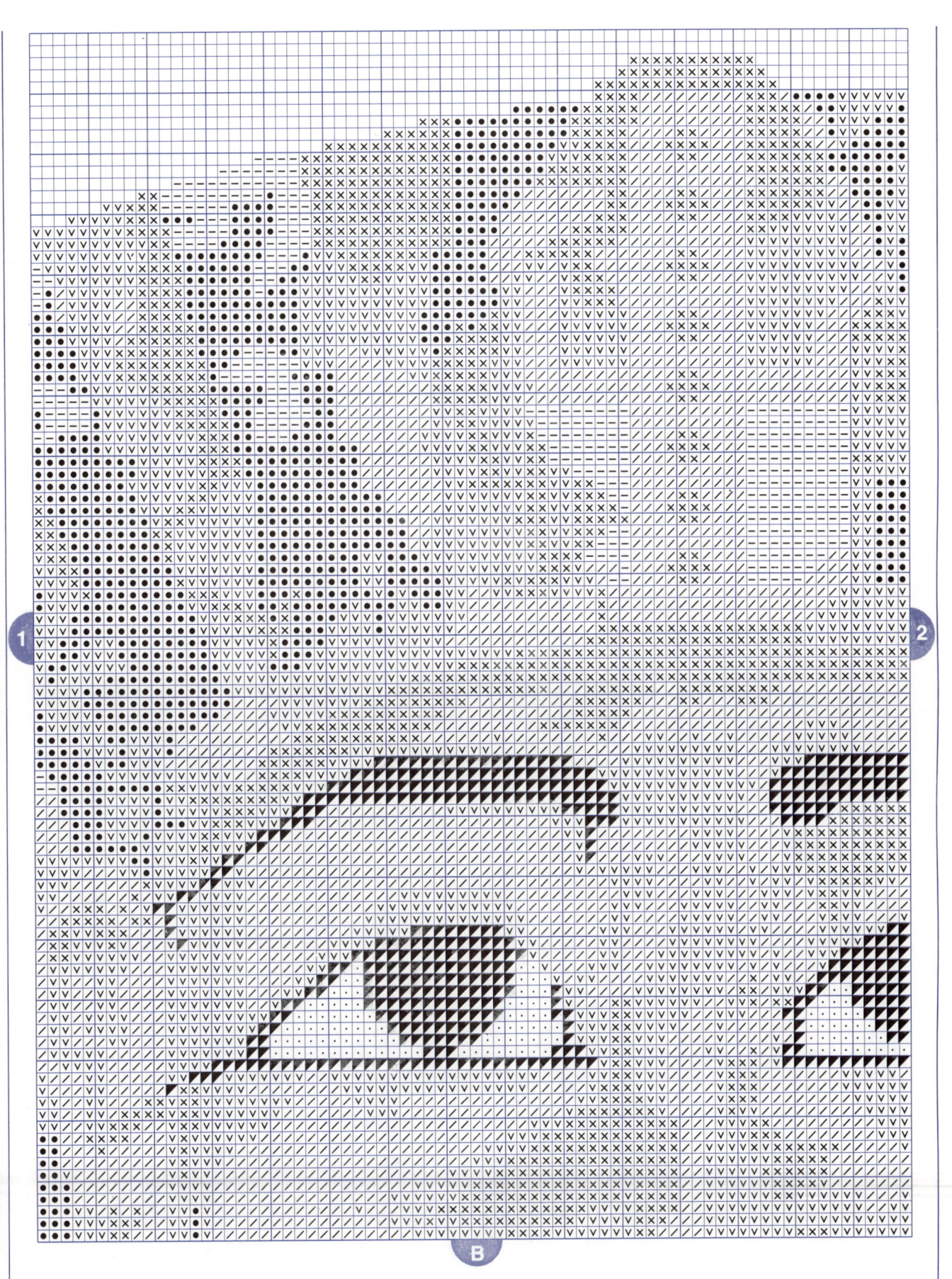

FACES

141

TUTANKHAMEN

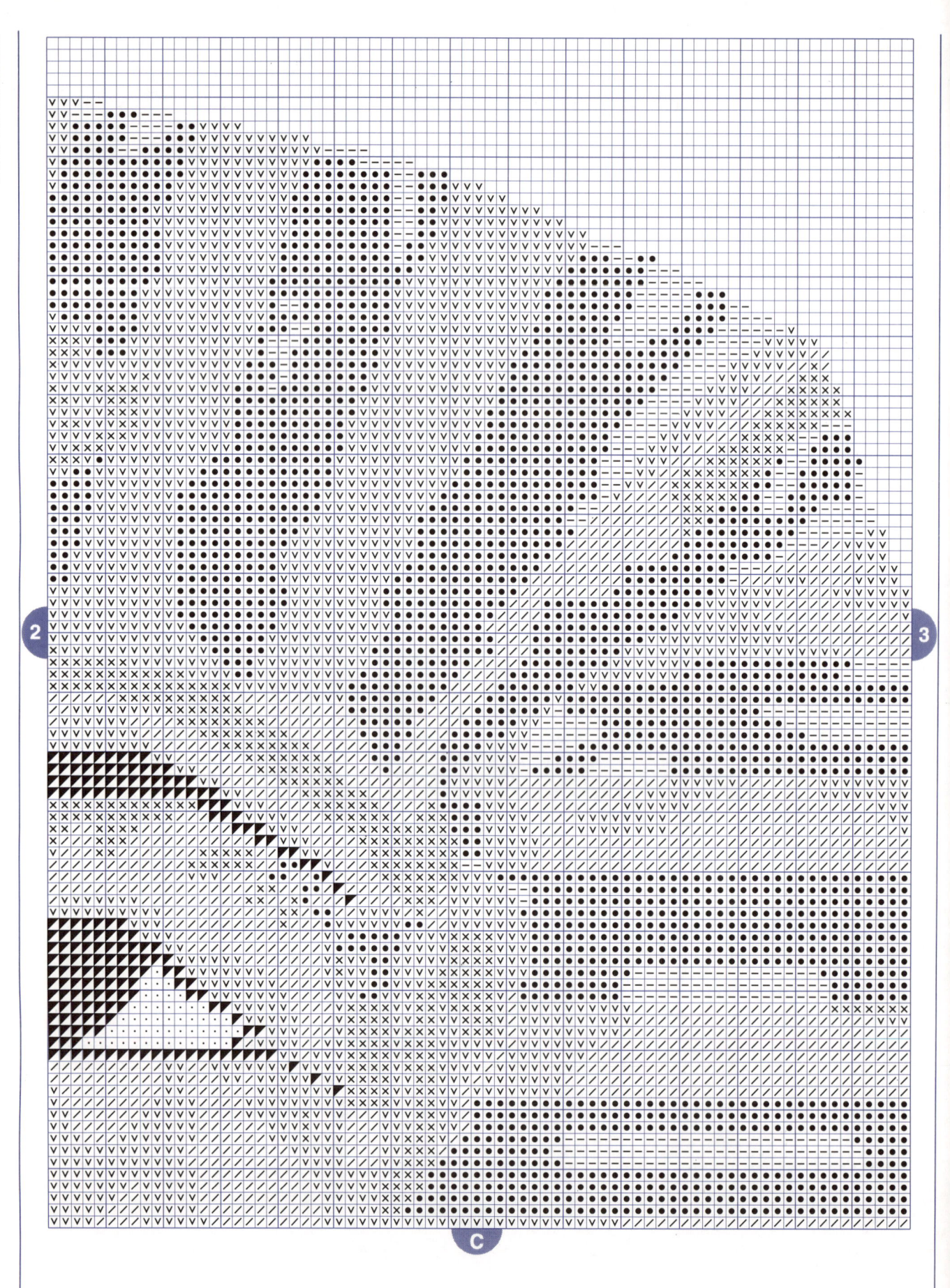

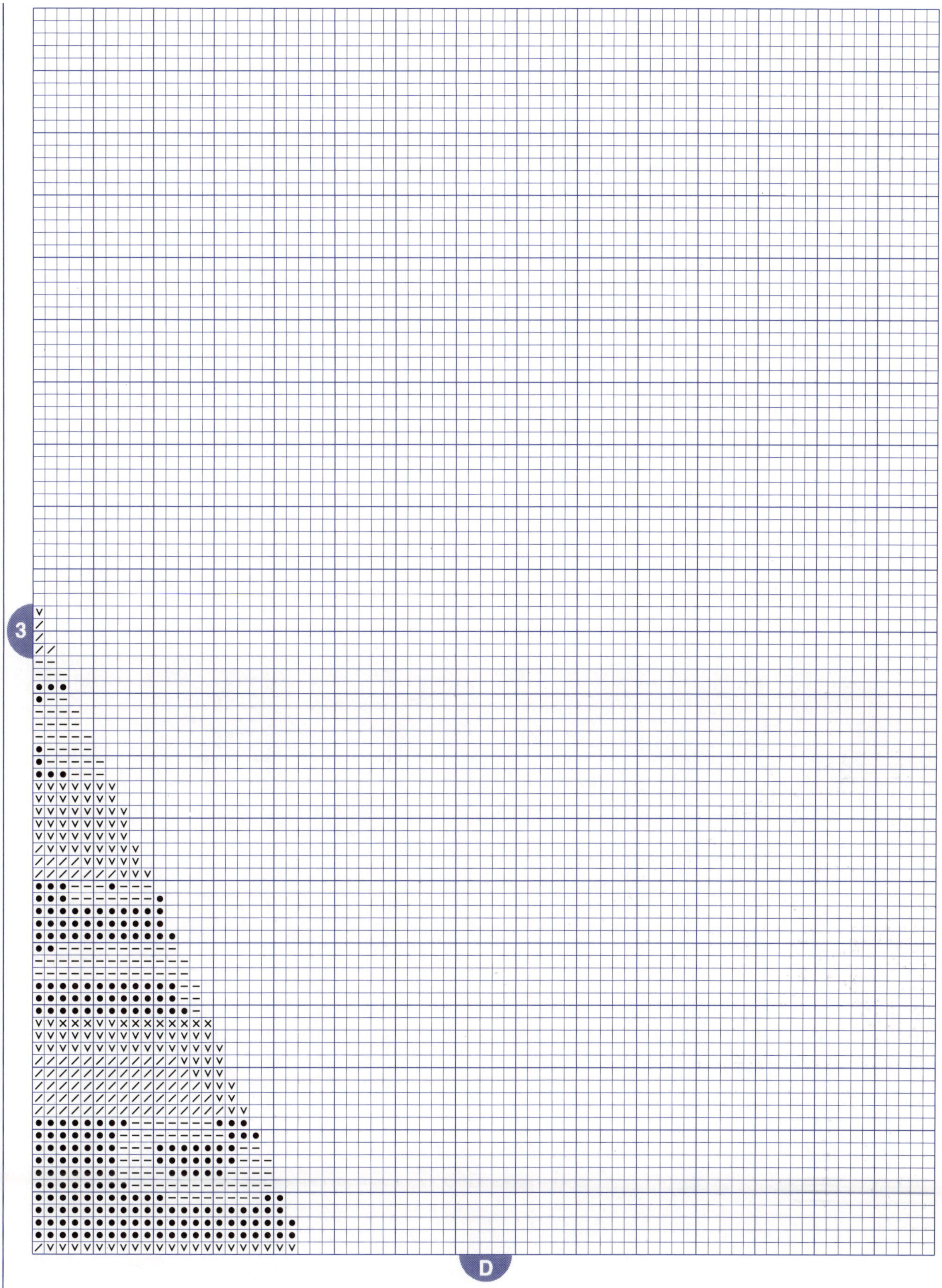

TUTANKHAMEN

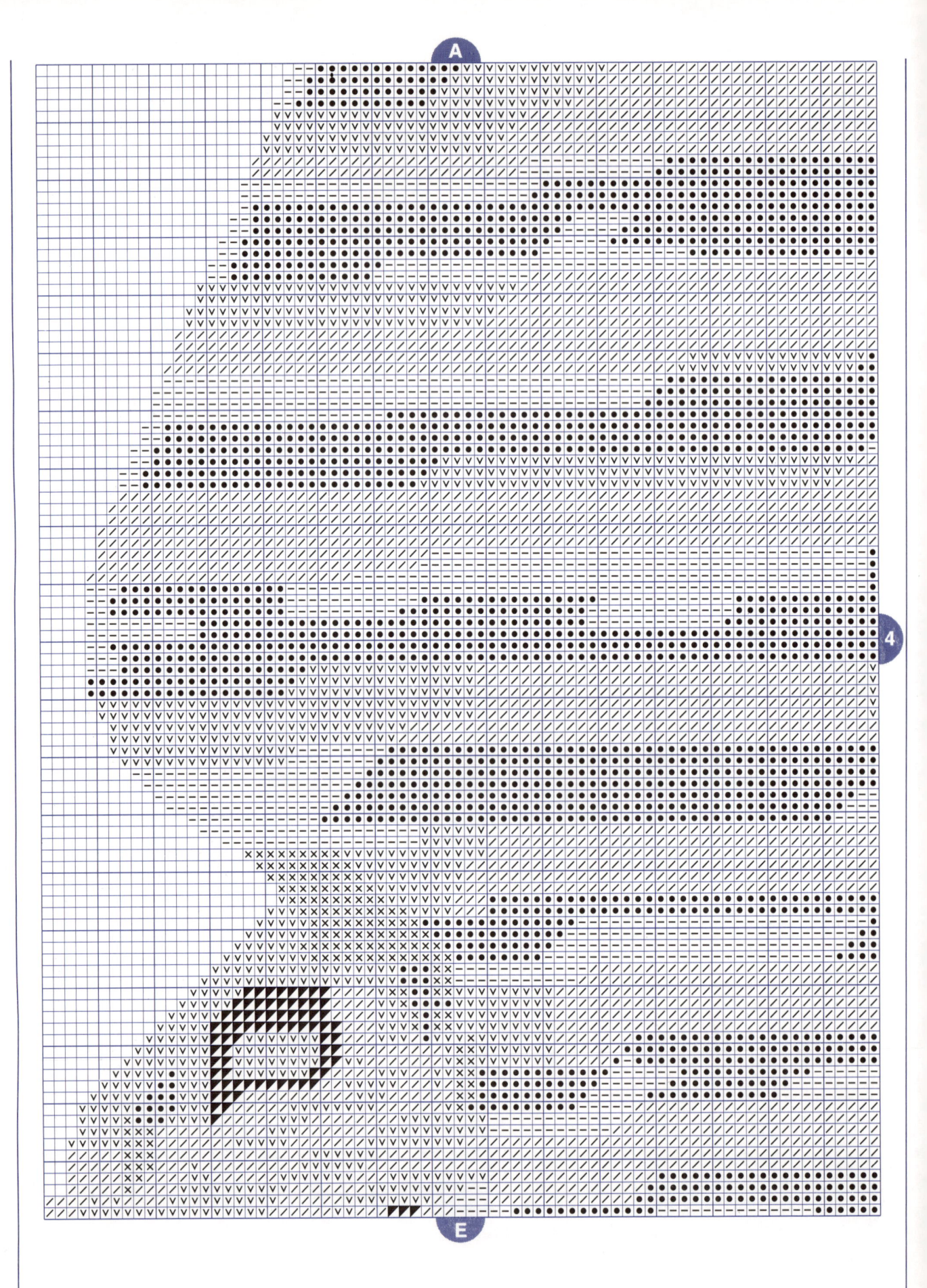

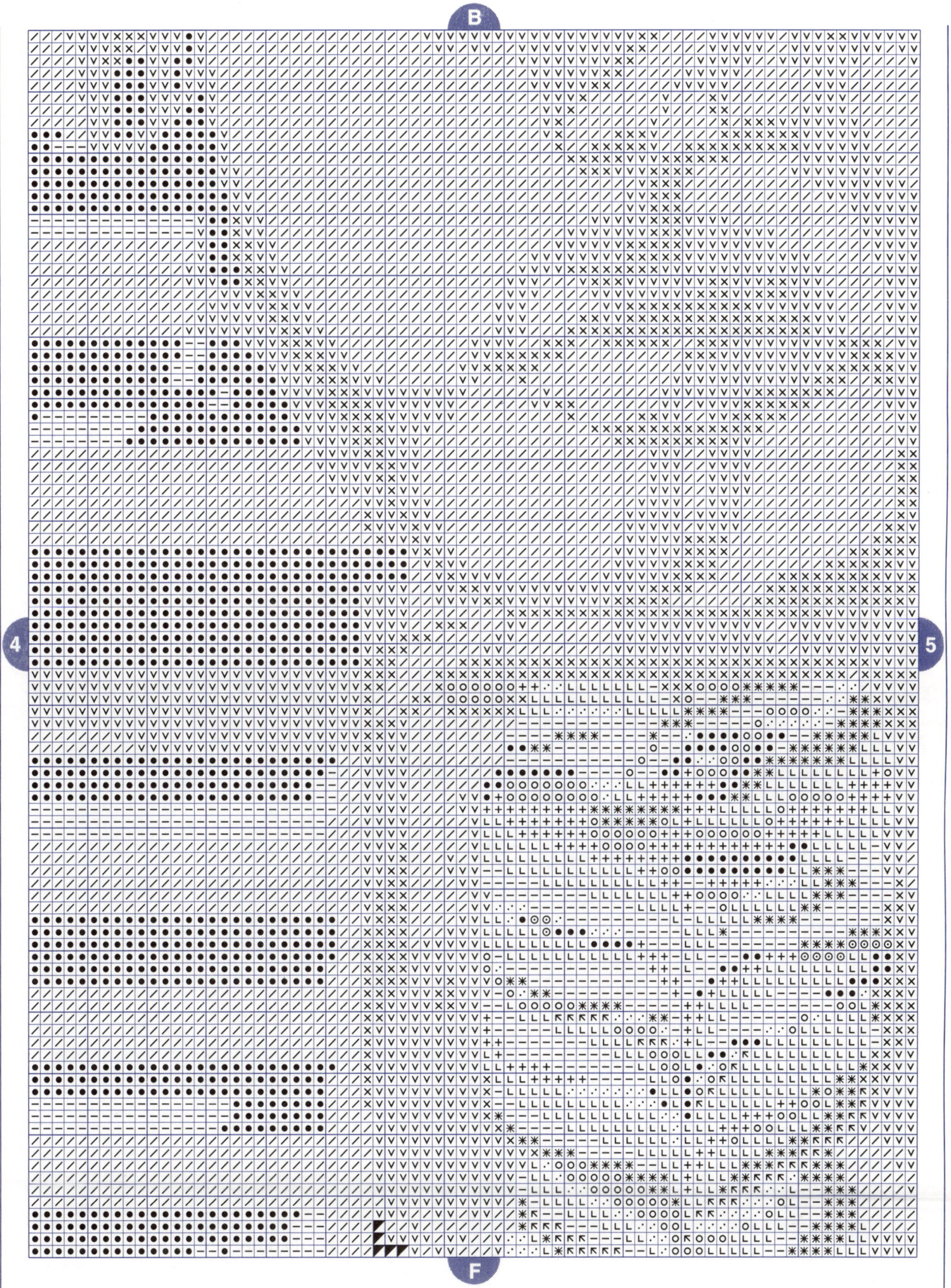
B
4
5
F

146 TUTANKHAMEN

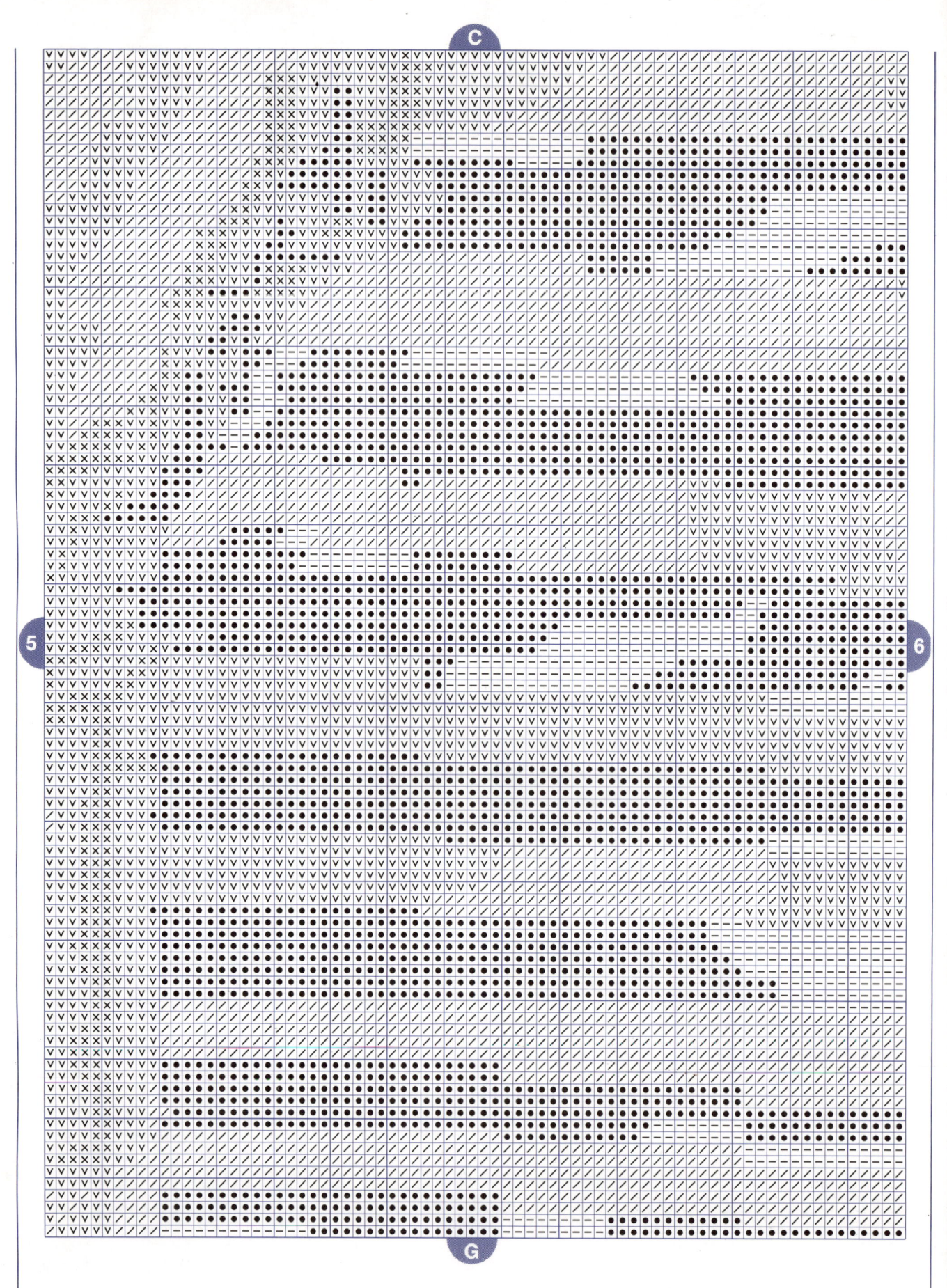

147

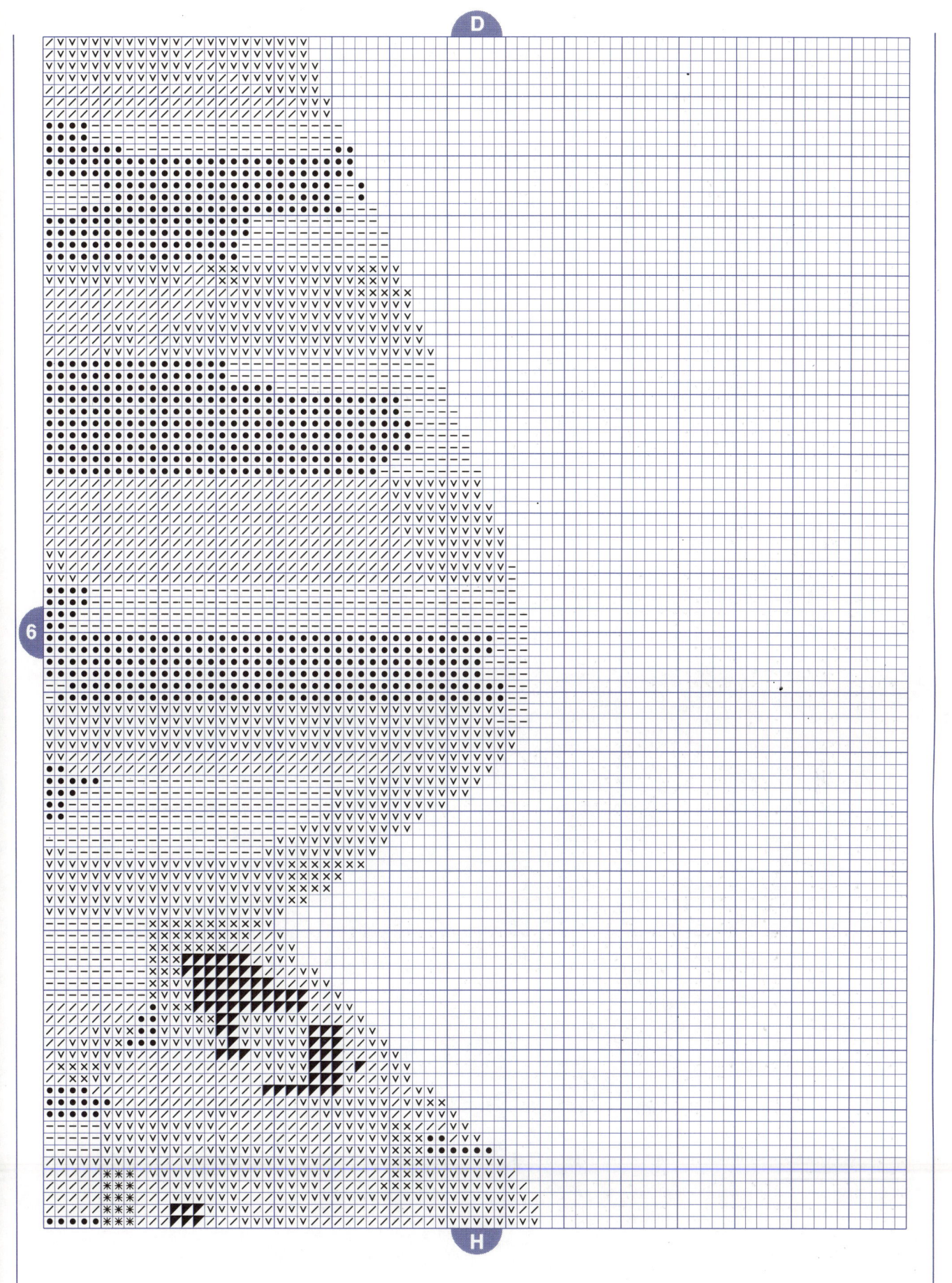

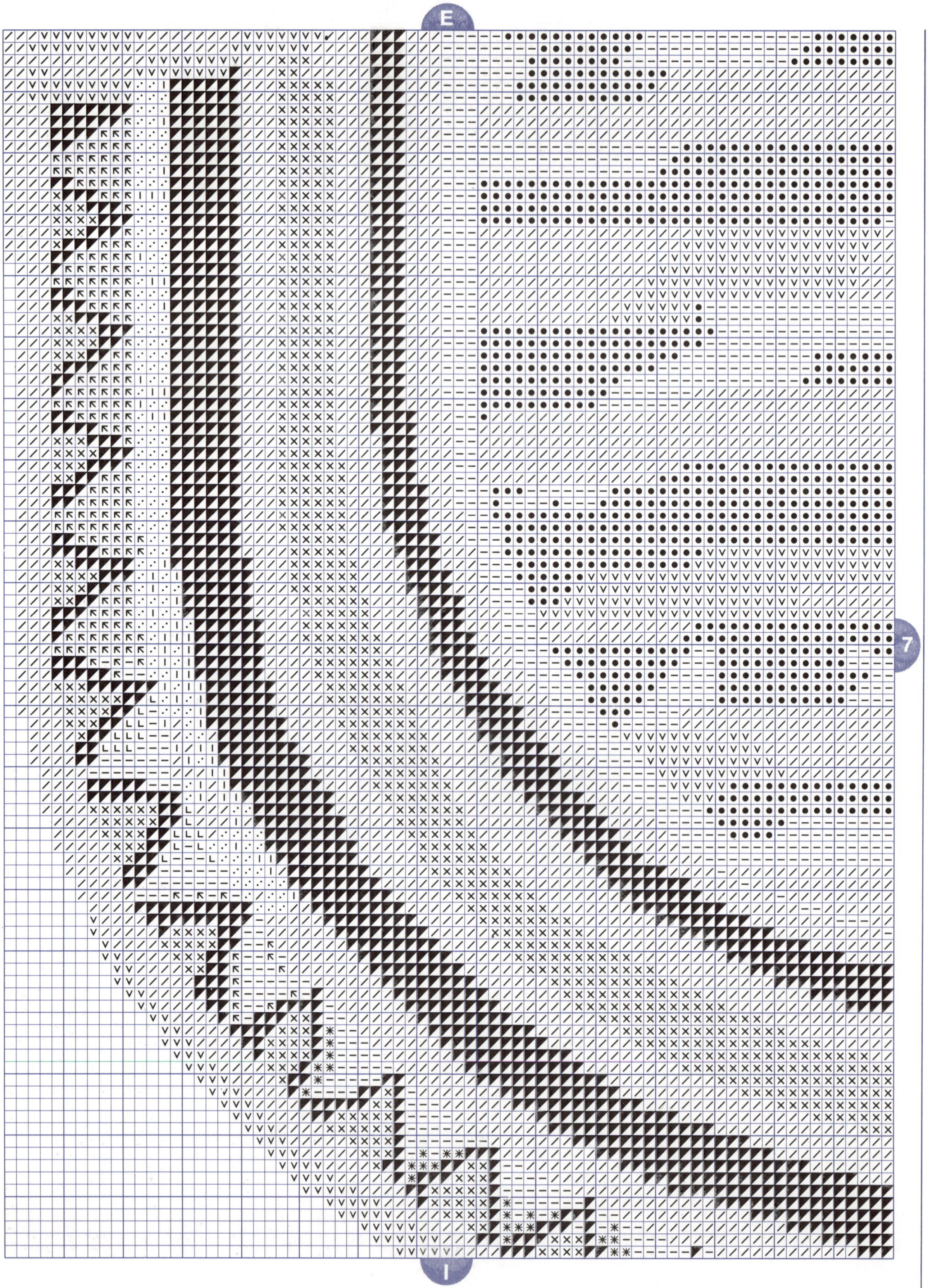
E
7
I

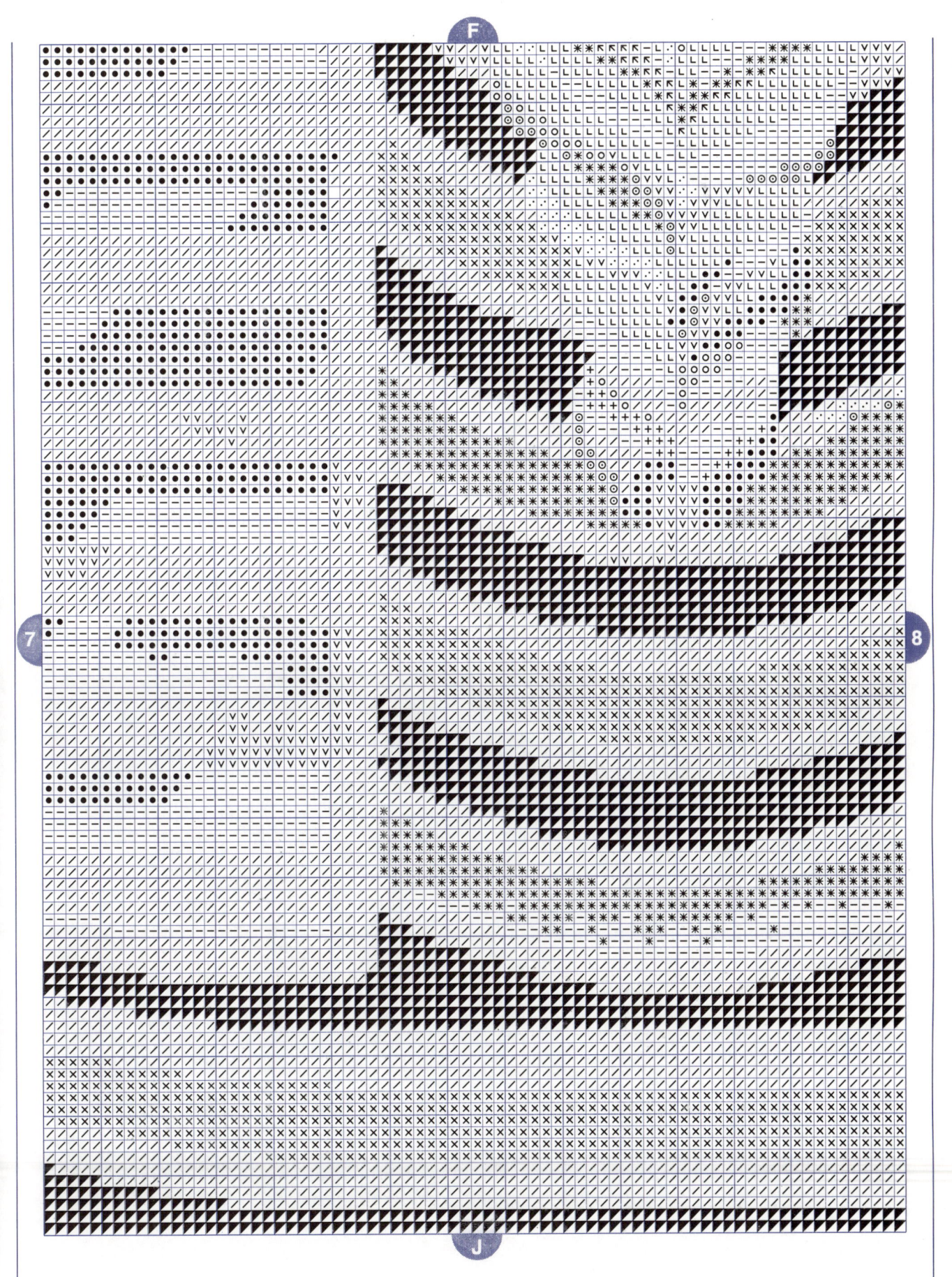

FACES

149

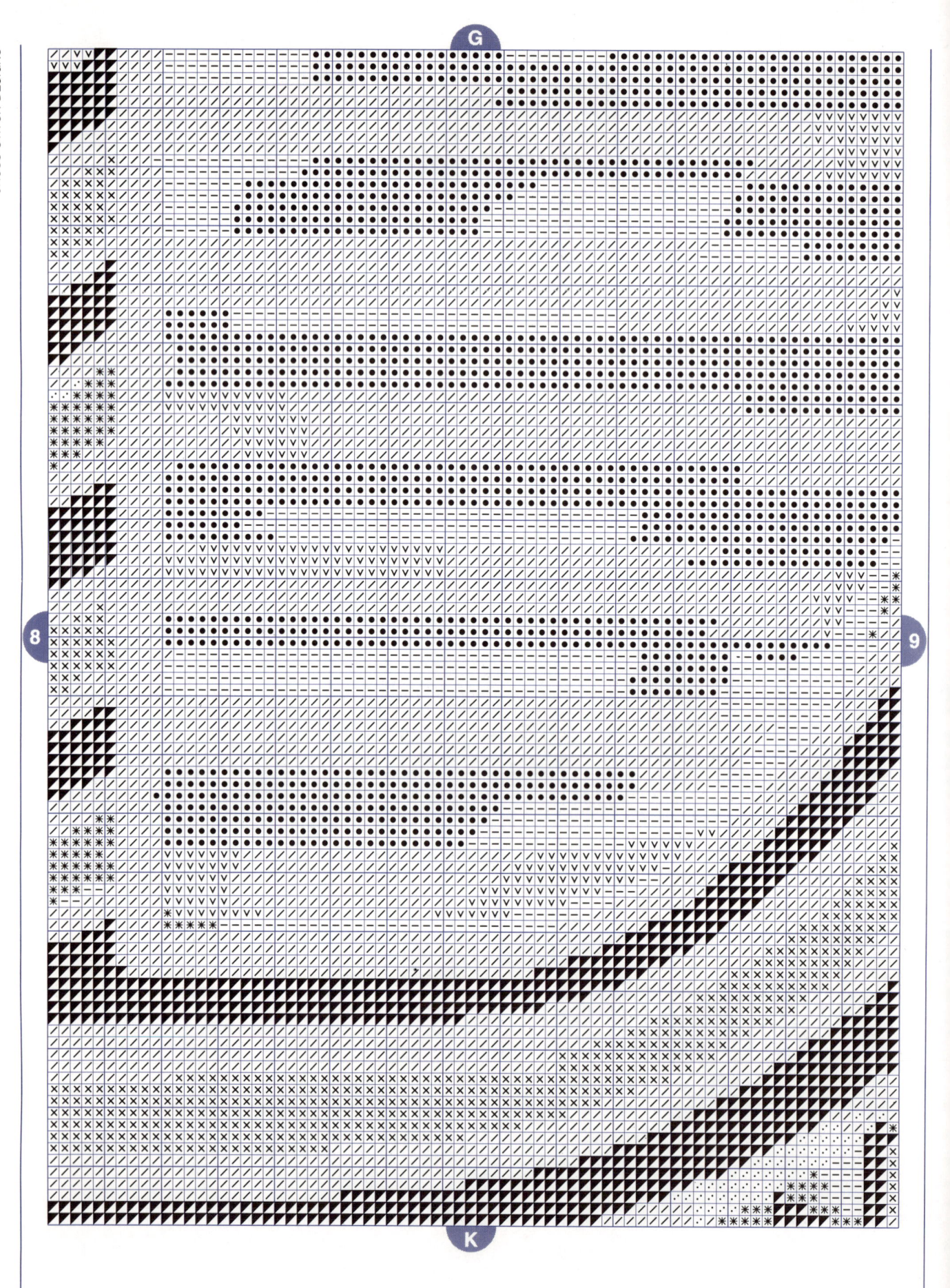

CROSS STITCH DESIGNS

150 TUTANKHAMEN

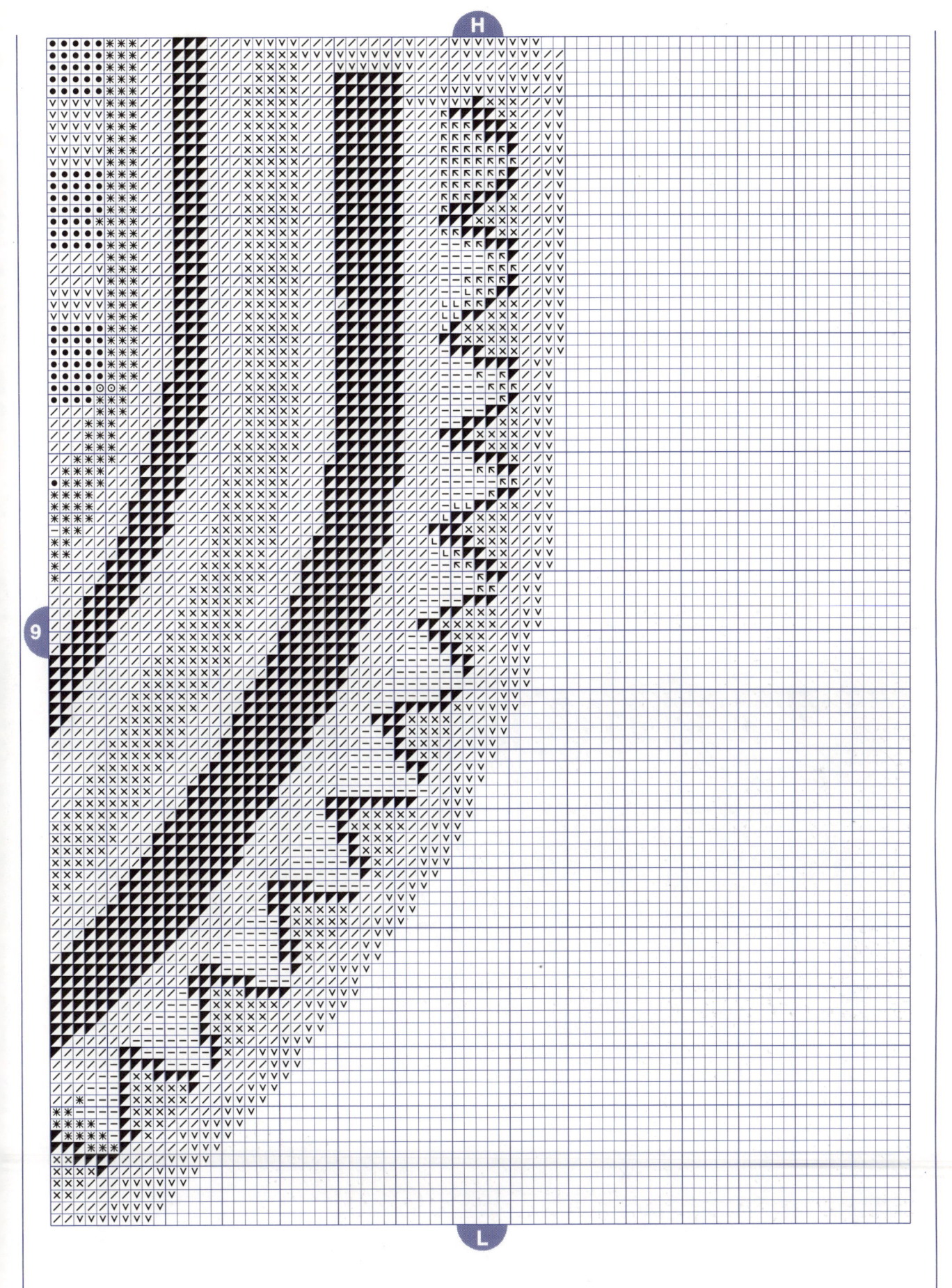

FACES

151

152 TUTANKHAMEN

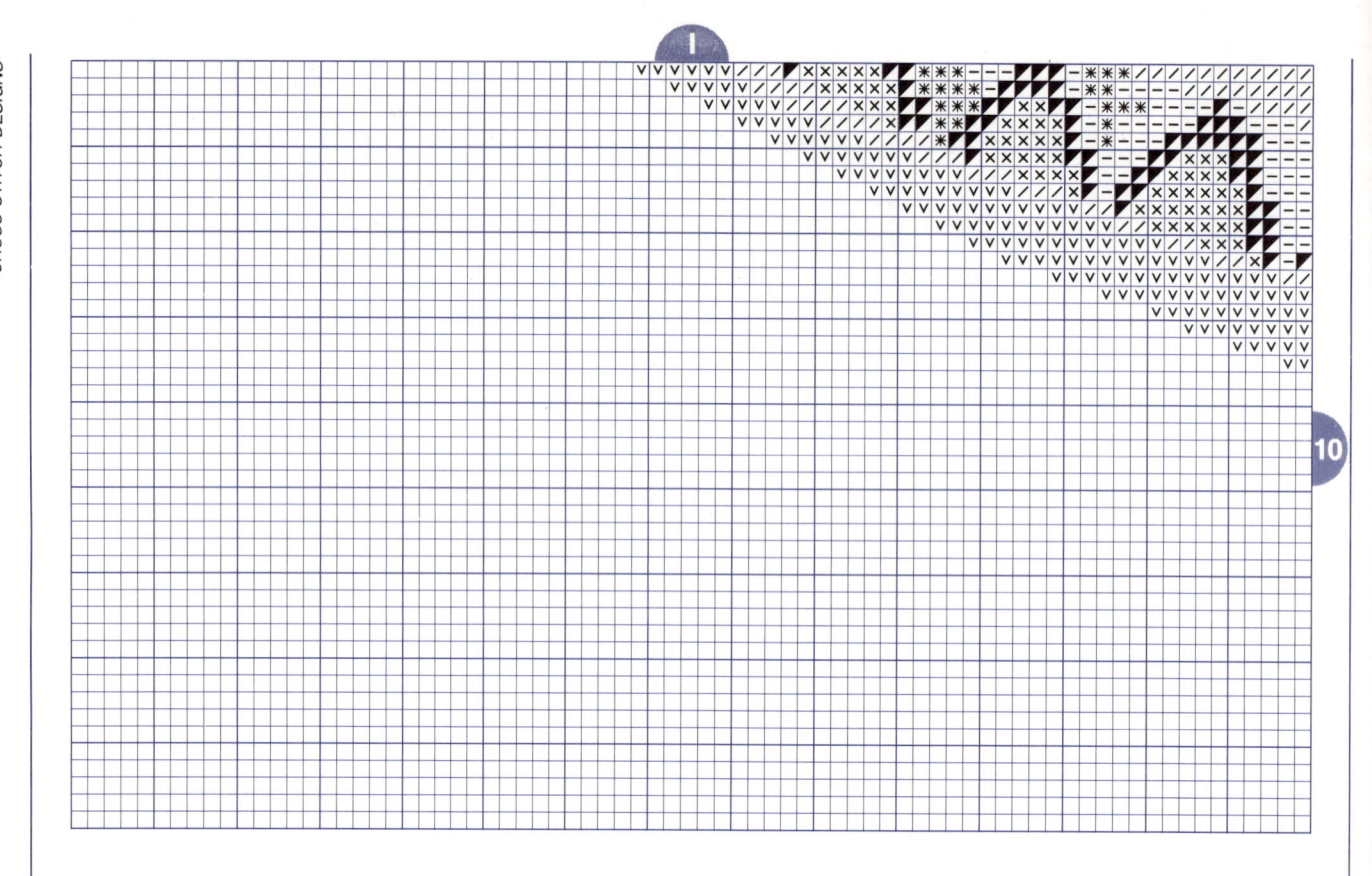

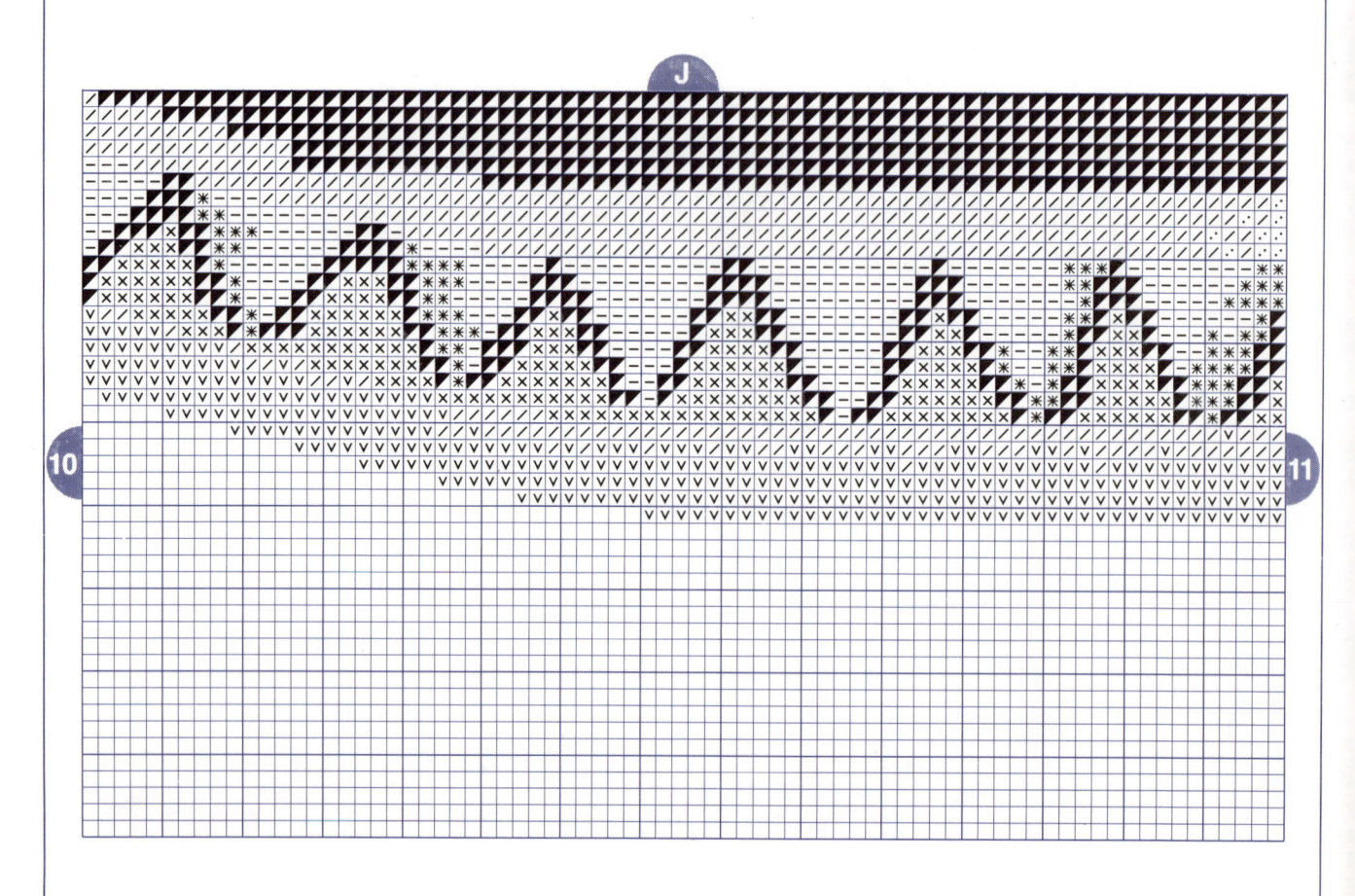

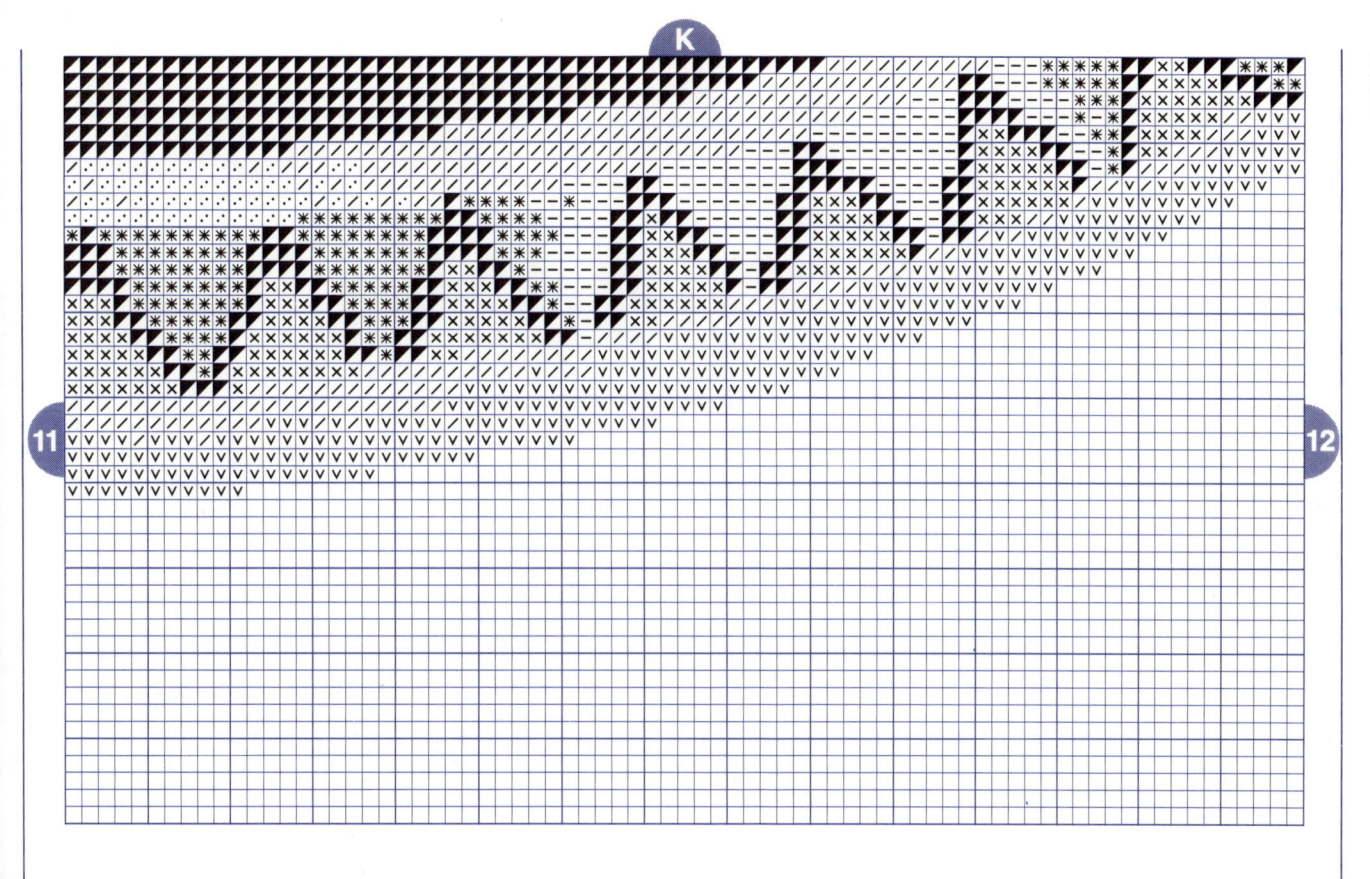

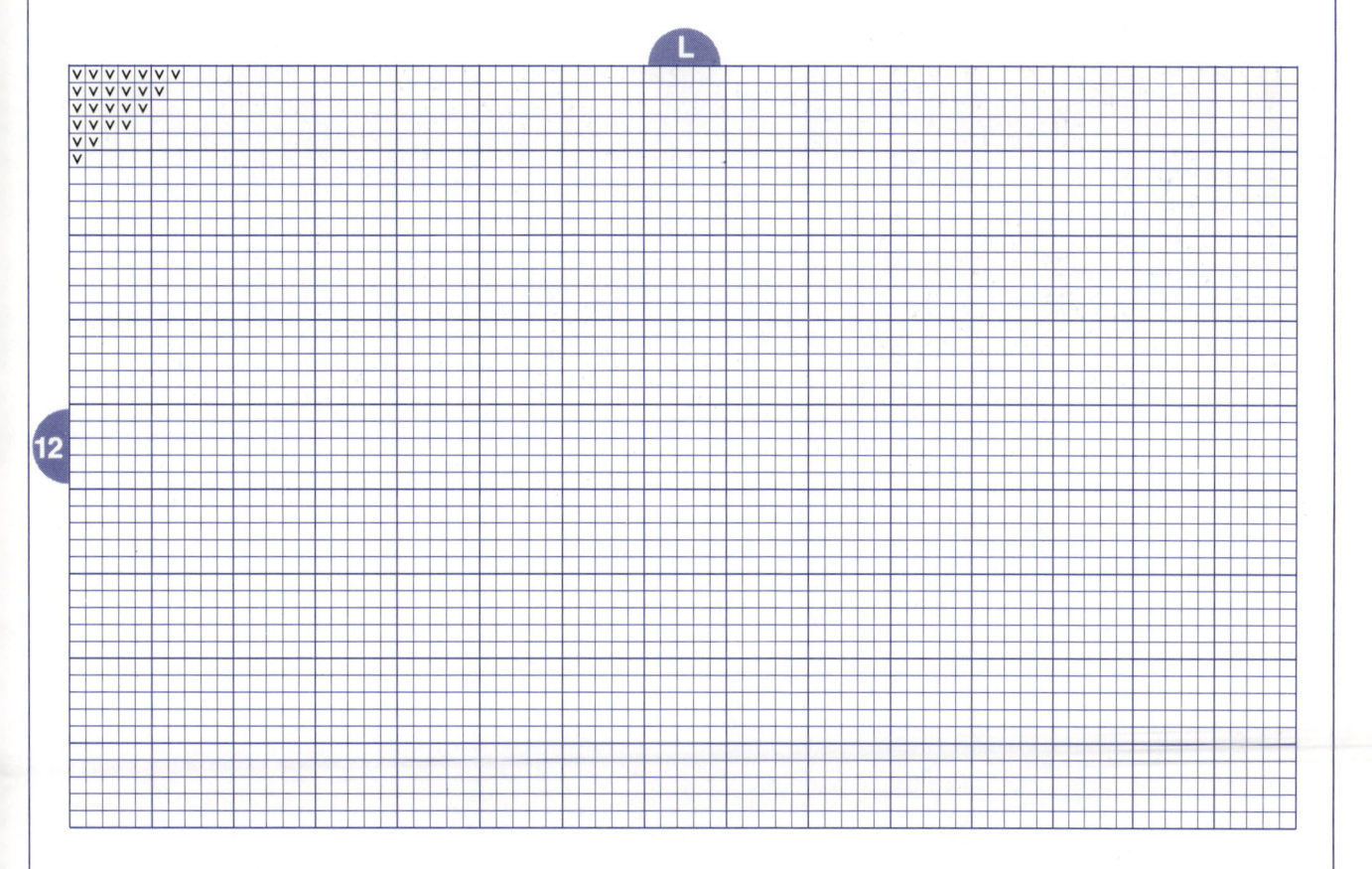

FACES

153